CRISIS' REPRESENTATIONS

Studies in Critical Social Sciences Book Series

Haymarket Books is proud to be working with Brill Academic Publishers (www.brill.nl) to republish the *Studies in Critical Social Sciences* book series in paperback editions. This peer-reviewed book series offers insights into our current reality by exploring the content and consequences of power relationships under capitalism, and by considering the spaces of opposition and resistance to these changes that have been defining our new age. Our full catalog of *SCSS* volumes can be viewed at https://www.haymarketbooks .org/series_collections/4-studies-in-critical-social-sciences.

CRISIS' REPRESENTATIONS

Frontiers and Identities in the
Contemporary Media Narratives

EDITED BY
CHRISTIANA CONSTANTOPOULOU

Haymarket Books
Chicago, IL

First published in 2020 by Brill Academic Publishers, The Netherlands
© 2020 Koninklijke Brill NV, Leiden, The Netherlands

Published in paperback in 2021 by
Haymarket Books
P.O. Box 180165
Chicago, IL 60618
773-583-7884
www.haymarketbooks.org

ISBN: 978-1-64259-615-1

Distributed to the trade in the US through Consortium Book Sales and
Distribution (www.cbsd.com) and internationally through Ingram Publisher
Services International (www.ingramcontent.com).

This book was published with the generous support of Lannan Foundation and
Wallace Action Fund.

Special discounts are available for bulk purchases by organizations and
institutions. Please call 773-583-7884 or email info@haymarketbooks.org for more
information.

Cover design by Jamie Kerry and Ragina Johnson.

Printed in the United States.

10 9 8 7 6 5 4 3 2 1

Library of Congress Cataloging-in-Publication data is available.

Contents

Figures and Tables

Figures

Tables

Notes on Contributors

Christiana Constantopoulou
is Professor of Sociology of Communication, Dept. of Sociology Panteion University of Social and Political Sciences (Athens, Greece). Author of many scientific articles and monographic works (mostly in Greek, French and English but also translated in Portuguese and Bulgarian), focusing essentially on the "communicational structures of the contemporary societies". Active member of the "Association Internationale des Sociologues de Langue Française", and elected member of the executive board (1996–2000, 2000–2004 and 2008–2012, 2012–2016); President of RC 14 "Sociology of Communication, Knowledge and Culture of the International Sociological Association" (2006–2010, 2010–2014, 2014–2018, 2018–2022, www.rc14-isa.com); member of the board of ISA-RC 13 "Sociology of Leisure" 2010–2014; member of organizational and scientific committees of many conferences in several countries such as Brazil, Canada, France, Greece, Italy, Morocco, South Africa, Spain, Sweden, Tunisia, Turkey, etc. Editor/or member of the Scientific Committee of scientific journals (such as Sociétés, Socio-Anthropologie, Sociologies, OJSS, etc.). Knight of the Academic Palms (French Ministry of Education) since 2012. Head of the Center of Studies of the Contemporary Communication in Europe (EURCECOM, eurcecom.webs.com).

Amalia Frangiskou
is Researcher—Grade A' Functional Scientific Personnel—in the National Centre for Social Research, since 1994. Master Degree in Communications Policy Studies from the City University of London. She also holds a Law Degree from the Law School of Athens University and a Diploma in Journalism from the Athens Institute for Professional Journalism.
Her research interests belong to the field of communication systems (policies, power, structures, transformation strategies, international interrelations), and their implications and the fields of social inclusion, minorities, institutional and legal integration framework, stereotypes through media, discrimination, structural inequalities of "info-com society". She has been particularly involved in research methods such as content analysis, discourse analysis, semiotics, biographical interviews, semi structured interviews and focus groups.

Evaggelia Kalerante
is Associate Professor in Education Policy, in the Preschool Teachers Department at the University of Western Macedonia. She is a graduate of the Policy Department, Law School of Athens, of the Faculty of Pedagogy in Athens and

of the Faculty of Preschool Education Teachers. She completed her Postgraduate studies in Sociology at the University of Athens. The topic of her Doctoral Thesis was on Education Policy. Her scientific interests focus on Education Policy, Sociology of Education and Political Sociology.

Dimitra Laurence Larochelle

is PhD Candidate on Sociology of Media and Cultural Studies at the Communication Department of the University Sorbonne Nouvelle—Paris 3. She is currently working as a Research and Teaching assistant (ATER) at the University Sorbonne Nouvelle—Paris 3. She has two master degrees on Sociology (University Paris Descartes) and on Communication (French Institute of Journalism, Panthéon-Assas University). She has worked as a teaching staff at the University of Burgundy Franche-Comté, at Paris Descartes University, at Saint-Denis University and at the University Paris XII. She has published papers in French, in English and in Greek and she has worked as a researcher in France as well as in Cyprus. Since 2018 she is member of the board of the Research Committee 14 (Sociology of Communication, Knowledge and Culture) of the International Sociological Association and since 2019 she is Associate Editor of the Art and Culture International Magazine.

Debora Marcucci

is research collaborator at the University of Trento (Italy). She completed a MA on Linguistic Mediation in the Department of Humanities at the University of Trento and a short specialization programme on global marketing and communication. Her main research interests include intercultural communication, local and regional development, and cultural heritage.

Valentina Marinescu

is Professor Habilitated at the University of Bucharest, Romania. Her main research interests are communication and media studies in Eastern Europe, with a special focus on Romania.

Albertina Pretto

PhD, is a sociologist at the University of Trento (Italy). Her research interests focus on the study and development of qualitative methods and mixed methods, and on their application in different research areas such as the sense of belonging and related values and symbols.

Maria Thanopoulou

is Research Director at the National Center for Social Research in Greece. She has studied Law in Greece (University of Athens), as well as Sociology and

Social Anthropology in France (University René Descartes-Paris V) obtaining a PhD in Sociology of memory (University Paris VII—Jussieu). Her books and articles refer to collective memory, biographical method, qualitative research, especially on issues of gender equality and integration of socially excluded groups.

Calliope Tsantali
is English Language Teacher and a certified Adult Educator. She holds a degree in English Language and Literature from the Aristotle University of Thessaloniki. She completed her Postgraduate studies in Continuous Education and Lifelong Learning at the Open University of Cyprus. She is currently a Doctoral Candidate in Education Policy at the University of Western Macedonia. Her scientific interests focus on English Language Teaching Methodology, Adult Education, Technical and Vocational Education.

Joanna Tsiganou
is Director of Research at EKKE. She has been appointed as administrative and/or scientific director in many national and European research projects (more than 40) in the field of social institutions, law, crime and deviance, discrimination and social exclusion. She has been author and co-author of scientific journal articles and book chapters (more than 80) as well as of 26 books in Greek and English languages. She also teaches as invited professor at Panteion University, and Law School of Athens, post-graduate Studies in Criminology.

Vasilis Vamvakas
is Associate Professor at the department of Journalism and Mass Media of the Aristotle University of Thessaloniki. His research interests lie in the areas of sociology of communication, popular culture and political communication. Books in Greek: *Elections and communication in the post-dictatorship period. Politics and Spectacle*, Savalas, Athens; *Greece in the 80s. Social, political and cultural dictionary*, Epikentro, Thessaloniki (co-editor with Panayis Panayiotopoulos); *The discourse of the crisis*, Epikentro, Thessaloniki; *The American series in the Greek TV*, Papazisis, Athens (co-editor with A. Gazi).

Eleni Zyga
is PhD Candidate on Sociology of Media at the Sociology Department of the Panteion University of Social and Political Sciences, (Athens). She holds two master degrees on Social Exclusion and Human Rights (Panteion University, Athens) and on Health Informatics (National and Kapodistrian University of Athens).

CHAPTER 1

Frontiers and Identities in the Contemporary Media Storytelling

Christiana Constantopoulou

1   Why the "Narratives of the Crisis" Are Important to the Sociological Analysis?

Why a volume on ongoing "narratives" of the crisis (either in media discourse or in filmic creations) could be very interesting for the sociological analysis of the contemporary everyday life?

We should at first remind that narratives are present in all societies: in myths, legends, news, rumors, in historical and artistic texts, in politics, in everyday conversation; giving specific sense to the social "reality" they can thus construct it (Castoriadis 1975), in the sense that they provide a "frame" of understanding and of living in it. Since Durkheim (1915), collective representations (or "social representations" for S. Moscovici, 1960) were considered important as the beliefs which gave meaning to the "being together" in any society. As Roland Barthes suggested (1957; 1966) an important issue is to describe the code by which the "narrator" and the "reader" are signified in a narrative; in this sense, an "author" is not the one who invents a narrative but the one who possesses best the code used by the participants. The dominant social discourses are supposed to reveal what a society considers as "natural", as requiring no further explanation (the kind of usual perception which is called "common sense" and which is "normally" used by media). This kind of narrative coincides with the *social representations of the audience* and even if this is not always the case, the social subjects normally try to reduce the distance between the information received and their attitudes: strategies are thus elaborated in order to maintain a dominant way of thinking.

This is why narrative analysis can be fundamental for the social sciences, and especially for sociology (although the narrations are often assimilated to the "mythic discourse"). Yet, in a sociological perspective, *myths and mythology express a culture's worldview* (where symbols become dominant). Consequently, when the term "myth" is used in this volume, it is to describe dominant and interacting worldviews in the frame of globalization. Of course, this kind of secular myths are less sacred than the religious ones, although when social representations are involved the separations are not always possible (or relevant).

Stories are part of everyday life and constitute means for actors to express and negotiate experience. For researchers, they provide a site to examine the meanings people, individually or collectively, ascribe to lived experience. Narratives are not transparent renditions of "truth" but reflect a dynamic interplay between life, experience and the story. Placed in their wider socio-political and cultural contexts, stories can also provide insights into different social conditions (for instance how forced migrants seek to make sense of displacement and violence, re-establish identity in ruptured life courses and communities, or bear witness to violence and repression).

We should also remind that it is impossible to grasp the nature of conscious collective life in any epoch without an understanding of the material forms and processes through which its ideas were transmitted—the communication networks that enable thought to have a social existence. The works of many theoreticians insist on the *importance of the image* in the contemporary perception of the world. In this sense, R. Debray (1992) explains the collapse of the *graphosphere* which has forced it to pack up its weapons and join the *videosphere*, whose thought-networks are fatal for its culture. A practical example: to find out what is going on one has to watch TV, and so stay at home. The symbolic authority for the logosphere was the invisible; for the graphosphere, the printed word; for the videosphere, the visible; status of the individual: subject; citizen; consumer; maxim for personal authority: "God told me"; "I read it"; "I saw it on TV".[1]

---

1   Régis Debray (2007) explains: "the successive stages of development of these means and relations of transmission—whose ensemble we might term the mediasphere—suggest a new periodization for the history of ideas. First, what we may call the *logosphere:* that long period stretching from the invention of writing (and of clay tablets, papyrus, parchment scrolls) to the coming of the printing press. The age of the *logos*, but also that of theology, in which writing is, first and foremost, the inscription of the word of God, the "sacred carving" of the hieroglyph. God dictates, man transcribes—in the Bible or the Koran—and dictates in his turn. Reading is done aloud, in company; man's task is not to invent but to transmit received truths. A second period, the *graphosphere*, runs from 1448 to around 1968: from the Gutenberg Revolution to the rise of TV. The age of reason and of the book, of the newspaper and the political party. The poet or artist emerges as guarantor of truth, invention flourishes amid an abundance of written references; the image is subordinate to the text. The third, still expanding today, is the era of the *videosphere*: the age of the image, in which the book is knocked off its pedestal and the visible triumphs over the great invisibles—God, History, Progress—of the previous epochs. A bourgeois house arrest, for beneath "a man's home is his castle" there always lurks, "every man for himself". *The demobilization of the citizen begins with the physical immobilization of the spectator.* What further implications for social thought might we draw from the "three estates" of logosphere, graphosphere, videosphere—the

To the above analysis (which in a sense seems to join Mac Luhan's theory (1964), but without so much insisting on the technological factor) we could add that mass culture could be seen as a culture that homogenizes, standardizes, simplifies and sentimentalizes, producing myths and dreams of comfort, leisure, success, happiness and love, all of which were designed to integrate people into capitalist society associated with the power of cultural industries and their worldwide impact (according to the scholars of the Frankfurt School). E. Morin's (1956; 1962) touch to all this, was the interesting conclusion that mass culture created "heroes wearing sleepers" (meaning that any adventure could be "lived imaginarily" by the means of *viewing*); a "maxim" that made him the precursor of the analysts of the nowadays *virtual social participation* (particularly promoted by the so called social media); it is the mass culture that created the "mood" of pleasures taken by viewing, mood which seems to characterize the contemporary "consumers".

Associating the importance of "narratives" (as expressing the most meaningful social representations of the ongoing world), of the "videosphere" (the dominant recitative sphere nowadays) and of the impact of "cultural industries" conveying a kind of "modern" culture very similar to the mass culture as described above, we can understand the importance of media and filmic storytelling narrating a dominant social phenomenon: the economic crisis. As argued above, the symbolization of reality is the most important factor of "living together";[2] the crisis, described by the established media literature (in close relation with political discourses) had specific effects to the audiences, thus shaping their social reality; media and political discourses can be "understood" as parameters of the "rational explanation" of the contemporary "being together", leaving a big part of existence (such as feelings, insecurities or phobias in relation with the dominant "rationale") to the domain of art.

The phenomenon of the late economic crisis could be described (in "realistic economic terms") as the sudden collapse of the 150 years old banking house Lehman Brothers in 2008 which made a global "financial crisis" manifest that soon spiraled into the "Great Recession". United States homeowners saw real estate prices rise ever higher and could not resist bank advertisements to use their homes as a kind of cash-machine by taking out ever higher mortgages. Banks profited through fees and refinance-charges; their management

---

word, the press, the screen? It would be possible to tabulate a series of norms and functions inherent in any social collectivity, and map out the particular modes and forms that have answered to them in each successive age".

2   We remind that even in the beginning of the existence of Sociology as science, Emile Durkheim (1915) had analyzed "religion" (the belief to a common value) as the unifying factor of being together.

rewarded itself with ever higher pays and bonuses. They bundled mortgages into larger packages that were mixed and re-mixed according to complex formulas aimed at distributing risk. Mortgage derivatives were seen internationally as safe investment opportunities with high yields. The demand drove the lending banks to ever more aggressive marketing of credit, often with very low initial interest rates, called "teaser rates", but variable market rates afterwards. Subprime mortgages were given out without concern whether the borrower could actually afford the terms of repayment on their salaries. The credit bubble grew until it burst. Confidence was shaken, interest rates went up. Since missed mortgages carried variable interest rates, the monthly payments would go up and up, increasing to unsustainable levels, thus causing mortgage defaults. Entire neighborhoods in the u.s. were becoming empty as their previous owners were evicted.[3] So this economic crisis originated in the u.s. but quickly spread around the globe. The specter of imminent economic disaster was used to bail out financial institutions in an unprecedented spending spree while new austerity measures were imposed on European countries too. *The rhetoric of "crisis"* has been very much employed as the new explaining "rationale", used by media discourse creating the narratives of crisis as major world interpretations.

2   Media Narratives

Media reflect the contemporary society (dominant ideas on everyday issues: life, work, liberties, obligations, "politically correct"—or not—expressions). If we had to "describe" these dominant ideas conveyed by the media, we could remark that they are characterized (on the cognitive level) by some *profound contradictions*; these contradictions are mainly due to the kind of *absence of adequacy* between *social representations* (which are essentially diffused by *media discourse*) and the changing social reality (based on the "laws of the market"—practically overcoming the up to now binding liberal principles on human rights—declared in most modern constitutions). Nonetheless, these principles are still "valid" as central arguments shaping the communication (including the understanding and justification of the world, giving at the same time signs and symbols for the communication among humans on important issues such as the questions of identities and borders—which finally influence almost all the aspects of everyday life). Although a "plenitude" of information can be possibly given because of the technological potentialities, information remains (as always) politically selected worldwide and dominated by:

---

3   In this sense, Markus Schulz (2017).

(1)   The current *modern myths*: these myths, consider as "irrational" any discourse which differs from the technocratic point of view (which monopolizes the "correct" knowledge). Technocratic narrative takes the dominant discourse as the only "scientifically based" one. Many sociologists and analysts such as Jean Baudrillard,[4] Michel Foucault,[5] Edgar Morin (1999) or Lucien Sfez (1988) have already analyzed in detail this point concerning the reference to the "correct" knowledge (which is based on an ideology perceiving technology as an "independent" parameter in social dynamics). Other analysts like Pierre Bourdieu (1996) focusing on media discourse explain how it is based on a dominant way of thinking taken as undoubtable. We can give examples of the everyday agenda press analysis indicating this way of understanding reality by the mass audience of the "civilized world"[6] on essential definitions of "right" and "wrong", of "good" or "evil"; our world is given as modern and rational; nevertheless, if an analyst sees objectively the political statements

---

4   Jean Baudrillard (1974, 1981), argued that the excess of signs and of meaning in late 20th century "global" society had caused (quite paradoxically) an effacement of reality. In this world neither liberal nor Marxist utopias are any longer believed in. We live, he argued, not in a "global village", to use Marshall McLuhan's phrase, but rather in a world that is ever more easily petrified by even the smallest event. Because the "global" world operates at the level of the exchange of signs and commodities, it becomes ever blinder towards *symbolic* acts such as, for example, terrorism. He characterized the terrorist attacks on the World Trade Center in New York City as the "absolute event". Seeking to understand them as a reaction to the technological and political expansion of capitalist globalization, rather than as a war of religiously based or civilization-based warfare, For Baudrillard, the end of the Cold War did not represent an ideological victory; rather, it signaled the disappearance of utopian visions shared between both the political Right and Left. Giving further evidence of his opposition toward Marxist visions of global communism and liberal visions of global civil society, Baudrillard contended that the ends they hoped for had always been illusions; indeed, as *The Illusion of the End* argues, he thought the idea of an end itself was nothing more than a misguided dream: if there are no more dustbins of history, this is because History itself has become a dustbin. It has become its own dustbin, just as the planet itself is becoming its own dustbin.

5   Michel Foucault (1969) criticizes the notion that Reason is synonymous with truth and that it offers the solution to all social problems. He notes that repressive systems of social control are usually highly rational. The notions of rationality and irrationality, as they were posed by the Frankfurt School, became a fashionable topic of discussion in the late 1970s. In this context Foucault notes the dangers of describing Reason as the enemy and the equal danger of claiming that any criticism of rationality leads to irrationality.

6   For example, the journalistic current description of the January 2015 terrorist attack in Paris: when "we" are involved, the horror and the injustice towards "innocent victims" is projected; when it's about the "others", in the name of the "war" for democracy and human rights, no horror and no slaughter terms, are ever involved!

constituting the titles of the media, he/she can easily understand the part
of mythology and irrational belief of the different everyday stories.

(2)   Despite the generally indisputable technocratic rationality *a rather "fig-
       ural" than "discursive" way of signifying society becomes more and more
       "current"*:

(a)   *The virtual "emotion" becomes primordial.* In his famous and now "classi-
       cal" analysis of the mass culture, Edgar Morin (1956, 1962) explains that
       many social "activities" become "virtual" (it is the case of the "adventurers
       in sleepers"—people watching action films on TV—and of feelings cre-
       ated by fiction, e.g. the miseries of a poor child on screen and not by a
       poor child in the neighborhoods: thus the planet may "cry" on the loss of
       a refugee child shown in a reportage and not being aware on an eventual
       child abuse nearby). This "virtual social link" followed by "virtual solidar-
       ity" somehow characterizes the contemporary "globalized" society. Be-
       cause as Jean Duvignaud (1970) explained, human beings are "naturally
       dramatic" (in the sense that they need emotion), the part of emotion
       needed, is nowadays given by spectacle; spectacles sell better if they can
       provoke emotions and tears, and because our world is mostly narrated by
       televisual discourse, "emotion" often plays the dominant role (implying
       anger against the "bad other", fear of "invasion of savages", or lately—and
       because of the general acceptance of the importance of the "scientific
       explanation"—of a biological war due to covid-19); elementary myths of
       survival continue to be live in the frame of the "rational era".

(b)   *Cultural industries* contribute to the everyday "prosperity" based on the
       "western way of life"; nevertheless, this way of life, cannot easily include
       the criticism of *contemporary inequalities* (although the consumption of
       products showing "prestige" does not really signify an "ascension" to the
       "rich class", as remarked years ago Adorno and Horkheimer;[7] yet, this

---

7   The term "culture industry" (German: *Kulturindustrie*) was coined by the critical theorists
     Theodor Adorno and Max Horkheimer (1972), and was presented as critical vocabulary in the
     chapter "The Culture Industry: Enlightenment as Mass Deception", of the book *Dialectic of
     Enlightenment* (1944), wherein they proposed that popular culture is akin to a factory pro-
     ducing standardized cultural goods—films, radio programs, magazines, etc.—that are used
     to manipulate mass society into passivity. Consumption of the easy pleasures of popular cul-
     ture, made available by the mass communications media, renders people docile and content,
     no matter how difficult their economic circumstances. The inherent danger of the culture
     industry is the cultivation of false psychological needs that can only be met and satisfied
     by the products of capitalism; thus Adorno and Horkheimer especially perceived mass-
     produced culture as dangerous to the more technically and intellectually difficult high arts.
     In contrast, true psychological needs are freedom, creativity, and genuine happiness, which
     refer to an earlier demarcation of human needs, established by Herbert Marcuse (1966).

consumptions helps to attenuate the consciousness of the difference). We can easily understand the impact of this "life style", not only in the (mass and social) media narration but also in other narratives (as in serials,[8] or popular films) but also of their impact on "different" cultures worldwide.[9]

3   The Contemporary Rhetoric of Crisis

In this frame, it is not an exaggeration to claim that in 2015 the major headline news in European media were about the South European countries (called PIGS[10] by northern political discourse) and more specifically about the "Greek crisis" and the stand-off in negotiations between the Greek government, the troika of the European Commission (EC), the European Central Bank (ECB), and the International Monetary Fund (IMF). Many stories (and myths) appeared (mostly in the media, whose analyses are mostly quite schematic) interpreting the Southern "underdevelopment" and "incapacity" (with special reference to Greek decadence) to integrate the European Economic Project – the most essential element of the European Union Project. Stories (and myths) appeared in order to explain, "interpret" and sometimes "justify" obvious inequalities and reclassifications in the European society, not as an inevitable consequence (even necessity) of the global economic system (the crisis being the main growth factor of capitalism)[11] but as a local deficiency. Many issues

---

8   See for instance the lifestyle promoted in a famous American serial "Sex and the City" but also the influence of this lifestyle (accompanying "western archetypal women kinds") to a whole generation, since the nineties.

9   For instance, there are fashion shows for "veiled women" where the "modernity" does not by any means concern the liberation from the obligatory veil but the inclusion of the veil in modern lifestyle rules!.

10   From the acronyms Portugal, Italy, Greece, Spain.

11   As Bruno Péquignot (2017) explains: The use of the word crisis is recurring in the economic and political literature since, at least 19th Century, and occupies a central place among different frightening stories. Friedrich Engels and Karl Marx had already in 1847 used this word in order to make "fun" of it (Communist Manifest) as follows: "a ghost haunts Europe : the communist ghost". The powers of the old Europe were united in a "Holy Alliance" to hound this ghost. Then came the 1929 "crisis" and new stories emerged. And then again came the 1974 "crisis", known as "oil crisis", and then ... there is no end to the enumeration all these "crises", narrated by politics and media, justifying all political agendas, even causing fears, including the fear of "the end of capitalism". One of the foundations of these stories is the idea that crisis would be an "accident" in history, due eventually to overproduction, oil crisis, national debt, and so on. Relying on Karl Marx's analysis, we will try to show that in order to analyze political and media "crisis" narratives, we

(and "mythic versions") necessitate to be investigated in order to understand how these representations reflect the contemporary values and ideas. Contemporary narratives of different aspects of the "crisis" "reinvent reality" in terms related to "economic" or "political" aspects of the "power" and define relations among nations and in supranational organizations.

The narration of the crisis, apart the strict economic analyzes (but we know how much the economic analysis depends on ideology) has mobilized all the aspects of social storytelling during the last decade, and dominated the political and media discourse as well as the artistic creations; we should remind though that the artistic creations nowadays are primarily related to the cultural industries: it is not strange that as far as the artistic creations are concerned, even in a period of economic crisis (like the one lived in the European South), the audiences are not very "friendly" towards productions criticizing the social inequalities which reflected best the everyday life (but we will return to this point, later on, in the text below).

3.1   The Political Discourse in the European Media

The European Union is a central issue for European politics which had to affront the economic crisis as well as the immigrants' issue in the last decade; the flow of migrants (mainly Syrians because of the war but also from other neighboring countries) arriving from the Balkan route and the Mediterranean Sea, represents one of the most complicated humanitarian challenges in history; since 2011, with the beginning of the Syrian crisis and the Arab Springs, these flows have been increasing and have affected especially Greece and Italy. While the left wing of both countries is in favour of immigrants' accommodation, the right wing is against the opening of borders and strongly expresses its *disappointment in Europe* and its poor management of the accommodation and redistribution of migrants in the European territory. On this huge problem, strong economies (e.g. Germany) let the "countries of the frontiers" (for instance Greece and Italy) deal with practical accommodation details. The goal is to let the local authorities in the "frontier countries" observe the rules of choosing people who correspond to the demand of main d'oeuvre of the "central counties"; it is only these people who are allowed to travel towards the dreamed lands of Northern Europe. Despite the "humanitarian programs" migrants are kept in "hot spots" in bad conditions (overcrowded areas) and only few are "chosen" to escape misery. One can understand that the citizens of the

---

should use an alternate story, which is different to the story that presents the crisis as "accidental": and realize that "once upon a time there was a productive system whose main growth factor was 'crisis'".

"frontier lands" do not identify themselves as citizens of the European Union;[12] under these circumstances, and because of the lack of convincing oppositional discourses, the discourses on the crisis are vested with the old mantles of Right and Left jargons which: (1) are unable to describe the ongoing reality and/or (2) are unable to express an effective oppositional argumentation (which could really include "humanitarian" aspects without using any stereotypical slogans[13]); this is true for Italy and for Greece, as there is left and right radicalization in all Europe, not only in the televisual discourse but also in the "debates" in social media (which do not "have" to be "politically correct"); in social media, the "hate speech" decompresses but also at the same time destroys all the oppositional potentials; "hate speech and conspiracy theories were the basic means to try and keep connection to the vulgar, offensive and political incorrect discourse that gave extraordinary political influence in the public sphere of the debt crisis".[14]

On the issue of "identities" and "frontiers" the dominant discourse becomes thus ambiguous and disorienting. The European Unionist political ideologies embraced by most parties in the South of Europe only hid the geopolitical inequalities between "center" and "periphery"; the main argument of "being European" (a reassuring identity) "integrated" in the European family the European South which "integrated" the European South "separating" it from the "rest of the neighboring periphery" (the Arab and Muslim countries). In this frame, and although a political discourse could "express" this ambiguous situation (given the peripheral economic role of the European South), the Southern European political parties focused on the Right/Left radicalization, which in fact was oppositional only on issues that were not "central" as far as it concerned the historical situation. Thus, the economically "peripheral" countries like Greece, Italy or Spain, embraced the role of the "strong economic center" which included the clear separation from the "peripheral countries" (the "Others"—"underdeveloped" and/or Muslim people—who came to invade the European tranquility and who ought to remain at the—European—borders!). Apart the economic crisis, this situation created an identity crisis (Greece is an example) which was not at all included in the current political discourses. This lack, was "recompensed" by some fictional representations.[15] We have to notice that in modern societies, where reigns the ideological distinction of different

12   See A. Pretto and D. Marcucci's chapter, on this point.
13   "Langue de bois".
14   See V. Vamvakas's chapter in this volume.
15   For instance, in an extremely interesting work (Chapter 4) analyzing the relation between the ambiguity of the Greek national identity and the viewing of Turkish serials, Laurence Larochelle explains the importance of this kind of reference to the traditional values

ways of thinking in "rational" (such as science and politics) and "irrational" (such as religious, mythical, artistic, etc.) categories, when the "rational" discourses fail to make understand the social reality, other narratives can be successful (even if not considered as socially "plausible" and even if they differ from those belonging to the official versions of reasoning). This is why, the "storytelling" of popular shows is necessary to be taken under consideration in order to understand the issues of identities and borders (the relation to the "others" in time and in space).

3.2   Contemporary Storytelling in Popular TV Serials

As argued above, much of the weekly televisual schedule can be qualified as a myth (in the sense that it is generally "recognized" as a myth, which is not the case with the "official" storytelling). Westerns, thrillers and soap operas have a social function in our societies similar to that of myths among many non-industrial peoples (meaning that they reflect popular culture in relation with the contemporary everyday life in symbolic terms). Given that contemporary history demonstrates many characteristics of "hybridity", the definition of "identity" (being essentially "national" in modernity, roughly during the 18th, 19th and 20th centuries) changes.[16] What Jean-François Lyotard[17] (1979) had named "postmodern condition" is characterized by the coexistence of different "visions of reality"[18] and thus by a certain "hybridity" of thought; in this context we observe the deconstruction and reconstruction of "identities" all over the

---

      which better reflect the feeling of being peripheral—an argument almost inexistent from the official political discourses.

16   Certainly, the idea of "identity" as defined in the Western countries, being very much attached to a concrete "person" is very different from what "identification" meant in other societies; for instance, many anthropologists as Roger Bastide (1970) or Louis-Vincent Thomas (1982) had explained that in the traditional African societies a "person" was not distinguished from his/her society; under the Ottoman Empire, the notion of "family" was more powerful than the individuals constituting it, and the titles of nobility in France characterized a whole family during the period of "Ancien Régime".

17   For Lyotard, reality consists of singular events which cannot be represented accurately by rational theory; this fact has a deep political import, since politics claim to be based on accurate representations of reality. Lyotard's philosophy exhibits many of the major themes common to poststructuralist and postmodernist thought. He calls into question the powers of reason, asserts the importance of irrational forces such as sensations and emotions, rejects humanism and the traditional philosophical notion of the human being as the central subject of knowledge, champions heterogeneity and difference, and suggests that the understanding of society in terms of "progress" has been made obsolete by the scientific, technological, political and cultural changes of the late twentieth century.

18   Translation in English of the Greek word "Κοσμοθεωρία", or the German term *Weltanschauung*, which are more appropriate.

world incorporating many aspects of Western modernity and of show biz life style, while essential archetypes—of love, courage and success—continue to be strong, keeping their important place in the popular storytelling world-wide.[19] Especially during times of "crisis" (when insecurity becomes essential), the "narration" of presumed safe—or plausible as successful—values tries to interpret the traumatic reality either by means of reassuring myths or by means of contesting ones.

Thus, analyzes of TV serials during the period of economic crisis (dealing with successful stories conveyed by TV serial industries all over the world) have raised some essential identity issues which try to respond to questions unanswered by the "official" ("rational", "realistic", scientific or political) discourse. As far as it concerns this volume, three case studies reveal different aspects of the contemporary "mythology" (the imaginary of fiction) which deal with modern and traditional identities, the fusion of narratives from different cultures, the questioning of current values (such as the meaning of "goodness" or "badness").

More specifically: During the period of economic crisis, media narratives play a significant role in presenting the European society; as the crisis hit mostly the European South and especially Greece, the Greek attitude against the oppressive "West" (the ongoing American/North European economic supremacy) searching cultural elements opposite to it (the "Oriental" past under the Ottoman Empire) found many components of the tradition in the Turkish serials' storytelling. As a consequence of the hybridity of the modern-Greek identity,[20] especially during periods of crisis, a back and forth between these two traditions can be observed: *the viewing of Turkish soap operas is a symptom of the identity negotiation operated by a part of the Greek audience* during this period of financial crisis, despite the fact that Turkey is considered an "enemy nation" for modern Greece.[21]

---

19 Jean-Claude Kaufmann (1999) has explained this ambiguity of modern identities, analyzing the relation of modern women to the "romantic love": The number of one-person households is rising steeply all over the world and a growing proportion of these "new singles" are women. It is estimated that one woman in three lives on her own. This development reflects general social trends, ranging from rising divorce rates to the growing professionalization of women and their dissatisfaction with a traditional model that offers them a future organized solely around "husband–baby–home". At the same time, the attractions of that model still linger, and the fairytale prince is by no means a figure from a story or a remote past. Even in an age in which the internet promises that love is "just a click away", many women still wait for their prince to come.

20 Details of this hybridity are given in Chapter 4.

21 See L. Larochelle's chapter on soap operas.

Another important contemporary aspect is the "adaptation" of American (originally) cultural expressions in different cultures; the case study here, refers to the ability of South Korean culture and media industry to translate Western or American culture to fit Asian tastes something which is as a key-factor that explains the success of Hallyu in Eastern Europe;[22] it is considered as a possible "effective bridge or buffer functioning between the West and Asia"; the hybrid cultural products' consumption (American products "adaptation" and exportation of the "adapted" version by South Korea products, exported to the "West"[23]) is brought along not only by new consumption motivations (polyvalent) but also by new abilities to decode them (derived especially from the mix of media "genres" made possible through the technological and digital process). What is quite important is that the analysis of Hallyu' spread in Central and Eastern Europe could open the way towards new questions related to the appearance of a new "cultural identity" in the case of postmodern public for various cultural products. As identities are important (first of all because they create borders which define societies and affinities), the understanding of nowadays cultural identities could explain priorities and mobiles of action (we could then understand the nodal part played by the "inspiration" of "passive vigilance" or by "spiritual activities" in the internet forums, which leave the "corporal materiality" behind, in the same way explained half a century ago by Edgar Morin—op. cit.).

A third case study, concerns the serial "Breaking Bad"[24] trying to analyze the reasons of a successful story all over the world. Undoubtedly, this "story" shows how a genius professor and good father being in desperate need of money for health reasons, uses his intelligence to produce a "bad product" well sold all over the world, the only possibility to make much (and quick) profit. The market needs (even "illegal") seem to be the organizing agent for nearly all social, political, economic, and personal decisions. From one point of view the story seems to be a "critical reflection" of contemporary society: the power to contest injustice is a very appealing element in every storytelling (although belonging to the sphere of "fiction" and thus unable to find a role in political action). This reminds the anthropological "subversive rituals"[25] allowed during special

---

22   See V. Marinesu's chapter on the success of Hallyu in Easter Europe.
23   Although it is necessary to underline here, that (1) the American influence because transmitted by Korea is accepted more easily to ex-Eastern European countries (a fact that validates the idea that dominant discourses still take into consideration older divisions—such as West/East—which have no more the same meaning as in past years).
24   See A. Frangiskou's chapter in this volume.
25   As Georges Balandier (1967) explains so well for African traditional societies.

periods contesting the power but at the same time consolidating it. In the contemporary world, this function is very appealing in the popular storytelling (all
of our three case studies deal with aspects of this function). Thus, in these
terms, the global economic crisis has been attributed—even in technical
terms—to the totally uncontrolled financial system and to a speculative market driven by the "world money leaders" who have crossed the line regarding
the regulated rules of the game. In the story of "Breaking Bad", the real "bad",
are world money leaders! Market sovereignty, indolent wealth, unbridled
stockbrokers, ineffective politics, fragmented identities, meet together in a
"liquid world".

Liquidity and hybridity become the sustaining base of a universal popular
ideology (contesting the dominant one, and yet unable to make it taken seri-
ously, because of its simple categorization as "storytelling").

3.3   Films on Crisis: an Uneven Fight of Realistic Representations against Popular Fairytales

The filmic language has become dominant for the representation of western
everyday values and concerns in the 20th century, replacing the primordiality
of the romans of the 19th century. Yet, films with the bigger success are roughly
those who "advance" the archetypal fairytales: everlasting love, sudden change
of fate, miraculous subversion of a miserable reality, etc. Normally the "happy
end" is a very appealing factor (the aspect nearest to the fairytale) although
many times, the accordance of a myth with what is called "popular wisdom" is
also successful. This concerns for instance either the defeat of an honest hero
in an unequal social system or the fears against problems not or little taken
into consideration by the official discourses.[26]

The economic crisis was "represented" in European films: either in documentaries (such as those of Avgeropoulos on the "Agora"[27]) or in fiction very

---

26   Louis-Vincent Thomas in his very interesting analyses (1979, 1982, 1988) on Science-Fic-
      tion films (which he characterizes as the modern mythology) explains, how the fears of
      people about the bad effects of unthoughtful progress of technology (such as environ-
      mental disaster, the robotization of society, the inequality in front of illness and death,
      etc.) and the catastrophe of money accumulation against any other value, are expressed
      in films of "catastrophe" (showing desperately the extreme need to change quickly the
      "deadly" contemporary economic organization).
27   See Chapter 7.

much approaching reality.[28] There were also documentaries (for instance Matthew K. Firpo on the "Refuge Project"[29]) or protesting films.[30]

The common element in all these creations is the will to "wake up" people from the dominant culture promoting comfort for everybody. In this sense, we could analyze this kind of films as ways to inform (using the very powerful language of images) on aspects not "evident" in the dominant political discourses and at the same time as ways of "contestation" of the global (although considered as local) social inequalities.

Unfortunately, another common element is the "little success" these creations have to the audiences. Of course, when the question of audiences appears, the vicious circle of the powerful cultural industries (diffusing films all over the world) is revealed: cultural industries invest on productions which would have a sure success and audiences massively prefer the fairytale storytelling (not only because it is promoted by cultural industries' advertisement and because the rich productions are often very "spectacular"—"fairy"—but also because audiences seem to "need" fairytales after all—may be as their time to reverse reality in order to be able to live in it).

It is interesting to question the final remark in Chapter 10: could education "change" the contemporary viewing situation (as suggested by different writers but also the Information Resources Management Association?[31]). It is argued that the cinematic political discourse should be based on the educational discourse developed in formal education; new readings about democracy, globalized values and humanism should be enhanced by education. Therefore, this kind of cinematic discourse could be instrumentally integrated into teaching methods about democratic values in all educational grades. On this point, we could remark that: Of course, education provides skills in order to permit primarily young people to be well socialized embracing the values of modernity and promotes the scientific "objectivity" in order to make "understand" the world and the social system in which they would function at the end of the studies, giving social meaning to any specific knowledge. This thesis reminds that the provided knowledge also includes values and ethics more or less dominant (in accordance with the common sense).

The contemporary "turn" of the educational system (almost all over the world), in adequacy with the inspiration of modern science and technology,

---

28 As "The Law of the Market", film of Stephane Brizé, described in Chapter 8, or the five Greek films described in Chapter 9.

29 As analyzed in Chapter 10: Mathew Firpo "tells stories" about the largest worldwide forced migration since World War II.

30 "Survivor" is a short film produced in 2016 by Mazen Haj Kassem, a Syrian film director (this film is also described in Chapter 10).

31 Analysis in Chapter 10.

consists in becoming (1) particularly technical accentuating the value of digital skills and technological application (instead of critical theory) and (2) mostly unable to incorporate other ethical orientations apart the necessity to "be adapted" to the market leaving in this way behind (or just in schematic and insufficient approach) all the vital questions related to the existence (such as the meaning of friendship, of love, of feelings, of other needs than digital skills and mostly of the understanding that technocracy is only one possible paradigm of society and not a "divine law"); the "answers" of all these vital questions, young people can find nowadays in the media (including the new media) which narrate in a way or another the dominant common sense.

Is it possible to imagine an educational institution which would explain the relativeness of technocracy (introducing more critical theory in the program and softening the digital skills from their educational importance)? This is totally related to the political decision of permitting to citizens to be really "critical": utopic? May be (given the general frame and the different guidelines); but it seems as the only possibility to change the failure of school to "produce" thinking citizens. Yet, criticism or "humanitarian" values cannot be part of the educational program if they are not in accordance with the existing communicational system (because "education" only reflects the dominant values although many educators believe in its "capacity to change things").

Answering the question if education can change the contemporary viewing situation, we must underline that the popular culture determines the audiences' options and not the educational institutions (the school teaching is blocked between "what should be" and "what it is"—in other words the values taught differ from the everyday culture and young people understand this "gap").

Then, the sociological questions on this situation concern not only the low influence of "protest movies" (also called "qualitative" or experimental and apparently addressing only a very specialized "public") which have a rather "marginal" role (being unable to suggest subversive behaviors); they come also to concern what was suggested above on the influence of the mass culture, the insufficiency of political discourses to include different values and the quite general conviction that the need to change is impossible to be realized.

4   Identities and Frontiers in Modern Myths

The Greek example seems to be a good one: in 2008 (government of "Nea Dimokratia"—of the so called "right" inspiration) crisis was foreseen in Europe (and people suffered economically). G. Papandreou (Center) had promoted the slogan "money exists" (meaning that the government did not manage well the distribution); he was elected and no change was brought (guiding Greece under International Monetary Fund's supervision); governments of coalition were "elected" under this supervision, taking extreme measures of austerity. The results are known:[32] unemployment, suicides, poverty were evident. As a reaction, Greeks voted for "Suriza" (a party belonging to the "communist" tradition[33]) claiming independence from the European Union (most specifically the German) oppression: elected in January 2015 this party too imposed a Memorandum with very austere conditions, in July 2015. After this outcome, the "belief" to a possible political change becomes less and less probable, verifying the popular attitude of unwillingness to fight "from the low".

The general "frame" reflects the following issues (characterizing the current mentalities and attitudes): The ongoing political insufficiency as far as it concerns (1) urgent social needs[34] (apart the ones dictated by the laws of the market) and (2) an appropriate language to describe the ongoing reality. The political antagonism may be brutal but remains "superficial" towards the important aspects of social organization (remaining essentially the same with one political side or the other).

On the other hand, we can observe popular mistrust in the capacity of politics to "change things" and much despair due to the official narratives describing the ongoing reality, because of the lack of satisfactory explanations.

It is quite revealing to observe the Covid-19 political measures all over the world and the accompanying literature (arguments in favor of the "confinement at home", the prohibition of meetings, the discourage of human contacts without mask, gloves, antiseptic, restrain to the absolute necessary transports, necessary distance of two meters from one person to another; an initial guideline that a mask is not necessary if one is healthy because it does not really protect changed to the guideline of "obligatory wear of mask" when the market

---

32   In 2016 and 2017, we have also published 3 different volumes (in English, French and Greek) on the Greek crisis (see references); of course they are not the only ones.

33   Greece is a very special case: after the Second World War and the repartition of the Balkans under the influence of the United States and the Soviet Union, Greece was (after a terrible Civil war) the only state belonging to the "American" alliance (and NATO). Because Greek communists felt that the Soviet Union had "sold" them, the communist party was divided (pro-soviet, faithful to Moscow and pro-Greek, opting for a kind of national independence). The Greek communist parties were illegal roughly up to the end of the Military Dictatorship. Suriza is the "descendant" of the "pro-national" communist party!

34   Such as the (dangerous for humans as well for life in general in the planet), climate change, major inequalities towards health, growing inequalities among countries of North and South, etc.; these issues only grow despite the different measures taken by governments and dictated by international organizations.

had the possibility to sell them in a sufficient quantity). The main "justification" of all this ambiguous information is the argument that "this virus is very new, we don't have sufficient knowledge on it, data can change from one moment to the other because of new research results". Of course, when information is not sufficient, rumors become dominant[35] and people are wondering if this collection of restrictions is not dictated by political and economic power to easily construct docile people ready to be electronically spied all the time and be kept "prisoners".

On this aspect, Jeanne Wolff Bernstein[36] wrote an interesting essay[37] that runs roughly as follows: "there is not any appropriate language to describe the Corona virus pandemic which determines the contemporary political measures almost all over the world. How can we find an appropriate language when there is so much human misery and death during global pandemic? In order to find a language, a symbolic system, to grasp linguistically the Real and to integrate the current catastrophe, Jeanne Wolff Bernstein questioned how Sigmund Freud himself, at the beginning of the last century, might have reacted to the then extremely devastating pandemic of the Spanish flu, and how he might have integrated it into his own writings. In contrast to today's Covid-19 pandemic, Freud seems to have viewed the Spanish influenza as a difficult, but less prominent "side-show" (Nebenschauplatz) in light of all the other hardships and fatalities he had had to endure. There are innumerable parallels between the Spanish influenza and today's pandemic, starting with the symptoms and the course of the disease.

Europe does not even consider itself able to help the few thousands of refugees who have to remain in Greek refugee camps to flee the Syrian war. We are not fighting famine (yet), our chances of survival are far higher than in the 1920s thanks to newly acquired safety measures and to newly found medicines and vaccinations which may be on their way in the coming year.

The difference between those who died in the pandemic and those who died of other reasons cannot always be distinguished. In addition, human-staged death—like a war that could be avoided—would require a more complex analysis of human lust/unwillingness to use violence, in contrast to the consequences of an invisible pandemic, which renders one relatively helpless and frightened by the unknown. Freud's words "si vis vitam, para mortem—if

---

35   As indicated long ago by Jean-Noël Kapferer (1987).

36   Dr. Jeanne Wolff Bernstein is chairwoman of the advisory board of the Sigmund Freud Foundation.

37   Entitled "THE SPANISH FLU, COVID-19 AND SIGMUND FREUD What can we learn from history?".

you want to endure life, prepare yourself for death" seem then appropriate to decompress the phobia we live in (Freud 1915: 355)."

This text could be qualified as "simplifying" (because it does not follow a dominant rationale but a rather "premodern" way of thinking which takes into consideration human "materiality" and mortality—parameters which are ideologically rejected from the prevailing "progressive" thought—the dominant contemporary way of thinking which deifies technology and science). This does not mean of course that humanity does not have to fight for better life conditions: on the contrary, the necessity is to recognize the "physical" part of any human being (implying necessarily death) and to overrun the huge inequalities in front of health and in front of death in the planet. For hundreds of years, death was a part of life for human societies; when modernity replaced gods by science, the western imaginary privileged the image of "mastery" of this fatality; this image is so strong that somehow overshadows the existence of death (which remains extremely dominant—as some kind of counter balance—in rumors and art creations). This is the reason why these creations are sometimes more eloquent than the rationalized discourses of everyday life: this could also explain why documentaries showing how deadly the contemporary society is, are weaker to express this fact, compared to the popular shows of the TV series and spectacular films of the show biz. An element which seemed very important in premodern societies' beliefs, is the factor of "fate" in the sense of "chance". Erving Goffmann, with his "game theory" tried to explain that this factor (in strategic terms) can always be possible for human relations (which cannot be totally planned) and thus for societies.

These aspects of the present-day expressions seem major for the analysis of the contemporary societies. The texts in this volume try to question some of them (resulting mainly after the economic crisis felt particularly in the South of Europe) related to reshaped identities and frontiers. But it is challenging to analyze how forthcoming new realities can last, vested with old myths (narratives); of course history has shown that myths often remain powerful even if "realities" change.

Bibliography

Balandier, Georges. (1967). *Anthropologie Politique*. Paris: PUF.

Barthes, Roland. (1957). *Mythologies*. Paris: Seuil.

Barthes, Roland. (1966). "Introduction à l'analyse structurale des récits". *Communications* 8: 1–27.

Bastide, Roger. (1970). *Le prochain et le lointain.* Paris: Cujas.

Baudrillard, Jean. (1974). *La société de consummation.* Paris: Gallimard.

Baudrillard, Jean. (1981). *Simulacres et Simulation.* Paris: Galilée.

Castoriadis, Cornelius. (1975). *L'institution imaginaire de la société.* Paris: Seuil.

Constantopoulou, Christiana (ed.). (2012). *Barbaries Contemporaines.* Paris: L'Harmattan.

Constantopoulou, Christiana. (2016). "Narratives of the Crisis". *French Journal for Media Research* 5/2016. http://frenchjournalformediaresearch.com/lodel-1.0/main/index.php?id=613.

Constantopoulou, Christiana. (2017). *Récits de la crise, mythes et réalités de la société contemporaine.* Paris: L'Harmattan.

Debray, Régis. (1992). *Vie et mort de l'image, une histoire du regard en Occident.* Paris: Gallimard.

Durkheim, Émile. (1915). *Les formes élémentaires de la vie religieuse.* Paris.

Duvignaud, Jean. (1970). *Spectacles et sociétés.* Paris: Denoël.

Foucault, Michel. (1969). *L'archéologie du savoir.* Paris: Gallimard.

Freud, Sigmund. (1915). "Thoughts for the Times of War and Death". *The Standard Edition of the Complete Psychological Works of Sigmund Freud*, Volume XIV: 273–302.

Goffman, Erving. (1969). *Strategic Interaction.* University of Pennsylvania Press.

Horkheimer, Max and Adorno, Theodor. (1972). *Dialectic of Enlightenment.* New York: Herder & Herder.

Kapferer, Jean-Noël. (1987). *Rumeurs : le plus vieux média du monde.* Paris: Seuil.

Kaufmann, Jean-Claude. (1999). *La femme seule et le prince charmant.* Paris: Nathan Pocket.

Lyotard, Jean-François. (1979). *La condition postmoderne.* Paris: Éditions de Minuit.

McLuhan, Marshall. (1964). *Understanding Media, the Extensions of Man.* Mc Graw Hill.

Marcuse, Herbert. (1966). *Eros and Civilization, a Philosophical Inquiry into Freud.* Boston: Beacon Press.

Morin, Edgar. (1956). *Le cinéma ou l'homme imaginaire.* Paris: Éditions de Minuit.

Morin, Edgar. (1962). *L'esprit du temps.* Paris: Grasset Fasquelle.

Morin, Edgar. (1999). *Relier les connaissances.* Paris: Seuil.

Moscovici, Serge. (1960). *Étude sur la représentation sociale de la psychanalyse.* Paris: PUF.

Péquignot, Bruno. (2017). "Un récit pour faire peur : la crise du capitalisme". In Christiana Constantopoulou (ed.). *Récits de la Crise, mythes et réalité de la société contemporaine.* Paris: L'Harmattan, pp. 39–50.

Schulz, Markus. (2017). "La crise et les politiques de l'avenir". Preface in Christiana Constantopoulou (ed.). *Récits de la Crise, mythes et réalité de la société contemporaine.* Paris: L'Harmattan, pp. 9–19.

Sfez, Lucien. (1988). *Critique de la Communication.* Paris: Seuil.

Thomas, Louis-Vincent. (1979). *Civilisation et Divagations.* Paris: Payot.

Thomas, Louis-Vincent. (1982). *La mort africaine, idéologie funéraire en Afrique Noire.* Paris: Payot.

Thomas, Louis-Vincent. (1988). *Anthropologie des Obsessions.* Paris: L'Harmattan.

CHAPTER 2

The Value Image of Europe through Images

Albertina Pretto and Debora Marcucci

1   What Is Europe?[1]

The research study presented in this chapter focuses on the image of Europe which this entity transmits to European citizens based on some specific values and the image that Italian citizens have of Europe. This ongoing study has been conducted using a particular type of narrative analysis focused mainly on images rather than texts.

The ties that individuals feel towards communities and places in which they live are a relevant issue for many academic disciplines (e.g. Low and Altman 1992; Giuliani 2003; Scannell and Gifford 2010) and are analyzed on different territorial levels (Lewicka 2011a). This theme is even more crucial in this era, which is characterized by strong instability (Tomaney 2015) that consequently seems to intensify in people the need to belong to a certain place (Tizon 1996; Savage, Bagnall, and Longhurst 2005). With the development of postmodernity, globalization, and consequently, internationalization of markets, migrations, urbanization, and creation of new technologies, socio-territorial units tend to multiply, intersect and combine into larger entities. As a consequence, the territorial social structures also grow and become more articulated (Faludi 2013), so that the ties that people feel towards them become more complex to define and understand (Gubert 2000).

All the more, in the case of the ties that people feel (or not) towards Europe, these are affected not only by the economic and political issues (Lewicka 2011b) but also by the set of values that this supranational entity intends to advocate. As Scriven and Roberts (2001) suggest, it is necessary to remember that people tend to identify Europe through its prevailing institution, i.e. the European Union (EU). The EU is at present an economic and political institution of twenty-seven countries, and was incepted in 1951, the year in which Belgium, France, West Germany, Italy, Luxembourg, and the Netherlands

---

1   This paper is the result of the constant exchange of views between the authors; specifically, pars. 1 and 4 were written by Albertina Pretto, whereas pars. 2 and 3 were written by Albertina Pretto in collaboration with Debora Marcucci.

established the European Coal and Steel Community. Its path proceeded with the creation of the European Economic Community and later these projects were integrated and developed in 1992 through the foundation of the present EU, giving to Europe also political and institutional power to create a network of relationships among internal and external countries, in trying to guarantee peace and prosperity.

Thanks to these dynamic processes, Europe has continued to transform also as a territorial space: it has grown exponentially, in particular after the expansion in 2004 during which the EU opened towards the eastern part of the European continent. Nevertheless, after the accession of Croatia in 2013, this expansion process seems to have ceased (many candidate countries are waiting to enter the EU: Turkey since 2005, Montenegro since 2008, Macedonia and Albania since 2009, Serbia since 2014) or even inverted in view of the Brexit.

The parameters and procedures to access membership and remain in the EU entail countries taking radical paths and changes. But numerous benefits are also acquired because becoming a Member State means being part of a stable political system able to face the global market. So, in order to obtain EU membership, countries must attain and observe the so-called Copenhagen criteria related to political and economic standards and conditions concerning, for instance, democracy, and financial and monetary issues.

However, the European geopolitical and economic project is not based solely on power dynamics and the network of relationships which derives from it: Europe is also a wide value and symbolic container, well-defined since the dawn of the European Community (Rovisco 2010; Triandafyllidou and Gropas 2015). Indeed, the EU requirements do not only concern economic or political issues but also the ones related to values: to cite only some, countries have to pay attention and guarantee respect for minority and human rights. Thus, to be part of Europe, these values—and the symbols representing them—must be accepted and respected by the Member States and all citizens.

Since values drive social action, they are embedded in a dimension that is wider than the individual one: in fact, already at the beginning of the previous century, Weber (1904–1905; 1922) assigned values with a normative connotation, as they were considered as essential in orienting and addressing choices and behaviors of a society and its members. According to Weber (1904–1905), values are so integrated in the social fabric that they even contribute to the economic success of a society and/or organization; an example is the importance given to work as a value by the Calvinist Protestants who, over time, determined the success of the capitalist economy model (Pretto 2019). Therefore, the existence of Europe is based also on values and symbols which it creates and promotes (Lehning 2001; Tselios and Tomaney 2019).

Every community incorporates its own values in a symbolic pattern which constitutes cultural loyalty, the second dimension of the model of socio-territorial belonging (Pretto 2018). Some authors (e.g. Parsons 1959; Pollini 2005; Pretto and Battello 2016) describe the analytical system of belonging as constituted by four dimensions: attachment, cultural loyalty, institutionalized solidarity, and sense of affinity (see Figure 2.1).

Attachment is a form of subjective investment in a social object that, besides being identified with community, can also refer to territory (Lewicka 2005). To explain attachment, Parsons (1959) uses the Freudian notion of cathexis—that is, a long-lasting relation that individuals create with a social object being the source of gratification/deprivation.

When attachment is organized and structured into a symbolic pattern shared by the community, cultural loyalty arises. This dimension is the sphere in which the community assigns value and symbolic meanings to specific social and territorial elements (whether material or immaterial, natural or human), which make up the symbolic-cultural system (Pretto and Battello 2016). In other words, a social object becomes a symbol on the basis of the meaning that is attributed to it, and is consequentially, recognized, accepted, and shared by the community that refers to it (Pollini 2005).

Solidarity can be defined as the institutionalized integration of community, since inclination toward values and symbols created in the dimension of loyalty are transformed into institutionalized obligations in accordance with roles that individuals have in their community (Stjernø 2004). It distinguishes itself from loyalty because it entails that community-orientation converts this

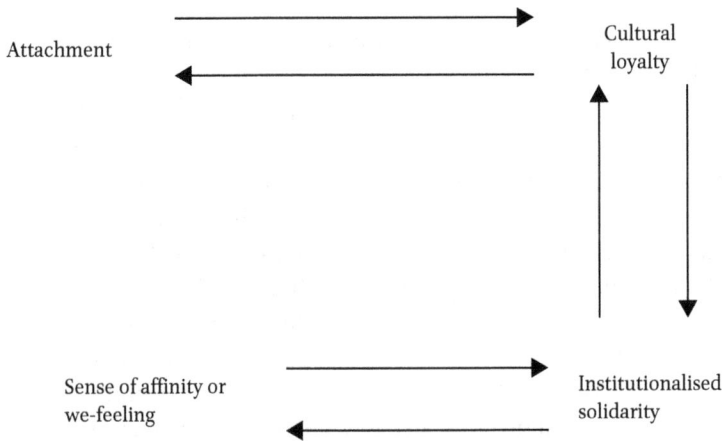

FIGURE 2.1   The analytical system of socio-territorial belonging.
OUR ELABORATION OF THE ORIGINAL POLLINI 2005

propensity into an institutionalized obligation of the role expectation. Then whether the actor "feels like it" or not, he/she is obliged to act in certain ways and risks the application of negative sanctions if he/she does not (Parsons 1959).

Finally, the sense of affinity (or we-feeling) is both the final outcome of attachment, loyalty, and solidarity and the dimension that controls and legitimizes the others and which therefore performs the function of holding the system of socio-territorial belonging together (Pollini 2005).

For the development of the willingness to belong to a socio-territorial unit like Europe, cultural loyalty is then particularly important because here, the relationship between the individuals and the social unit of which they are members is created and strengthened through the value and symbolic elements and their acknowledgement, acceptance and sharing.

Starting from these theoretical premises, our study tries to understand the symbols and values through which Europe defines and narrates itself and its way of acting. Furthermore, it investigates how these values and symbols are mediated in Italy by political parties and how they are received and reproduced by citizens as final recipients. In this way, the aim is to reflect on how these values and symbols contribute to the creation of a less remote image of Europe (Biebuyck and Rumford 2012; Immler and Sakkers 2014), which is able to strengthen the sense of belonging of Italians towards this supranational entity.

2   Methods and Materials

To examine the values of Europe, a narrative analysis using images, photos and cartoons has been conducted.

As Somers affirms (1994: 614), "narrative is an ontological condition of social life". Indeed, narrative is not only a fundamental tool to comprehend reality and social dynamics, but also one of the most effective devices through which individuals create and transmit meanings, since it is through narrative construction that they interpret their experience, opinions, knowledge and social and cultural interactions (Bruner 1990, 1996; Smith 2016). This is possible because the process and the product of narrative "do not just index a relation between words and between texts, but between text and social reality" (Franzosi 1998: 547). Narrative, then, both as a representation and reasoning device (Richardson 1995), enables individuals to know, understand and make sense of history and the social reality in which they live and, as a consequence, to establish and structure their own identities (Breheny and Stephens 2015) in relation to the interactions that happened and occur over time and in space (Somers 1994). Somers (1994) claims that these processes are valid also for organizations, institutions and states and calls these shared stories "public narratives".

Despite its important role, the narrative approach has not often been adopted in the different areas of social sciences—especially as a tool for analysis—because it is generally considered limitative and useful only for discursive, non-quantitative and non-explicative types of research (Somers 1994). However, in the last decades, it seems that interest towards narrative and narrative analysis is increasing and affects different areas of inquiry (Holley and Colyar 2009; Prior 2014).

Considering what is affirmed by some authors (e.g. Clandinin and Connelly 2000; Holley and Colyar 2009; Prior 2014), three are the constitutive elements of narrative analysis:
- chronology: divides a narrative into three parts, beginning, middle and end;
- plot: brings together and adapts heterogeneous factors such as goals, means, interactions, events, circumstances, etc., and is a "synthesis of the heterogeneous" (Ricoeur 1984: 66) because it harmonizes, puts in relation and incorporates events, causes, choices and aims in a temporal unit of a whole action (Cobley 2001);
- characters: are most commonly thought as individuals, but they can be considered in much broader terms (a party, a government, an organization and so on) and in relation to the functions that they fulfil within a story.

Narratives can be transmitted in different ways: the stories and their meanings are told through words, images, movements, sounds or even combinations of these different elements (Breheny and Stephens 2015) and, for this reason, Keats (2009) describes how to carry out a narrative analysis not only for oral and written texts, but also for visual ones. After all, images are everywhere in modern and postmodern societies: they are an integral and fundamental part of daily practices, collective visual conscience and culture (Jenks 1995; Dahmen, Mielczarek, and Morrison 2019). Thanks to their persuasiveness and easy memorization, they represent and simplify reality, facilitate the processes of understanding, analysis and interpretation of more complex and articulated concepts and models (Harper 1998; Earnest and Fish 2014), and consequently convey meanings of the social world that are etched in people's mind even more than words (Ewbank et al. 2009; Corrigall-Brown 2012; Pretto 2018). Furthermore, images, being the result of negotiation between their production and their interpretation, are in actual fact a social and cultural construct (Burri 2012). In other words, images represent and reflect attitudes, values and beliefs of the society in a broader sense, the perspective of the creator and the idea and interpretation of the observer (Foss 1992; Meidani 2015).

Because of their diffusion and characteristics, images become fully part also of the field of social sciences: about fifteen years ago Clark-Ibáñez (2004) wrote that the Sociological Abstracts database contained one hundred forty studies which mentioned the keyword "photo" in their abstract, eighty of which used photographs as an integral part of the study. Ten years later the Sociological Abstracts database contained more than a thousand publications that included the keyword "photo" in their abstract (Pretto 2015). These simple figures can confirm the importance that images have acquired in social research.

However, one should not erroneously think that images are only photographs. The same previous considerations are valid—and perhaps even more so—also for cartoons. The strength and meanings of cartoons are carried not only by the message that the author wants to transmit, but also, and especially, through the way in which they are actively perceived and understood by people (Meidani 2015). As affirmed by Caswell (2004: 14), they are, in actual fact, "both opinion-molding and opinion-reflecting". Then, the analysis of cartoons within social sciences can be fundamental to comprehend individual opinions and attitudes (Kasen 1980; Brabant and Mooney 1999), social structures (LaRossa et al. 2000), and cultural models (Chavez 1985; Brabant and Mooney 1999).

On the basis of these premises, a study on images, photos, and cartoons of different sources has been carried out in order to identify and analyze values and symbols that are narrated by the EU and their reception and interpretation in the Italian context. We have been using narrative analysis considering its three key points:

- chronology: we consider the moment when a given symbol or value appeared in a European communication as the beginning, the diffusion or increasing of that communication as the middle, and the view of Italian citizens on the same topic as the end;
- plot: we analyse it on the basis of events, politics or policies that took place in the world, Europe or Italy, and that influenced communication of Europe on specific topics;
- characters: we consider the EU as the first communicator and vehicle of specific values and symbols, the Italian political parties seen as mediators of this communication and the Italian citizens as recipients who, in turn, communicate their own view on Europe.

To do this, we have been working on the official websites, Instagram and Facebook profiles of the EU and its institutions, and of the Italian political parties. And for the Italian citizens' point of view, we have been examining the cartoons they created for competitions reserved for these types of images, such as "Una vignetta per l'Europa" (A cartoon for Europe) and their various editions, organized throughout the years by the Representation of the European

Commission in Italy in collaboration with the *Internazionale* magazine, and the participation of *VoxEurop* (a European news and debate website). The aim of these contests was to make professional and amateur cartoonists illustrate Europe and issues that involved it; citizens could vote for the cartoon they considered the most representative in relation to a specific theme.

3   Symbols and Values

On the EU official website, the Euro is defined as the most concrete evidence of European integration: being used every day by more than 340 million people, it is the second most-used currency in the world. Its benefits are clear and tangible, for example in relation to travelling and shopping—even online commerce—in other EU countries (European Union 2020a). The EU regards the Euro as a symbol, but it is not exactly the case. In reality, some Member States (Bulgaria, Croatia, Czech Republic, Poland, Sweden, and Hungary) still have not adopted the single currency, even if they will be joining the Euro area once the required conditions have been met. Furthermore, albeit occasionally, Member States can negotiate a non-participation clause for parts of the EU legislation or treaties and agree not to join certain sectors and domains as, for example, the single currency. This is the case of Denmark, which has kept its national currency after becoming an EU Member (European Union 2020a) and even the United Kingdom, while still a Member State, continued to use the pound sterling. In addition to this, in 2002, the year in which the Euro entered into circulation, the sense of attachment European citizens felt towards Europe suffered a strong decrease (Antonsich and Holland 2014). Even if it is widely recognized, the Euro is actually not accepted and shared by all EU States and citizens and, therefore, according to literature (see e.g. Pollini 2005), it cannot be considered a symbol. As a matter of fact, it is rarely used in images created by Italian political parties and cartoonists.

Currently, the only European element recognized, accepted and shared everywhere seems to be the blue flag with the yellow stars, which was created in 1955 when the Council of Europe, engaged in the defense of human rights and promotion of European culture, chose its configuration and design, which are at present still maintained. In the 1980s, the European Parliament decided that the flag already adopted by the Council of Europe should be the emblem of the European Community, later to become the EU. On the EU website, it is claimed that the flag represents the unity and identity of Europe in general and that the circle of twelve yellow stars on a blue background symbolizes the values of unity, solidarity, and harmony among peoples of Europe (European Union

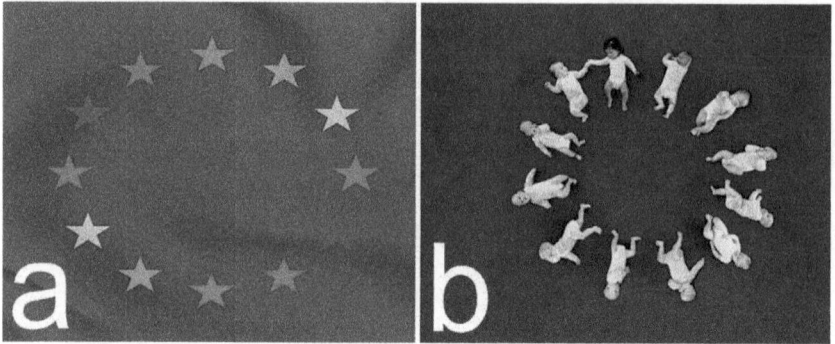

FIGURE 2.2 The European flag. On the left (a), the flag with LGBT-colors, 2017; on the right (b), the flag with the Erasmus babies, 2017.

NOTES: THE IMAGE WAS PUBLISHED BY THE EUROPEAN COMMISSION ON ITS FACEBOOK PROFILE (@EUROPEANCOMMISSION, 17 MAY 2017). AVAILABLE AT: HTTPS://WWW.FACEBOOK.COM/EUROPEANCOMMISSION/ PHOTOS/A.169236379790517/1381804995200310/?TYPE=3&THEATER; THE IMAGE WAS PUBLISHED BY THE EUROPEAN COMMISSION ON ITS INSTAGRAM PROFILE (@EUROPEANCOMMISSION, 13 JUNE 2017). AVAILABLE AT: HTTPS:// WWW.INSTAGRAM.COM/P/BVR7ENBDSEF/.

2020b). So, the flag or its colors or its stars are used by the EU to represent and spread different values and related projects which this entity wants to promote and/or support. For instance, as we can see in Figure 2.2,[2] it is used (with appropriate graphic modifications) to affirm its strong commitment to the equality and dignity of all human beings irrespective of their sexual orientation and gender identity (coloring the stars with the rainbow of the LGBT flag, see Figure 2.2a) and to celebrate the million babies born to couples who met while on Erasmus[3] during the thirty years of the program (depicting twelve babies instead of the stars, see Figure 2.2b).

Considering that the websites of the EU and its institutions were created in the mid-2000s, followed by the Facebook and Instagram profiles in the 2010s, one can note that at the beginning of this online communication, the flag was not used symbolically as often as in the last five years. Before the creation of the social profiles, the flag appeared above all as a stylized symbol which

---

2 All images taken from EU websites and profiles and used in this paper are offered free of charge for EU-related information and educational purposes. Available at: https://audio visual.ec.europa.eu/en/copyright.

3 Being a synthesis of seven previous programmes, the present Erasmus+ programme addresses a wide range of people and organizations in order to offer European citizens the opportunity to study, train, acquire experience, and do volunteer work in the EU countries (European Commission n.d.).

marked the homepage and the publications of the European Commission. In the 2000s, the emblem was mainly depicted through photos which accompanied written texts referring to the general values of the EU. In more recent years (and as can be seen in Figure 2.2), the flag has been subject to numerous graphic modifications and creative representations and the circle of stars has been often associated with and/or replaced by other elements that draw attention to particular topics, anniversaries, awareness campaigns, and so on.

As shown below, also in the communication of the Italian parties as well as in the citizens' cartoons, the flag, its stars or colors are often used symbolically to represent the EU and to express orientations, ideas, and opinions on European policies and the actions of the Member States and of the EU itself. With regard to the images created and spread by the Italian parties, we must specify that in this paper they will only be described. Despite the fact that we contacted several parties of both the left wing (left and center-left) and the right wing (right and center-right) by email and by telephone in order to use some of their images, nobody gave us permission to publish them. Refusals (and non-responses) were not motivated.

Focusing on values, we could say that unity and solidarity have always been what the EU tries to promote the most.

The value of unity is well summarized in the EU motto "United in Diversity" adopted since 2000. However, the unity of Europe is not a simple matter since, to make it real, the EU must be able to make people and countries, often very different from each other, feel tied. Thus, for this unity to be fully achieved, it is not sufficient that people perceive themselves as merely retaining rights and fulfilling obligations, but citizens should also recognize themselves as such, acquiring awareness of belonging to a supranational entity and feeling united in a common identity, which is not so simple considering the diversities of the EU Member States (Lehning 2001; Tselios and Tomaney 2019). Europe, as an entity whose existence is founded on the value of unity, has always created and published images aimed at communicating and spreading it, as can be seen in Figure 2.3, below. Since 2006, year in which the European Commission website was opened, the unity of Europe is narrated mainly through objectives accomplished or goals to be achieved, focusing on the importance and advantages of being together: together as regards free travels, climate, human rights, battle against racism, and so on.

In analyzing the images and narratives produced and communicated by Italian political parties, we can notice that, similarly to other European countries, the value of unity is seen from two different points of view. On the one hand, the left wing is favorable to Europe and tends to underline the advantages that derive from being a Member State. For instance, in the period of the

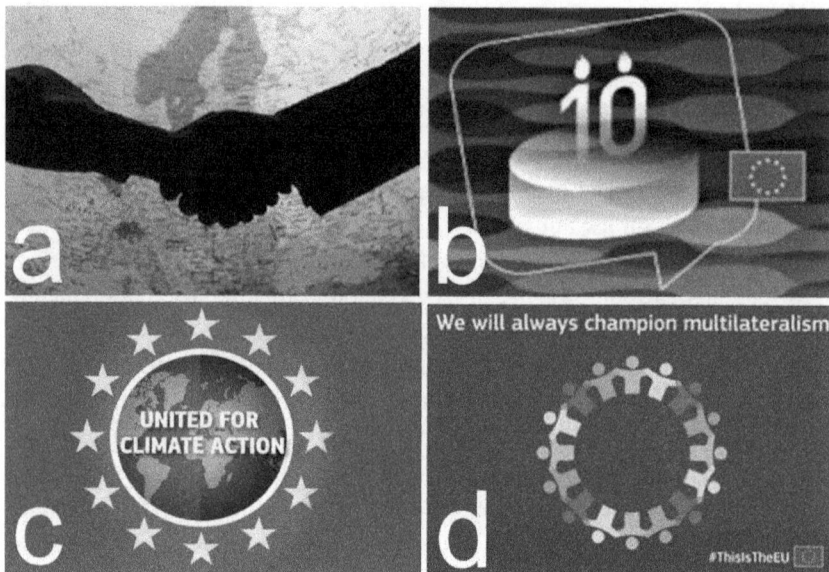

FIGURE 2.3 The EU value of unity. At the top left (a), shaking hands for the diplomatic protection of EU citizens outside the EU, 2006; at the top right (b), the celebration of the 10th European Day of Languages, 2011; at the bottom left (c), united for the climate, 2019; at the bottom right (d), united for multilateralism, 2019.

NOTES: THE IMAGE WAS PUBLISHED BY THE EUROPEAN COMMISSION ON ITS OFFICIAL WEBSITE (EUROPEAN COMMISSION, 30 NOVEMBER 2006) AND IS RETRIEVED FROM AN INTERNET ARCHIVE. AVAILABLE AT: HTTPS://WEB. ARCHIVE.ORG/WEB/20070410062245/HTTP://EC.EUROPA.EU/NEWS/ JUSTICE/061130_1_IT.HTM; THE IMAGE WAS PUBLISHED BY THE EU ON ITS OFFICIAL WEBSITE (EUROPEAN UNION, 11 OCTOBER 2011) AND IS RETRIEVED FROM AN INTERNET ARCHIVE. AVAILABLE AT: HTTPS://WEB.ARCHIVE.ORG/ WEB/20111215194506/HTTP://EC.EUROPA.EU/LANGUAGES/NEWS/20110912- EDL2011_IT.HTM; THE IMAGE WAS PUBLISHED BY THE EUROPEAN COMMIS- SION ON ITS INSTAGRAM PROFILE (@EUROPEANCOMMISSION, 19 FEBRUARY 2019). AVAILABLE AT: HTTPS://WWW.INSTAGRAM.COM/P/BUEIFTSAVJN/; THE IMAGE WAS PUBLISHED BY THE EUROPEAN COMMISSION ON ITS INSTAGRAM PROFILE (@EUROPEANCOMMISSION, 15 AUGUST 2019). AVAILABLE AT: HTTPS://WWW.INSTAGRAM.COM/P/B1LLP5QH928/

European elections in May 2019, *La Repubblica* (an Italian center-left oriented newspaper) urged its readers to vote, promoting an image of a united and protective Europe. The well-known cartoonist, Altan, who has been publishing his works in this newspaper for many years, created for that occasion a cartoon in which a man standing in front of a ballot box marked with the European flag

says "Remember folks, Europe is always Europe, just like a mother", paraphras-
ing a traditional Italian idiom.[4]

On the other hand, the right wing underlines the negative effects of belonging to Europe, highlighting its dominant position especially over economy, culture, and the general well-being of Italy and Italians. On the occasion of the
2019 European elections, the leader of *Lega* (an Italian center-right political
party), Matteo Salvini, blamed the pro-European position of the left wing and
reaffirmed the predominance of Italy as a sovereign state over Europe. The slogan used to narrate this position was "For the left more Europe, for us more Italy", accompanied by an image of an Italian flag covering the European one.[5]

We believe that this political dualism and the communication of the right-
wing parties have an influence on the opinions and sense of belonging that the
Italians feel towards Europe even beyond individual political orientations. Indeed, in the cartoons presented and voted for in the examined contests, the
position of Italy within the EU context is often perceived and illustrated as
subdued to other nations. Moreover, the unity of Europe is represented as a
problematic issue and, according to the winning cartoon of the 2012 edition of
"Una vignetta per l'Europa" drawn by Agim Sulaj, this is due to the lack of agreement among European countries: in Figure 2.4, some EU States are represented
through their heads of government who, wanting to prevail, row against each
other on the same raft and, in doing so, they do not go in any direction.

According to the cartoonists, this problem has further intensified through
the construction of walls—both symbolic and physical—in Europe: walls hin-
der dialogue and collaboration and, rather than unifying, create both internal
and external divisions. Considering that 2015 was the year in which most of the
present European walls were built (Akkermann 2019), it is no surprise if in the
2016 editions of the contests[6] the theme of the wall was taken up by many
cartoonists. For example, Carlo Casaburi in *"Bende"* (Blindfolds) represents
Europe as a woman with her eyes blindfolded with a brick-patterned cloth.[7]

---

4   The cartoon was published by *La Repubblica* on its Facebook profile (@Repubblica, 26 May
    2019). Available at: https://www.facebook.com/Repubblica/photos/a.196989226150/10158924
    516991151/?type=1&theater.

5   The image was published by Matteo Salvini on his Facebook profile (@salviniofficial, 25 May
    2019). Available at: https://www.facebook.com/salviniofficial/photos/a.278194028154/101566
    39978668155/?type=1&theater.

6   An example is the whole photo album "*Una vignetta per l'Europa 2016*" shared by *Internazionale* on
    its Facebook profile (@Internazionale, 15 July 2016). Available at: https://www.facebook.com/
    pg/Internazionale/photos/?tab=album&album_id=10154228323201760&ref=page_internal.

7   The cartoon was published by *Internazionale* on its Facebook profile (@Internazionale, 15
    July 2016). Available at: https://www.facebook.com/Internazionale/photos/a.10154228323
    201760/10154228350096760/?type=3&theater.

FIGURE 2.4 *"Europa in alto mare"* (Europe in the deep seas).
          NOTE: THE CARTOON WAS PUBLISHED IN THE VOLUME *"UNA
          VIGNETTA PER L'EUROPA : EDIZIONE 2013"* (VISSOL AND ACCARDO
          2013: 9). AVAILABLE AT: HTTPS://EC.EUROPA.EU/ITALY/SITES/
          ITALY/FILES/DOCS/BODY/2013_VIGNETTE.PDF. THIS CARTOON IS
          OFFERED FREE OF CHARGE FOR EDUCATIONAL PURPOSES BY
          COURTESY OF THE AUTHOR, AGIM SULAJ.
          BY AGIM SULAJ, 2011

Or again, as Figure 2.5 shows, Giuseppe La Micela writes that a wall cannot
represent Europe, recalling *"La Trahison des images"* (The Treachery of Images)
by René Magritte, and underlines the error that the EU is making in building
walls, as this clashes with the values it promotes.

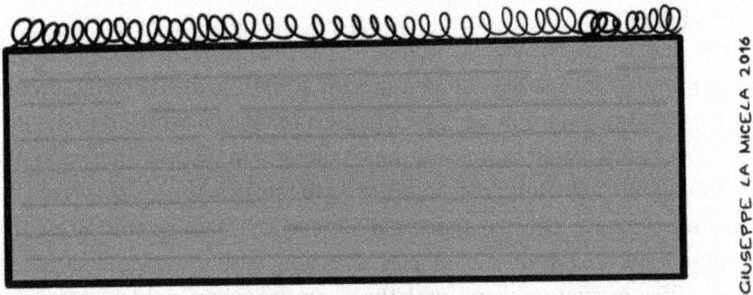

GIUSEPPE LA MICELA 2016

Ceci n'est pas une Europe

FIGURE 2.5 "La Trahison" (The Treachery).

NOTE: THE CARTOON WAS PUBLISHED BY *INTERNAZIONALE* ON ITS
FACEBOOK PROFILE (@INTERNAZIONALE, 15 JULY 2016). AVAILABLE AT:
HTTPS://WWW.FACEBOOK.COM/INTERNAZIONALE/
PHOTOS/A.10154228323201760/10154228372036760/?TYPE=3&THEATER. THIS
CARTOON IS OFFERED FREE OF CHARGE FOR EDUCATIONAL PURPOSES BY
COURTESY OF THE AUTHOR, GIUSEPPE LA MICELA
BY GIUSEPPE LA MICELA, 2016

In addition, the 2016 Brexit referendum and the following events on the terms
for the United Kingdom to leave the EU not only shocked Italy but also further
strengthened the sense of precariousness of this unity among Italians. The cartoons about Brexit were numerous and this event was illustrated in different
ways in many cartoons.[8]

---

8   An example is the whole photo album *"Una vignetta per l'Europa 2017"* shared by *Internazionale*
    on its Facebook profile (@Internazionale, 14 July 2017). Available at: https://www.facebook

Another value that has always been supported by the EU is solidarity, which is displayed through programs, interventions, incentives, and funds both to Member countries facing situations of crisis or natural disasters, and to foreign countries dealing with any humanitarian emergency or the violation of human rights (see Figure 2.6). As a matter of fact, Europe has played a central role in tackling different types of crises and disasters, also through the initiatives of the European Solidarity Corps[9] and promotion of volunteer work among young people.

The consistency of the EU in relation to this value has been put to the test particularly in the last decade by a specific situation: the flow of migrants arriving from the Balkan route and the Mediterranean Sea, which represents one of the most complicated humanitarian challenges in history. Since 2011, with the beginning of the Syrian crisis and the Arab Springs, these flows have been increasing and have affected especially Greece and Italy. For the latter, this phenomenon became dramatic on 3 October 2013 with the tragedy of Lampedusa when a boat of migrants sank, with three hundred sixty-eight reported dead and about twenty missing. However, the EU communication on this issue was poor until 2015 and only afterward it intensified showing mainly the rescue operations at sea coordinated by Frontex (the European Border and Coast Guard Agency) and the major European refugee registration hotspots (e.g. Lampedusa, Lesbos, Idomeni, Malta, Passau).

On the basis of the various political orientations which alternated in the government, initially Italy implemented different operations to welcome the flows of foreigners and avoid deaths at sea, then closed the borders and finally reopened them. While the left wing is in favour of accommodation, the right wing is against the opening of borders and strongly expresses its disappointment in Europe and its poor management of the accommodation and redistribution of migrants in the European territory. A typical expression of this disappointment, for example, is conveyed by the party *Fratelli d'Italia* (right): in 2018, it shared the image of a boat in the middle of the sea with about forty black men on board accompanied by the sentence "Stop European diktat, stop illegal migration".[10]

.com/pg/Internazionale/photos/?tab=album&album_id=10155414956391760&ref=page_internal.

9   The European Solidarity Corps is an EU project which gives young people opportunities to do volunteer work in their own country or abroad, in order to support and help communities and people around Europe (European Union n.d.).

10   The image was published by Fratelli d'Italia on its Facebook profile (@FdI.paginaufficiale, 16 May 2018). Available at: https://www.facebook.com/FdI.paginaufficiale/photos/a.5058 87899510509/1633395913426363/?type=3&theater.

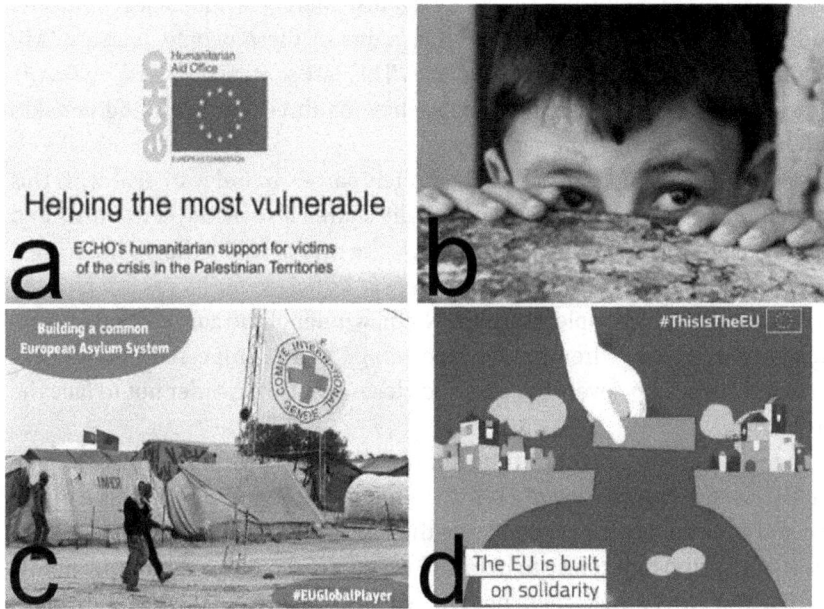

FIGURE 2.6   The EU value of solidarity. At the top left (a), solidarity for the most vulnerable
            people, 2003; at the top right (b), solidarity for the children affected by conflicts,
            2013; at the bottom left (c), solidarity for a common European asylum system,
            2014; at the bottom right (d), EU solidarity, 2019.
            NOTES: THE IMAGE IS A FRAME TAKEN FROM THE VIDEO "HELPING THE
            MOST VULNERABLE" PUBLISHED BY THE EUROPEAN COMMISSION ON ITS
            OFFICIAL WEBSITE (EUROPEAN COMMISSION 2003) AND IS RETRIEVED
            FROM AN INTERNET ARCHIVE. AVAILABLE AT: HTTPS://WEB.ARCHIVE.ORG/
            WEB/20070707051321/HTTP://EC.EUROPA.EU/ECHO/INFORMATION/MEDIA/
            CLIPS_EN.HTM; THE IMAGE WAS PUBLISHED BY THE EU ON ITS OFFICIAL
            WEBSITE (EUROPEAN UNION, 12 FEBRUARY 2013) AND IS RETRIEVED FROM
            AN INTERNET ARCHIVE. AVAILABLE AT: HTTPS://WEB.ARCHIVE.ORG/
            WEB/20130406033913/HTTP://EEAS. EUROPA.EU/TOP_STORIES/INDEX_IT.
            HTM; THE IMAGE WAS PUBLISHED BY THE EUROPEAN COMMISSION ON ITS
            FACEBOOK PROFILE (@EUROPEANCOMMISSION, 25 APRIL 2014). AVAILABLE
            AT: HTTPS://WWW.FACEBOOK.COM/EUROPEANCOMMISSION/
            PHOTOS/A.682276651819818/682277088486441/?TYPE=3&THEATER; THE
            IMAGE WAS PUBLISHED BY THE EUROPEAN COMMISSION ON ITS INSTAGRAM
            PROFILE (@EUROPEANCOMMISSION, 2 MAY 2019). AVAILABLE AT: HTTPS://
            WWW.INSTAGRAM.COM/P/BW9GRBYAU4_/

Italian politics, on the one hand, is split in two in relation to accommodation
but, on the other hand, both the right wing and the left wing turn to Europe for
help to deal with this emergency. In this sense, the left-wing parties solicit a
common management of European borders, fair distribution of migrants

among Member countries, sanctions against Members that reject refugees, and the protection of the fundamental rights of these people, because "Migrants arriving in Italy arrive in Europe". This last sentence is used by *Partito Democratico* (center-left) on an image showing three hands of different skin colors united over the European flag.[11]

The request for help made by the Italian parties in order to deal with this humanitarian emergency seems to be fully shared also by the cartoonists and citizens who voted for their works. In 2015, the year in which the EU intensified its communication on this issue, Europe was criticized for its passive attitude to this regard. For example, Marilena Nardi, winner of the 2015 edition of *"Una vignetta per l'Europa"*, drew the *"Vecchia Europa"* (Old Europe, see Figure 2.7) as an elderly lady who covers her ears and closes her eyes in order not to face the problem.

In the same edition, this attitude of the EU is also highlighted by Giuseppe La Micela in *"Unità di intenti"* (Unity of Intent, see Figure 2.8). In this cartoon the author is doubly ironic: depicting the European countries (represented by the twelve stars) that refuse to help and welcome a boat of migrants, he points out the unity that unifies them both in denying solidarity to the Member States that are dealing with this emergency, and in opposing respect for human rights, if it threatens their national interests.

Furthermore, if at a first stage Europe was accused of indifference, in the following years the criticisms became more severe and the cartoons often depicted the EU also as being responsible for the situation in the Mediterranean Sea. Andrea Lupo, for example, in the 2016 edition of the same contest, symbolizes Europe through two bloody hands collecting dead bodies from the sea in his cartoon *"SangEU"* (EU-Blood).[12] Or again, in the cartoon *"Doppio linguaggio"* (Double language), Ismail Dogan depicts Europe that pushes back a boat full of migrants with one hand, holding a bomb with the other.[13] The latter represents the European arms trade with countries in war which are often also those from which migrants are fleeing.

---

11   The image was published by *Partito Democratico* on its Instagram profile (@partitodemo-cratico, 11 May 2019). Available at: https://www.instagram.com/p/BxUsSOKnwXX/.

12   The cartoon was published by *Internazionale* on its Facebook profile (@Internazionale, 15 July 2016). Available at: https://www.facebook.com/Internazionale/photos/a.10154228323 201760/10154228343221760/?type=3&theater.

13   The cartoon was presented at the exhibition organized by Europe Direct Trentino with the Euro-Mediterranean Centre Librexpression—Fondazione"Giuseppe Di Vagno (1889–1921)", on the occasion of the festival *"Siamo Europa"* (We are Europe) in 2018 (Libex.eu n.d.). Available at: https://www.libex.eu/en/2018/05/25/libex-at-the-festival-we-are-europe-trento -25-27-may-2018/.

FIGURE 2.7 *"Vecchia Europa"* (Old Europe).

NOTE: THE CARTOON WAS PUBLISHED BY *INTERNAZIONALE* ON ITS FACE-
BOOK PROFILE (@INTERNAZIONALE, 21 JULY 2015). AVAILABLE AT: HTTPS://
WWW.FACEBOOK.COM/INTERNAZIONALE/
PHOTOS/A.10153345666126760/10153345666546760/?TYPE=3&THEATER. THIS
CARTOON IS OFFERED FREE OF CHARGE FOR EDUCATIONAL PURPOSES BY
COURTESY OF THE AUTHOR, MARILENA NARDI.
BY MARILENA NARDI, 2015

Many other cartoons underline the lack of solidarity by the EU both in general and towards some specific Member States—including Italy—not only in relation to migratory flows but also in relation to other crisis situations.

On the basis of this analysis, we can conclude that although the EU promotes certain values and symbols, the related communication and narration are not always consistent with its actual way of acting. In Italy, this discrepancy is highlighted in particular by the right-wing parties and in part also by the left-wing ones, and it is perceived and criticized also by the Italian citizens, as shown in the cartoons. As a further evidence of this, a recent survey conducted by the Political Observatory CISE (De Sio and Angelucci 2019) revealed that even though Italians are favorable to the EU, they are losing confidence in this supranational entity. In particular, it emerged that they perceive a lack of solidarity of Europe and other Member States not only in relation to this tragic

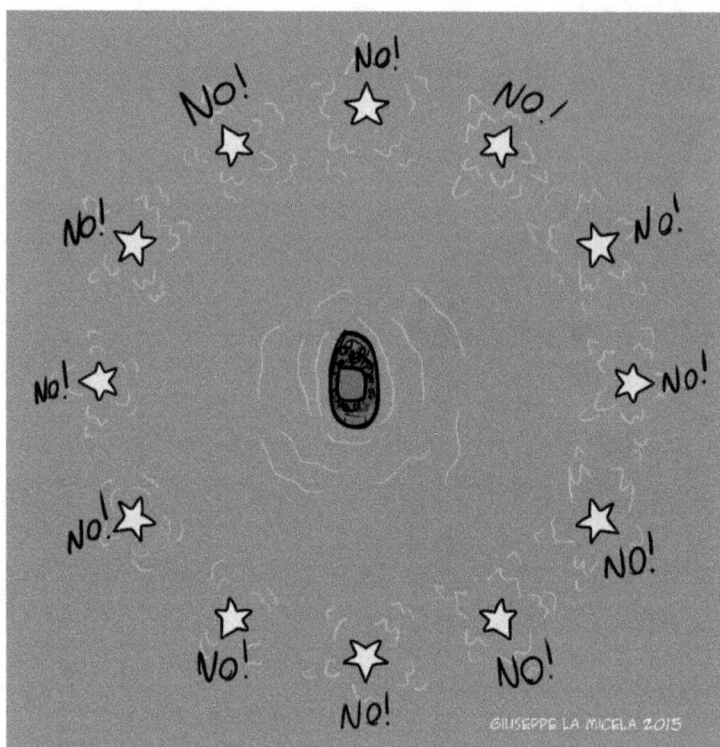

FIGURE 2.8 *"Unità di intenti"* (Unity of intents).
         NOTE: THE CARTOON WAS PUBLISHED BY *INTERNAZIONALE* ON ITS
         FACEBOOK PROFILE (@INTERNAZIONALE, 21 JULY 2015). AVAILABLE
         AT: HTTPS://WWW.FACEBOOK.COM/INTERNAZIONALE/
         PHOTOS/A.10153345666126760/10153345666706760/?TYPE=3&THEAT
         ER. THIS CARTOON IS OFFERED FREE OF CHARGE FOR EDUCATION-
         AL PURPOSES BY COURTESY OF THE AUTHOR, GIUSEPPE LA MICELA
         BY GIUSEPPE LA MICELA, 2015

emergency, but also regarding other issues. As a consequence, Italians believe that the EU is unlikely to implement economic and social policies which would be truly supportive of all EU Members.

4   Final Considerations

It is difficult to properly define what Europe is, not only because in literature, it is approached by different disciplines but also because its development is still ongoing and depends on different dynamic processes. For instance, Europe is a territorial space that has both internal and external boundaries that can vary according to the entry (or exit) of new Member States. At the same time, Europe is an economic, political, and cultural space and much more (Seton-Watson 1985; Delanty 1995; Shore 2000; Stråth 2002; Reale 2003; Richards and Wilson 2004; Delanty and Rumford 2005; Rovisco 2010; Immler and Sakkers 2014). Maybe for these reasons, when people talk about Europe they usually refer to its institutional unit represented by the EU (Scriven and Roberts 2001; Biebuyck and Rumford 2012; Triandafyllidou and Gropas 2015).

However, we must remember that this supranational entity is founded on the consensus of its Member States, which in turn base their consensus on that of their citizens. As a result, its existence is conditioned by the willingness to belong to this entity. As other studies show (e.g. Haesly 2001; Antonsich 2008; Lewicka 2011a; Chacha 2013; Antonsich and Holland 2014) the sense of belonging can develop not only toward local and national units but also toward supranational ones, like Europe. Cultural loyalty is particularly important for the development of this feeling, since, in this dimension, a pattern of symbols and values have to be created and acknowledged, accepted and shared by all components of the unit (Pollini 2005; Pretto and Battello 2016; Pretto 2018).

Our analysis shows that the EU has worked on the creation and dissemination of its symbols to a limited extent or, in any case, attempted to create them, but these have not always been accepted by the Member States. Article I-8 of the 2004 "Treaty Establishing a Constitution for Europe" identifies five symbols of Europe, which have remained unchanged to date: the blue flag with the twelve yellow stars, the "Ode to Joy" taken from the Ninth Symphony by Beethoven, the motto "United in Diversity", the Euro, and Europe Day which is celebrated on 9 May. As to the symbols that can be conveyed through images, the EU seldom uses the Euro for representative purposes, though it considers the single currency as "the most tangible proof of European integration" (European Union 2020a). After all, it would be senseless to use a medium of exchange as a symbol, when some Member States refuse to adopt it, and when even the EU itself prohibits others to adopt it. On the contrary, the narratives created through images that depict the flag in a symbolic way have always been numerous and have intensified over the years, also thanks to the concomitant increasing communication through social media from the EU and its various institutions. The use of flag, its colors or its stars seems to be more effective, because it allows Europe to communicate not only this emblem as a symbol, but also all the values associated with it.

The fact that the Euro is not considered a symbol by Italians—even though they adopted it as their national currency—is clear in the communication of parties and citizens, since it is rarely represented in the images they produce.

As seen in the previous section, the European flag is instead used in various ways by both to narrate different points of view on Europe in relation to its way of acting, also linked to the values it bears.

As essential elements of a society, values are recognized, accepted, and shared through two processes: institutionalization and internalization. The first occurs when values are structured to such an extent that they become generally accepted constructs of meaning, and are transmitted by a set of social institutions which, depending on their functions, can contribute to their maintenance and diffusion. The process of internalization refers to the ways in which a value is assimilated by a subject who will then simultaneously accept the orientation and attitudes of the reference group in which the value is recognized and shared. Internalization is therefore only possible when the institutionalization of the values has already occurred within the reference communities (Pollini 2012a; Pretto 2019).

As regards values, Europe has worked intensely in order to institutionalize those on which it is based and which it intends to promote. Already in the 1992 "Treaty of Maastricht", there was a reference to a set of values that the Member States "should" respect. This set of values has been modified and implemented over time and has been more precisely described in the 2012 "Consolidated Version of the Treaty on European Union". According to Art. 2 of this Treaty, the EU is founded on the values of respect for human dignity, freedom, democracy, equality, the rule of law, and respect for human rights, including the rights of persons belonging to minorities. These values are common to the Member States in a society in which pluralism, non-discrimination, tolerance, justice, solidarity, and equality between women and men prevail. Nowadays these values assume a normative function, as the violation of the same might lead to the suspension of some EU membership rights of the Member State that does not respect them (Art. 7).

Recalling the analysis of the previous section, we can note that the evolution of the institutionalization of values is accompanied also by the intensification of the EU communication of such values. In fact, while in the past communication only fulfilled functions related to marketing and commercial purposes, at present there is a growing tendency to communicate values and address social issues not only for companies but also for organizations and institutions of all kinds (Gadotti 2003). This is due to the fact that on the one hand, institutions and organizations (both public and private) are required to be efficient and righteous, and on the other hand, individuals are increasingly aligned with post-modern values and more oriented towards ethical attitudes and behaviors (Siano, Vollero, and Siglioccolo 2015; Papakristo 2016). In this perspective, the image of any type of organization is therefore the outcome of communication created internally and disseminated with the aim of being assessed and considered in a specific way by the external environment (Whetten, Lewis, and Mischel 1992; Gioia and Thomas 1996; Pretto 2019). However, it should be remembered that the communicated image is interpreted and evaluated by individuals also through their perceptions and considerations on the means and strategies the organization adopts to achieve its goals (van der Merwe and Puth 2014; Massey 2016). The communication of Europe that focuses on symbols and, above all, on values should therefore be consistent and also represent its actual way of operating.

What emerged from the analysis of the images produced by the Italian political parties and of the cartoons of citizens participating in the various contests is an ironic and sometimes openly critical judgement on the inconsistency they perceive between the image that Europe communicates and its way of acting. The communication of political parties (in particular those of the right wing) is frequently based on this lack of consistency and consequently affects citizens' perception of this supranational entity. The more the EU is presented as a social unit with which citizens do not identify themselves due to its inconsistency, the more the citizens' trust and sense of belonging towards it will decrease.

This consequence emerges also in the analysis of the cartoons, since those that reflect confident or hopeful attitudes towards Europe are rare. The cartoonists (and the citizens who voted for their works) seem to have actually internalized the symbols and values promoted by Europe, but they also underline how these values are absent in decisions and actions that concern various problematic situations, such as the lack of unity and harmony among the different States, the construction of symbolic and physical walls, the defective solidarity among Member States and regarding migratory flows, and much more.

It should be kept in mind that the process towards greater institutionalization and internalization of values, at least in specific cases and connected to moments of economic and political crisis, could be reversible (Pretto 2012). As a matter of fact, as values influence the behaviors and attitudes of each social actor, they are also affected by the specificity of the conditions and situations of the social context (Pollini 2012b). However, what we can hope for—especially today, when we are all afflicted by the Covid-19 pandemic[14]—is that it will not be values that change but rather, the attitudes and actions of everyone, including Europe.

---

14   This chapter was finalized between January and March 2020.

Bibliography

Akkermann, Mark. (2019). *The Business of Building Walls*. Transnational Institute. Available at: https://www.tni.org/files/publication-downloads/business_of_building_walls_-_full_report.pdf (consulted 10 January 2020).

Antonsich, Marco and Holland, Edward C. (2014). "Territorial Attachment in the Age of Globalization: The Case of Western Europe". *European Urban and Regional Studies* 21(2): 206–221. doi:10.1177/0969776412445830.

Antonsich, Marco. (2008). "EUropean Attachment and Meanings of EUurope. A Qualitative Study in the EU-15". *Political Geography* 27(6): 691–710. doi:10.1016/j.polgeo.2008.07.004.

Biebuyck, William and Rumford, Chris. (2012). "Many Europes: Rethinking Multiplicity". *European Journal of Social Theory* 15(1), 3–20. doi:10.1177/1368431011423567.

Brabant, Sarah and Mooney, Linda A. (1999). "The Social Construction of Family Life in the Sunday Comics: Race as a Consideration". *Journal of Comparative Family Studies* 30(1): 113–133. doi:10.3138/jcfs.30.1.113.

Breheny, Mary and Stephens, Christine. (2015). "Approaches to Narrative Analysis: Using Personal, Dialogical and Social Stories to Promote Peace". In: Bretherton, Diane and Law, Siew Fang (eds.). *Peace Psychology Book Series: Vol. 26. Methodologies in Peace Psychology: Peace Research by Peaceful Means*. New York: Springer International Publishing, 275–291.

Bruner, Jerome. (1990). *Acts of Meaning*. Cambridge: Harvard University Press.

Bruner, Jerome. (1996). *The Culture of Education*. Cambridge: Harvard University Press.

Burri, Regula Valérie. (2012). "Visual Rationalities: Towards a Sociology of Images". *Current Sociology* 60(1): 45–60. doi:10.1177/0011392111426647.

Caswell, Lucy Shelton. (2004). "Drawing Swords: War in American Editorial Cartoons". *American Journalism* 21(2): 13–45. doi:10.1080/08821127.2004.10677580.

Chacha, Mwita. (2013). "Regional Attachment and Support for European Integration". *European Union Politics* 14(2): 206–227. doi:10.1177/1465116512462910.

Chavez, Deborah. (1985). "Perpetuation of Gender Inequality: A Content Analysis of Comic Strips". *Sex Roles* 13: 93–102. doi:10.1007/BF00287463.

Clandinin, D. Jean and Connelly, F. Michael. (2000). *Narrative Inquiry: Experience and Story in Qualitative Research*. San Francisco: Jossey-Bass.

Clark-Ibáñez, Marisol. (2004). "Framing the Social World with Photo-Elicitation Interviews". *American Behavioral Scientist* 47(12):1507–1527.doi:10.1177/0002764204266236.

Cobley, Paul. (2001). *Narrative*. London: Routledge.

Corrigall-Brown, Catherine. (2012). "The Power of Pictures: Images of Politics and Protest". *American Behavioral Scientist* 56(2): 131–134. doi:10.1177/0002764211419358.

Dahmen, Nicole Smith, Mielczarek, Natalia, and Morrison, Daniel D. (2019). "The (in) Disputable 'Power' of Images of Outrage: Public Acknowledgement, Emotional

Reaction, and Image Recognition". *Visual Communication* 18(4): 453–474. doi:10.1177/1470357217749999.

De Sio, Lorenzo and Angelucci, Davide. (2019). "Italiani ancora europeisti, ma ormai critici e sfiduciati: il super-sondaggio CISE con 19 domande sull'Europa". *CISE— Centro Italiano Studi Elettorali*. Available at: https://cise.luiss.it/cise/2019/05/09/italiani-ancora-europeisti-ma-ormai-critici-e-sfiduciati-il-super-sondaggio-cise-con-19-domande-sulleuropa/ (consulted 20 January 2020).

Delanty, Gerard and Rumford, Chris. (2005). *Rethinking Europe: Social Theory and the Implications of Europeanization*. London: Routledge.

Delanty, Gerard. (1995). *Inventing Europe: Idea, Identity, Reality*. London: Macmillan.

Earnest, David C. and Fish, Jennifer N. (2014). "Visual Sociology in the Classroom: Using Imagery to Teach the Politics of Globalization". *Politics* 34(3): 248–262. doi:10.1111/1467-9256.12041.

What is Erasmus+? | Erasmus+. European Commission. (n.d.). Available at: https://ec.europa.eu/programmes/erasmus-plus/about_en (consulted 20 February 2020).

Which Countries Use the Euro | European Union. European Union. (2020a). Last published 1 February 2020. Available at: https://europa.eu/european-union/about-eu/euro/which-countries-use-euro_en (consulted 20 February 2020).

The European Flag | European Union. European Union. (2020b). Last published 18 March 2020. Available at: https://europa.eu/european-union/about-eu/symbols/flag_en (consulted 20 March 2020).

European Solidarity Corps: What is the European Solidarity Corps? | European Youth Portal. European Union. (n.d.). Available at: https://europa.eu/youth/solidarity_en (consulted 20 February 2020).

Ewbank, Michael P., Barnard, Philip J., Croucher, Camilla J., Ramponi, Cristina, and Calder, Andrew J. (2009). "The Amygdala Response to Images with Impact". *Social Cognitive and Affective Neuroscience* 4(2): 127–133. doi:10.1093/scan/nsn048.

Faludi, Andreas. (2013). "Territorial Cohesion, Territorialism, Territoriality, and Soft Planning: A Critical Review". *Environment and Planning A: Economy and Space* 45(6): 1302–1317. doi:10.1068/a45299.

Foss, Sonja K. (1992). "Visual Imagery as Communication". *Text and Performance Quarterly* 12(1): 85–90. doi:10.1080/10462939209359638.

Franzosi, Roberto. (1998). "Narrative Analysis—Or Why (and How) Sociologists Should Be Interested in Narrative". *Annual Review of Sociology* 24: 517–554. doi:10.1146/annurev.soc.24.1.517.

Gadotti, Giovanna. (2003). *Pubblicità Sociale. Lineamenti, Esperienze e Nuovi Sviluppi*. Milano: Franco Angeli.

Gioia, Dennis Arnold and Thomas, James B. (1996). "Identity, Image, and Issue Interpretation: Sensemaking during Strategic Change in Academia". *Administrative Science Quarterly* 41(3): 370–403. doi:10.2307/2393936.

Giuliani, Maria Vittoria. (2003). "Theory of Attachment and Place Attachment". In: Bonnes, Mirilia, Lee, Terence, and Bonaiuto, Marino (eds.). *Psychological Theories for Environmental Issues.* Aldershot: Ashgate, 137–170.

Gubert, Renzo. (2000). "Territorial Belonging". In: Borgatta, Edgar F. and Montgomery, Rhonda J.V. (eds.). *Encyclopedia of Sociology.* New York: Macmillan, 3128–3137.

Haesly, Richard. (2001). "Euroskeptics, Europhiles and Instrumental Europeans: European Attachment in Scotland and Wales". *European Union Politics* 2(1): 81–102. doi:1 0.1177/1465116501002001004.

Harper, Douglas. (1998). "An Argument for Visual Sociology". In: Prosser Jon (ed.). *Image-Based Research: A Sourcebook for Qualitative Researchers.* Philadelphia: Falmer, 20–35.

Holley, Karri A. and Colyar, Julia. (2009). "Rethinking Texts: Narrative and the Construction of Qualitative Research". *Educational Researcher* 38(9): 680–686. doi:10.31 02/0013189X09351979.

Immler, Nicole L. and Sakkers, Hans. (2014). "(Re)Programming Europe: European Capitals of Culture: Rethinking the Role of Culture". *Journal of European Studies* 44(1): 3–29. doi:10.1177/0047244113515567.

Jenks, Chris (ed.). (1995). *Visual Culture.* London and New York: Routledge.

Kasen, Jill H. (1980). "Whither the Self-Made Man? Comic Culture and the Crisis of Legitimation in the United States". *Social Problems* 28(2): 131–148. doi:10.2307/800147.

Keats, Patrice A. (2009). "Multiple Text Analysis in Narrative Research: Visual, Written, and Spoken Stories of Experience". *Qualitative Research* 9(2): 181–195. doi:10.1177/1468794108099320.

LaRossa, Ralph, Jaret, Charles, Gadgil, Malati and Wynn, G. Robert. (2000). "The Changing Culture of Fatherhood in Comic-Strip Families: A Six-Decade Analysis". *Journal of Marriage and Family* 62(2): 375–387. doi:10.1111/j.1741-3737.2000.00375.x.

Lehning, Percy B. (2001). "European Citizenship: Towards a European Identity?" *Law and Philosophy* 20: 239–282. doi:10.1023/A:1010681009751.

Lewicka, Maria. (2005). "Ways to Make People Active: The Role of Place Attachment, Cultural Capital, and Neighborhood Ties". *Journal of Environmental Psychology* 25(4): 381–395. doi:10.1016/j.jenvp.2005.10.004.

Lewicka, Maria. (2011a). "Place Attachment: How Far Have We Come in the Last 40 Years?" *Journal of Environmental Psychology* 31(3): 207–230. doi:10.1016/j.jenvp.2010.10.001.

Lewicka, Maria. (2011b). "On the Varieties of People's Relationships with Places: Hummon's Typology Revisited". *Environment and Behavior* 43(5): 676–709. doi:10.1177/0013916510364917.

Libex.eu. n.d. LIBEX at the festival "We are Europe"—Trento 25–27 May 2018. Available at: https://www.libex.eu/en/2018/05/25/libex-at-the-festival-we-are-europe-trento-25-27-may-2018/ (consulted 27 February 2020).

Low, Setha M. and Altman, Irwin. (1992). "Place Attachment". In: Low, Setha M. and Altman, Irwin (eds.). *Place Attachment. Human Behavior and Environment (Advances in Theory and Research)—Vol. 12*. Boston: Springer, 1–12.

Massey, Joseph Eric. (2016). "A Theory of Organizational Image Management". *International Journal of Management and Applied Science* 2(1):1–6. doi:IJMAS-IRAJ-DOI-3810.

Meidani, Mahdiyeh. (2015). "Holocaust Cartoons as Ideographs: Visual and Rhetorical Analysis of Holocaust Cartoons". *SAGE Open* (July). doi:10.1177/2158244015597727.

Papakristo, Paola Costanza. (2016). "Comunicazione sociale: quando parlano le aziende". In: Sobrero Rossella (ed.). *I linguaggi della comunicazione sociale: Collana Comunicazione Sociale: Volume 5*. Milano: Fondazione Pubblicità Progresso, 47–49. Available at: https://www.pubblicitaprogresso.org/Uploads/Docs/i-linguaggi-della-comunicazione-sociale-def_22959.pdf (consulted 23 January 2020).

Parsons, Talcott. (1959). *The Social System* (2nd ed.). Glencoe: The Free Press.

Pollini, Gabriele. (2005). "Elements of a Theory of Place Attachment and Socio-Territorial Belonging". *International Review of Sociology* 15(3): 497–515. doi:10.1080/03906700500272483.

Pollini, Gabriele. (2012a). "Introduzione: per una sociologia dei valori". In: Pollini, Gabriele, Pretto, Albertina and Rovati, Giancarlo (eds.). *L'Italia nell'Europa: i valori tra persistenze e trasformazioni*. Milano: FrancoAngeli, 15–40.

Pollini, Gabriele. (2012b). "Conclusioni". In: Pollini, Gabriele, Pretto, Albertina and Rovati, Giancarlo (eds.). *L'Italia nell'Europa: i valori tra persistenze e trasformazioni*. Milano: FrancoAngeli, 511–516.

Pretto, Albertina and Battello, Veronica. (2016). "The socio-territorial belonging in a cross-border area: a sociological approach". *Space and Polity* 20(2): 177–193. doi:10.1080/13562576.2016.1157302.

Pretto, Albertina. (2012). "Gli orientamenti verso il lavoro". In: Pollini, Gabriele, Pretto, Albertina and Rovati, Giancarlo (eds.). *L'Italia nell'Europa: i valori tra persistenze e trasformazioni*. Milano: FrancoAngeli, 167–216.

Pretto, Albertina. (2015). "A Type of Interview with Photos: The Bipolar Photo Elicitation". *L'Année Sociologique* 65(1): 169–190. doi:10.3917/anso.151.0169.

Pretto, Albertina. (2018). "Different Landscape Perceptions of the Same Territorial Area". A Research Study in Italy. *Space and Culture* (September): 1–13. doi:10.1177/1206331218799619.

Pretto, Albertina. (2019). *Grandi eventi e valori. Il caso dell'Adunata degli Alpini 2018*. Bologna: Il Mulino.

Prior, Lindsay. (2014). "Content Analysis". In: Leavy, Patricia (ed.). *The Oxford Handbook of Qualitative Research*. New York: Oxford University Press, 359–379.

Reale, Giovanni. (2003). *Radici culturali e spirituali dell'Europa. Per una rinascita dell'uomo europeo*. Milano: Raffaello Cortina Editore.

Richards, Greg and Wilson, Julie. (2004). "The Impact of Cultural Events on City Image: Rotterdam, Cultural Capital of Europe 2001". *Urban Studies* 41(10): 1931–1951. doi:10.1 080/0042098042000256323.

Richardson, Laurel. (1995). "Narrative and Sociology". In: Van Maanen John (ed.). *Representation in Ethnography*. Thousand Oaks: Sage, 198–221.

Ricoeur, Paul. (1984). *Time and Narrative*. Chicago: University of Chicago Press.

Rovisco, Maria. (2010). "One Europe or Several Europes? The Cultural Logic of Narratives of Europe—Views from France and Britain". *Social Science Information* 49(2): 241–266. doi:10.1177/0539018409359844.

Savage, Mike, Bagnall, Gaynor and Longhurst, Brian. (2005). *Globalization and Belonging*. London: Sage.

Scannell, Leila and Gifford, Robert. (2010). "Defining Place Attachment: A Tripartite Organizing Framework". *Journal of Environmental Psychology* 30(1): 1–10. doi:10.1016/j. jenvp.2009.09.006.

Scriven, Michael and Roberts, Emily. (2001). "Local Specificity and Regional Unity under Siege: Territorial Identity and the Television News of Aquitaine". *Media, Culture & Society* 23(5): 587–605. doi:10.1177/016344301023005003.

Seton-Watson, Hugh. (1985). "What is Europe? Where is Europe? From Mystique to Politique". *Encounter* 65(2): 9–17.

Shore, Cris. (2000). *Building Europe: The Cultural Politics of European Integration*. London: Routledge.

Siano, Alfonso, Vollero, Agostino and Siglioccolo, Mario. (2015). *Corporate communication management. Accrescere la reputazione per attrarre risorse*. Torino: G. Giappichelli Editore.

Smith, Brett. (2016). "Narrative Analysis". In: Lyons, Evanthia and Coyle, Adrian (eds.). *Analysing Qualitative Data in Psychology* (2nd ed.). London: Sage, 202–221.

Somers, Margaret R. (1994). "The Narrative Constitution of Identity: A Relational and Network Approach". *Theory and Society* 23: 605–649. doi:10.1007/BF00992905.

Stjernø, Steinar. (2004). *Solidarity in Europe: The History of an Idea*. New York: Cambridge University Press.

Stråth, Bo. (2002). "A European Identity: To the Historical Limits of a Concept". *European Journal of Social Theory* 5(4): 387–401. doi:10.1177/1368431027605139965.

Tizon, H. Philippe. (1996). "Qu'est-ce que le territoire?" In: Di Méo, Guy (ed.). *Les territoires du quotidien*. Paris: L'Harmattan, 17–34.

Tomaney, John. (2015). "Region and Place II: Belonging". *Progress in Human Geography* 39(4): 507–516. doi:10.1177/0309132514539210.

Triandafyllidou, Anna and Gropas, Ruby. (2015). *What is Europe?* London: Palgrave.

Tselios, Vassilis and Tomaney, John. (2019). "Decentralisation and European Identity". *Environment and Planning A: Economy and Space* 51(1): 133–155. doi:10.1177/030851 8X18785905.

van der Merwe, Adri W.A.J. and Puth, Gustav. (2014). "Towards a Conceptual Model of the Relationship between Corporate Trust and Corporate Reputation". *Corporate Reputation Review* 17: 138–156. doi:10.1057/crr.2014.4.

Vissol Thierry and Accardo, Gian Paolo (eds.). (2013). *Una vignetta per l'Europa: Edizione 2013*. Available at: https://ec.europa.eu/italy/sites/italy/files/docs/body/2013_vignette.pdf (consulted 17 January 2020).

Weber, Max. (1904–5). *Die protestantische Ethik und der Geist des Kapitalismus*. Tübingen: Mohr.

Weber, Max. (1922). *Wirtschaft und Gesellschaft*. Tübingen: Mohr.

Whetten, David A., Lewis, Debra and Mischel, Leann J. (1992). "Towards an Integrated Model of Organizational Identity and Member Commitment". Paper presented at the 52nd Annual Meeting of the Academy of Management, Las Vegas.

CHAPTER 3

Social Media and the Institutionalization of Hate Speech in Greek Politics

Vasilis Vamvakas

1   Introduction

This essay tries to investigate hate speech in contemporary Greek politics. It focuses on two ministers of the Greek government (2015–2019) and the use of social media they employed throughout their service. These two examples are very important in order to understand the necessity of researching hate speech beyond its usual definition as a synonym of racist expressions. The thematic analysis of the posts of the two ministers will give us a good picture of the multiple targets that political hate speech can be directed to – which do not have always as their content defenseless minorities – and also helps us to understand the passage of this discourse from an unofficial (and sometimes anonymous) to a fully institutionalized status. The national-populist ideological frame (Pantazopoulos 2017) served by the government that formed in Greece a radical left party (SYRIZA) and extreme right one (ANEL), during the period of the economic crises, is crucial in order to understand the political proliferation and nomination of the hateful political rhetoric diffused by social media.

2   The Public Sphere of Mistrust

Well before the advent of the economic crisis, Greek society had begun to question strongly the basic post-junta institutions of influence and power. First, the appearance of journalistic blogosphere and then of social media led to an unprecedented democratization of information, which, among others, had set as a primary objective the degradation of traditional media as unreliable. However, this development did not consist a peculiarity of Greece as it was assumed at the beginning of the crisis (Gonawela et al. 2018). The cases of the American elections with the win of Donald Trump and the referendum in Great Britain that led to Brexit, proved that the "global village of communication" instead of favoring cosmopolitan trends, transparency and democratic information, formulates a state of generalized deregulation in which fake news

(McNair 2018) and rumors create an unexpected return to archaic certainties and conspiracy theories (Bergman 2018).

During the 21st century the terms of communication and information have changed globally and therefore their known explanations seem inadequate. Almost throughout the Cold War period and until the end of the 20th century, media studies have been dominated by a model of interpretation that gave great importance to all those structures, institutions, inequalities that contributed to the effective control of the flow and influence of information (McNair 2006). This theoretical scheme, having the economic parameter as the main explanatory factor, highlighted the way in which media are controlled more or less by social elites and powerful media, through propaganda methods and public relations, towards the dissemination of values and prejudices that led to the strengthening of an ideological hegemony.

Brian McNair (2006) has pointed out that the conditions that this approach (control paradigm) was trying to explain have changed dramatically after the terrorist attack of September 11, 2001. From the control of communication within the national context (Hall et al. 1978), from the "brainwashing" techniques (Herman and Chomsky 1988), from central channels of communication, we passed on to, what McNair aptly calls, the "chaos of communication". During the era of globalization and new media technologies the notion of a dominant ideology (hegemony) of the socio-political elites, which in various ways were supported by mainstream media, is increasingly declining in favor of another condition in which dissatisfaction with these elites prevails in the inter-national public sphere. What characterizes today's cultural chaos is more ideological competition than ideological hegemony, more communication mechanisms which form harsh disagreements (dissensus) rather than acceptable agreements (consensus).

From another theoretical point of view we are talking about a very important aspect of the post-modern public sphere: the ability of the public opinion to control the political personnel, and the social elites in general, especially on moral issues, through the proliferation of surveillance capacities given by the new technological reality. The "synopticon" and not the "panopticon" is what dominates, since sensationalist journalism became the most influential genre of information and is being continually strengthened by the era of online platforms of social interaction (social media). We are talking about a situation under which the "audience" monitors the (media, political, economic, social) elites and not the other way round as Foucault suggested or Orwell has foreseen in his dystopia in *1984* (Bauman 1998; Doyle 2011; Mathiesen 1997).

The Greek public sphere followed very quickly this new development in which the main factors, dimensions and means of communication are constantly changing. Sensationalism, polarized representations, hostile confrontation of the adversary, doomsday staff, conspiracy theories (Skoulariki 2018), latent admiration of extremism, regeneration of national stereotypes and the aestheticization of misery are—according to various studies (Vamvakas 2014; Pantazopoulos 2013)—the elements that eventually prevail from 2009 until at least 2015 (referendum for Grexit), without neglecting that more reflective forms of public discourse appeared at the same time.

It is a fact that the bipolar or sensational public sphere is not an unprecedented event in the Greek reality. The Mediterranean or polarized pluralist model includes also the case of the Greek public sphere as Hallin and Mancini have shown (2004). Neither new technologies, nor economic crisis and globalization have been the generators of populism and nationalism and the violent vulgarization of public discourse in Greece. These elements have appeared throughout the post-junta period, either by the phenomenon of "Avriani" (a powerful trend in Greek press specialized in political scandals and blackmailing various members of the political or artistic elites) or by the radicalization of national and religious identities (Macedonian issue, religious identification on IDs). What has happened since 2009 in an unprecedented way is the intensification and dissemination of all these characteristics by the important contribution of the political and journalistic discourse articulated in the new media. The result of these extreme polarization and radicalization is the appearance of a massive and at the same time individualized mode of expression, that of hate speech.

3   Hate Speech beyond Racism

Although there are many ways to determine hate speech (MacAvaney et al. 2019) we could agree that by this term we mean the offensive public utterances caused by individual or collective biases against a certain social group or person, utterances which -indirectly or directly- call for the violent treatment of the undesired social entity (through the demand of restraint, exclusion, humiliation or annihilation of this entity). The efforts of controlling and constraining hate speech have led to a restrictive definition of the term, which ends up usually to its identification with right-wing extremism, that is, with every ideological expression involving violent discrimination and stigmatization of minority groups (basically religious and ethnic ones). Consequently, hate speech tends to become synonymous to racist perceptions and aggressive forms of public expression against immigrants or other defenseless social groups (Assimakopoulos 2017).

In the Greek case, the specific signification of the term was adopted, through the attempt to legally deal with hate speech during the period of the crisis in 2014. The rise of Golden Dawn was the most serious case of a political party that developed hate for immigrants at the heart of its ideology and practices. However the attempt to legally cope with right-wing extremism (Golden Dawn) which had grown in Greece during the last decade and any other racist expression, partly prevented the research of hate speech in all its range.

Recent studies have identified a significant diversity of hate speech concerning its targets. Nine categories of hate speech can be identified in reference to its targets: Hate against financial power, political rivalries, minorities-immigrants, religion, specific nations, specific persons, media, armed forces, individual behavior. We are going to clarify the definitions that are given to these kinds of hate speech by Salminen et al. (2018) by giving some important examples from the Greek internet (basically social media).

1. Financial power: Hatred toward wealthy people and companies and their privileges and their intentions to manipulate and commit crimes.

    In 2013 a small terrorist organization acted against the most popular Mall in Athens. The justification of their act is very illuminating of their hatred toward the "commercial" world in general: "*...our question is what degraded values and what misguided morals do tolerate the existence of monsters like Mall? The target of course is presented as an organized area of amusement, shopping, walks and unsalted entertainment. A small oasis in the modern nightmare*" (Motivators of Social Explosions, 24/1/2013).

2. Political issues: Hate toward government, political parties and movements, war, terrorism, the flaws of the system.

    During the economic crisis in Greece a lot of popular artists used social media (especially Twitter) in order to express their anger about the measures of austerity imposed by the Greek government under the memorandum signed with the European institutions and IMF (troika). The Greek governments (2009–2015) have been faced as a group of traitors and a lot of humiliating comments have been used against their members. Representative example is the comment of a very popular Greek comedian: "*You German fucking bastards, you will fall in the prison, without exceptions, you are all in deep shit up to your eyes*" (Harry Clin, on Twitter, 31/12/2014).

3. Racism and xenophobia: Racists comments toward black, white, Asian. Generalizations about some characteristics, and hateful comments regarding refugees.

"Refugees (illegal immigrants) ... of luxury" (31/8/2015) is the caption revealing the real status of immigration by the most hateful paper that the crisis generated in Greece, *Makelio*. The basic racist argument that was marginally expressed by Greek media about the refugee crisis since 2015, had to do with the fact that some refugees (especially from Syria) were not poor.

4.   Religion: Offensive comments for everything about religion, including Judaism, Christianity, Islam.

Although the hate against religious beliefs is not a usual phenomenon in Greece, apart from the case of extreme-right agents, the anti-terrorist stance was randomly exposed in terms of an overt or indirect anti-Islamism. Thanos Tzimeros, the leader of a new small party (supposed to support radical transformations) often expressed this hate: *"it smells of Mohammad's perfume. Prepare masks -or even better to open the windows (of our minds, our country, Europe)"* (on Twitter, 23/12/2012).

5.   Specific Nations: Hate towards different countries, their systems, people (if the nationalities are mentioned), and certain events, like immigration, territory, and sovereignty.

The rivalry between Greece and Turkey has been historic, but since the 1990s it has been replaced by a new animosity towards North Macedonia and its nationalist threat against the Greek (mostly ancient) cultural heritage. The hate against this nation has many aspects, the most common of them the argument that negates to recognize it as a real state-nation: An article in *liberal.com*—when the negotiations between the two states was reaching an agreement—consists a representative example: *"Tsipras [the Greek PM] send the fake Macedonians to elections"* (19/5/2019).

6.   Specific persons: Hate towards specific people who can be regular people, politicians, millionaires, celebrities, or some other related to specific news.

Another popular Greek comedian Pavlos Haikalis wrote on Twitter when PM became Lucas Papademos, leading a collaborative government in the pick of the Greek debt crisis (he previously served as Vice President of the European Central Bank from 2002 to 2010 and Governor of the Bank of Greece from 1994 to 2002): *"You fag, traitor, Papademos"* (3/12/2012). The certain comedian became a politician of the extreme right party ANEL (Independent Greeks), which made a coalition with the dominant left party SYRIZA after 2015 giving to the famous actor the position of Deputy Minister of Social Security.

7.   Media: Comments and emotional outbursts about bias and false state-
     ments made on purpose by the corrupted media.
         The traditional media and especially television, became a basic target
     of populist arguments which considered that professional journalism
     of the past and all its deficiencies consisted a proof of their suspicious
     role in consolidating the power of the old political and economic es-
     tablishment. Golden Down employed and radicalized this hate to-
     wards traditional media, organizing demonstrations against concrete
     enemies of the people and the nation, the TV channels. One of them
     considered unpatriotic the fact that Turkish Soap Operas were shown
     on *Mega Channel* (the most popular private Greek channel) and a
     member of the Greek parliament belonging to Golden Dawn pissed
     outside the entrance of its building while some others threw fish roe
     on its widows (26/2/2013).
8.   Armed Forces: Hate toward military, law enforcement, and the way they
     operate, which includes unethical behavior.
         The relationship of hate and love between the Greek anarchists and
     police is something *that characterizes the post-junta period and many
     incidents of street vi*olence between them. The anarchist slogan "*Cops,
     pigs, criminals*" has become so popular and familiar to everybody that
     even a group in Facebook brings this name.
9.   Behavior: Hate toward the world, humanity, immoral actions of some
     part of the society, ignorant people, people that committed certain
     actions, and that have certain habits.
         A very famous and significant musician in Greece, Stamatis Kraouna-
     kis, wrote in one of his comments on Facebook, captioning a photo-
     graph with a woman having the Greek flag as body make up: "*This is
     the daughter of Vicky Leandros [a known singer] to advertise Greece in
     Germany, I am wondering if Vicky doesn't have a slipper to slap her ...
     Come on, fucking idiots ... bring the prosecutor, it is an insult of the na-
     tional symbol*" (6/1/2016). Here we have a discourse of hate combining
     nationalism and a fashion police attitude, something that many times
     in Greek social media causes extremely insulting comments.
The language categories used in the examples of hate speech according
to Salminen et al. (2018) tend to be four:
     Accusation: Accusing someone of something, without relevant evi-
     dence to support it;
     Promoting violence: Calling people to deal with something using
     violence, asking for murders or threatening human life;
     Humiliation: Using words trying to degrade someone;
     Swearing: Using filthy language.

As we have already seen a lot of cases of these tropes of hate speech have appeared in the online public sphere of Greece during the last decade. The majority of them develops forms of hate speech not only against the usual groups of racist stigmatization (based on ethnicity, race, sexual choices) but mainly against a much broader range of targets which are employed by agents that can hardly be included in the far right political ideological context.

Hatred for democratic institutions and their representatives, hatred for the "system" and all its actors, hatred for the powerful (in political or economic terms) foreigners, are only some of the examples recorded with great frequency and severity during the recent years in the Greek public discourse (however, there is a gradual diminish after 2015). They are types of hate speech that go beyond the one expressed by Golden Dawn, although the latter's impact cannot be explained only because of its rhetoric against immigrants. Its influence was important because of articulating all the aforementioned targets in a common ideological platform of anti-systemic extremism (Dinas et al. 2013).

National-populism, conspiracy theories, secret admiration of terrorism, aesthetic evaluations are discursive patterns beyond racism that diffuse and deconstruct the traditional ideological identities of the past between left-right, socialism-liberalism, which have been responsible for the political polarization of previous decades. The idealized victimization of the people and the nation, the search for the hidden (from the institutional knowledge and basic information agents) truth, the legalization of non-state violence in response to the "violence" of the national and global establishment, make up communicating vessels invoking hate speech in the public discourse (Vamvakas and Dimitrakopoulou 2018). It is a critical parameter to investigate whether or not hate speech motivates acts of violence but even more important is the understanding of how this discourse is being composed, how it takes multiple forms and what is the variety of its targets. If we agree with the theory of speech acts that studies the performative (or illocutionary) function of the utterances rather than their truth value (Levin 2019), the crucial thing is to analyze the broader semantic environment created by the multiplication of hate speech and how this acquires steadily a nominated-institutional status.

4   The Institutional Hate Speech

In this direction we are going to focus on the use of social media (Twitter and Facebook) by two ministers of the former government of SYRIZA-ANEL (2015–2019) in Greece in order to see the ways and themes in which the personalized utterances of the Greek State (its ministers) employed often a discourse foul of elements of hate speech. The two cases are:

1.   Panos Kamenos the ex-Minister of National Defense and President of the Party "Independent Greeks" (ANEL) that created the coalition with the left Prime Minister of SYRIZA, Alexis Tsipras.
2.   Pavlos Polakis the ex-Alternate Minister of Health (SYRIZA's member).

It is the first time that ministers express various aspects of hate speech so overtly as far as they consisted exemplary cases of what has been seen as the national-populist[1] ideological hegemony in Greece during the years of the economic crisis (Vamvakas 2014; Pantazopoulos 2013). The use of social media (Twitter, Facebook) by these two ministers can be studied as a very interesting example of hate speech becoming a "state narrative" of the crisis.

It is true that we can find other examples of ministers being agents of hate speech in the past. A very interesting and quite well explored case is that of Andreas Loverdos (PASOK) as Minister of Health in 2012 when he publicized the names and pictures of 11 HIV positive women with the charge of intentionally infecting people while allegedly working as prostitutes. The criminalization of unprotected sex with prostitutes by Loverdos caused the outrage among rights groups. The Greek court finally acquitted these women of charges. This example of severe stigmatization of marginal social groups took a traditional direction of government and media moral panic and met a lot of criticism. The examples of Kammenos and Polakis are not the same. Their strategy of stigmatization is not concerning marginal groups and it is not following the traditional paths of media propaganda. It is usually diffused not by mainstream media but by their own social media or their personal interviews. It is also interesting that right groups have hardly spoken about them. Let's see the themes under which what we could call "ministerial hate speech" has appeared.

4.1   Personalized Attacks

The most common target category between the two cases under examination is that of specific persons. Although the political character of all targets of hate that the ministers have is quite obvious it is important to see and analyze their habit of "naming" as enemies specific people (politicians, trade unionists, artists, etc.).

---

1   National populists prioritize the culture and interests of the nation, and promise to give voice to a people who feel that they have been neglected, even held in contempt, by distant and often corrupt elites (Eatwell and Goodwin 2018: 7).

President of POEDIN, ..., UNDERSTAND THIS: You prove you're such a
disgrace as Giorgakis [the PM of PASOK] who brought IMF to the country
in which he was prime minister. You have finished, your position is in the
garbage of history.

POLAKIS AGAINST THE PRESIDENT OF THE TRADE UNION OF EMPLOYEES IN
PUBLIC HEALTH, 3/1/2017

Neo-liberal crow, old collaborator and advisor of Mitsotatakis family, in
the role of modern NIGHTMARE, modern traitor of the country with
one goal: to overturn Tsipras and SYRIZA. ONLY SPITTING AND PUB-
LIC HUMILIATION is WORTH TO THIS "EXCELLENT" woman who
for the sake of its bosses disparages and undermines GREECE AND its
PEOPLE.

POLAKIS AGAINST MIRANTA XAFA, AN ECONOMIST AND FORMERLY IMF REP-
RESENTATIVE OF GREECE, 6/11/2017

And now, Adonis fake photographer, you can kill yourself.... Even
Handelsblatt betrayed you.

KAMMENOS AGAINST GEORGIADIS, A MEMBER OF THE PARLIAMENT FOR NEW
DEMOCRACY, 6/11/2017

The groom-git A. Papadopoulos after kissing pissed clothes to keep me
away from searching the scandal of Alexia with Red Cross behaves
badly.

KAMMENOS FOR RELATIVES OF HIS POLITICAL ADVERSARIES, 22/6/2017

Dora, where are you? Are you making chicken soup? You just ran off like
a chicken from the courthouse. What they say about you "the old hen has
the juice" I do not accept it....

KAMMENOS AGAINST DORA BAKOGIANI, IMPORTANT MEMBER OF THE PARLIA-
MENT FOR NEW DEMOCRACY, 31/1/2019

These attacks against concrete persons by the two ministers—although including the element of political rivalry—are extraordinary. Swearing and humiliation is the basic language and representational means used. Especially
metaphors that characterize the female "enemy" as an animal (crow, hen, etc.)
should be underlined. The indirect or direct promotion of violence is also a
mode of this ministerial hate speech. In the case of Polakis is quite overt
("Adonis fake photographer, you can kill yourself", "ONLY SPITTING AND
PUBLIC HUMILIATION is WORTH TO THIS "EXCELLENT" woman")

while Kammenos interlinks his violent connotations with a sexualized language or pictures (bitches, masturbation, lovers). The interesting point here is that political hate speech refers mostly to personal (moral or psychological) characteristics of the political opponent and not pure references to their political affairs.

4.2   Media of Corruption

The second favorite theme of expressing hate for both ministers had been media.

> SKAI [TV Channel] worries that there are no casualties from the fire and keeps on calling the Lieutenant commander on the front with the ambulance crews to find out if there's any!!!!!!!! Trashy is a merciful term to describe the way they broadcast fires!!! The fires will fade, the organized anomaly plan will go to THE BOTOM once again....
>
>   POLAKIS, 14/10/2017

> Good morning, after three years of fight. You understand to whom the first photo is devoted (exceptionally to the shit channels of corruption that tonight were in grief and silence, along with the parties that bankrupted the country)....
>
>   POLAKIS, 22/6/2018

> The "publisher" yesterday decided to hit my 85-year-old mother. WE HOLD ON "bitch of the dealer" to the end.
>
>   KAMMENOS, 23/7/2017

> Overcoming the boundaries of directed journalistic masturbation [some journalists] support that I am in the national ballot of SYRIZA. Drink vinegar, ANEL will enter the parliament stronger and Alexis [Tsipras] will win.
>
>   KAMMENOS, 14/10/2018

There are a lot of examples like this, all being very aggressive towards the hypothetical fake news of media around the ministers themselves or the government in general. The language being used is very humiliating (shit channels, bitches, filthy journalists, masturbation, drink vinegar). The only difference is that Kammenos often uses pictures to illustrate his anger while Polakis is using mostly expanded texts in order to form his vague accusation about the propaganda ("diaploki"[2]) of media against him and the government. However, the whole notion of hate emitted is very close to that of President Tramp against the mainstream media in U.S.A. that criticize his administration.

4.3   Media Owners and Banks: the Real Financial Enemies

It is interesting enough that both ministers targeted financial power almost exclusively when they were talking about businessmen and owners of media, naming them or not. Hatred toward wealthy people and companies and their privileges is coming as a result of the influence rich people have on media politics.

> The newspaper EFSYN executes a contract of a specific political business center earning a lot of money to be revealed soon.
>
> KAMMENOS, 12/10/2018

> K. Mitsotakis, SHUTUP AND SILENCE about the air taxi of Kyriakou [owner of *Antı channel*] ... six hours of flight within 24 hours???... There in Skai-disgraced channel, are you angry that the air-taxi was not of Alafouzos [Skai's owner] and you decided to disappear the issue, eh????
>
> POLAKIS 20/8/2018

Something which is a very important element of the hate speech of the two ministers—and especially that of Polakis—is the often attacks they make against the bank system and its most important representative in Greece the Governor of the Bank of Greece, Yiannis Stournaras. Quite indicative of Polakis' despise for the "bankers" and "technocrats" is also the comment he made after the terrorist attack against the former Prime Minister and also ex-Governor of the Bank of Greece, Lukas Papademos:

> Congratulations independent justice with your great reflexes. Tzimeros calls for a coup via fb, Golden Dawn call for atrocities against refugees-imigrants via fb, and you are mobilized when Stournaras sued somebody [a journalist] who said that he won't be sad if a bomb exploded on his feet, as in the case of Papademos (he wrote, he didn't put the bomb)
>
> POLAKIS 25/10/2018

---

2   The Greek word "διαπλοκή" can be translated here as the "involvement" of the Media in Politics (note of the Editor).

4.4   Conspiracy Theories and Nationalism

The more impersonal mode of hate speech that the two ministers followed, referred to various general matters of politics: from justice to the old political "establishment" and unnamed traitors. Here the accusation becomes completely obscure and the theories of conspiracy clearly inspire the certain political protagonists.

> [Justice] is not blind. It is sightless and serves a plan (one serious part). If it was Akis, Christoforakos, a Novartis' executive, a killer of Golden Dawn, they would be out.
>
> POLAKIS FOR IRIANNA, A WOMAN AND HER BOYFRIEND ACCUSED FOR TERRORISM, 17/10/2017

> All you Gestapo men, remain Europe, sauble-hold, don't be happy ... WE ARE GOING TO WIN ... No matter how much extra time your leader plays ... he has not much more time.
>
> POLAKIS FOR SAUBLE AND TRAITORS, 24/5/2017

> Spread the message of national independence at Syntagma Square by humor and hate the German sympathizers [evzones].
>
> KAMMENOS, 19/3/2015

While in power the two political figures under examination did not express important tweets and posts of hate speech against immigrants, other religions or against armed forces. Although sometimes Polakis combined his accusations about the blind justice (not convicting his political adversaries) with some police practices and Kammenos in one of his interviews threatened to send migrants including jihadists to Europe (because of the cruel face they were showing during the negotiations with the government of Alexis Tsipras) their public utterances, connoting or denoting hate or underestimation or criminalization of groups because of their origins and behaviors, are quite unusual. The only significant exception as we have already seen is Germany, and especially German politicians who are considered as the incarnation of the evil forces (the regeneration of Nazism) during the whole period of the Greek debt crisis (Lialiouti and Bithymitris 2013).

By the end of this political coalition the threat of North Macedonia became a very important case for the nationalist indignation of the ultra-right partner, Kammenos, who recalled the known conspiracy theory about the businessman George Soros (as the basic factor persuading with money Tsipras and Zaef, the two PMs of Greece and North Macedonia to make an unpatriotic agreement) in order to picture the foreign enemies and the left traitors (like the ex-minister of Foreign Affairs, Nikos Kotzias):

> *The credentials of Zoran Zaef to George Sorros. He surrendered his country.*
>
> Kammenos' caption on Twitter of a picture of the PM of North Macedonia and the businessman, 25/1/2019

5 Conclusion

To conclude, we could say that the institutionalization of hate speech through two seminal ministers of the government SYRIZA-ANEL comes to cover basically 5 out of the 9 topics other studies describe as usual targets of hostile online verbal expressions. Concrete persons of the economic, cultural or political elite, political adversaries either in individual or collective form, media and business interests that serve the old establishment, nations of imperialistic power in Europe or threats of the national identity are targeted as the main reasons of Greece's crisis and the main enemies to be confronted at any cost. Humiliation, swearing, promotion of violence and general accusations strictly linked to conspiracy theories are energized in different analogies in each case in order to be achieved the stigmatization of certain political attitudes and upper social positions.

The government of SYRIZA-ANEL in Greece (2015–2919) consisted the ideal coalition of left and right radicalization in Europe, the ideal synchronization of right-wing nationalism and left-wing populism, the perfect example of national-populism that overpasses the known ideological boundaries of the past (Mudde 2017). The two ministers we examined here retained their anti-systemic profile even when they came in power. By using social media and not traditional media they achieved to maintain the radical discourse their audience and voters were expecting from them to utilize, although they were somehow confined by their official role. Hate speech and conspiracy theories were their basic means to try and keep connection to the vulgar, offensive and political incorrect discourse that gave them extraordinary political influence in the public sphere of the debt crisis. What really happened with these two cases is not an effort to control the public opinion through the known paths of the most important Greek agents of information and create a consensus around the ideological frame of the government they served. These two ministers kept on using intensively their social media while in power in order to attune themselves regularly with the angriest voices of their electorate and preserve the polemic mentality that made them important political figures of left and right radicalization.

The period of the debt crisis was for the Greek public sphere a phase of increasing a lot of its archaic inclinations. Symbolic and direct violence became an important part of the political game. The anti-systemic fashion was closely connected to rhetorical and stylistic incivility. The alternative or radical political stance meant abandonment of typical behavior, rudeness to the basic democratic institutions, identification with the underdog cultural behaviors. The left and right national-populism that prevailed at least until 2015 (referendum) took old ideological elements of aggressiveness and renewed them. The traditional American anti-imperialism became German and European anti-imperialism, the suspicion against state or market institutions became suspicion against international institutions and banks, the idealization of the people became a glorification of the nation's victimization. Politicians such as Kammenos and Polakis became the most representative political incarnation of hate speech. They gave it an unprecedented institutional form while in power. By using social media they transformed themselves to receivers and re-producers of a limitless and blind polarization full of abhorrence for their political adversaries in personal and in impersonal terms. They legitimized conspiracy theories and made swearing, insulting and threatening a mainstream mode of political communication.

In future research of the institutionalization of radicalism and hate speech interesting issues to be examined could be:

- The various forms in which political incorrectness is articulated (Zompetti 2019), the aesthetic frames used either in linguistic or iconographic terms. It is obvious that hate speech has a certain "grammar" which is not so much reflecting low cultural capital but mostly the authenticity of the haters' anger. In our examples we can notice a traditional, anti-technological, masculine expressions trying to violate (or ignore) the rules of Greek modern language or creating a new one.
- The significance of black or humiliating humor (Kuipers 2015; Stafylakis 2013). There is a trend of a political humor which tends to identify with the victimizers and not the victims. Panos Kammenos used often this entertaining and insulting political discourse, even as a minister.
- The influence that hate speech achieves in social media and online journalism. The general polarization is the most obvious result of this mode of individualized political communication but there is no evidence that this mode of expression is always the most effective. Especially in the case of Polakis the ineffectiveness of his posts on social media were proved when he hatefully attacked during the European Elections (2019) a disabled

candidate of New Democracy (Stelios Kipouropoulos) creating a wide support for him and giving him the most votes for the European Parliament.

Bibliography

Assimakopoulos, S., Fabienne Baider, F. and Millar, S. (2017). *Online Hate Speech in the European Union A Discourse-Analytic Perspective*. Cham: Springer.

Bauman, Z. (1998). *Globalization: The Human Consequences*. Oxford: Blackwell.

Dinas, E., Georgiadou, V., Konstantinidis, I. and Rori, L. (2013). "From dusk to dawn: Local party organization and party success of right-wing extremism". *Party Politics* 22(1): 80–92.

Doyle, A. (2011). "Revisiting the synopticon: Reconsidering Mathiesen's 'The Viewer Society' in the age of Web 2.0: 283". *Theoretical Criminology* 15: 283–299.

Eatwell, R. and Goodwin, M. (2018). *National Populism: The Revolt Against Liberal Democracy*. London: Penguin Books.

Gonawela, A., Pal, J., Thawani, U., van der Vlugt, E., Out, W., and Chandra, P. (2018). "Speaking their Mind: Populist Style and Antagonistic Messaging in the Tweets of Donald Trump, Narendra Modi, Nigel Farage, and Geert Wilders". *Computer Supported Cooperative Work: CSCW: An International Journal* 27(3–6): 293–326.

Hall, S., Critcher, C., Jefferson, T., Clarke, J. and Roberts, B. (1978). *Policing the Crisis: Mugging, the State and Law and Order*. London: MacMillan.

Hallin, D. and Mancini, P. (2004). *Comparing media systems. Three models of media and politics*. Cambridge: Cambridge University Press.

Herman, E.S. and Chomsky, N. (1988). *Manufacturing Consent: The Political Economy of the Mass Media*. New York: Pantheon.

Kuipers, G. (2015). *Good Humor, bad Taste: a sociology of the joke*. Berlin: De Gruyter Mouton.

Lialiouti, Z. and Bithymitris, G. (2013). "'The Nazis Strike Again': The Concept of 'the German Enemy', Party Strategies and Mass Perceptions Through the Prism of The Greek Economic Crisis". In: Karner, C. and Mertens, B. (eds.). *The Use and Abuse of Memory: Interpreting World War II in Contemporary European Politics*. New Brunswick-London: Transaction Publishers.

Levin, A. (2010). *The Cost of Free Speech Pornography, hate speech, and their challenge to liberalism*. New York: Palgrave Macmillan.

MacAvaney, S., Yao, H.-R., Yang, E., Russell, K., Goharian, N., and Frieder, O. (2019). "Hate speech detection: Challenges and solutions". *PLOS ONE* 14(8): e0221152.

Mathiesen, T. (1997). "The Viewer Society: Michel Foucault's "Panopticon" Revisited". *Theoretical Criminology* 1(2): 215–234.

McNair, B. (2018). *Fake News: Falsehood, Fabrication and Fantasy in Journalism*. New York: Routledge.

McNair, B. (2006). *Cultural Chaos. Journalism, news and power in a globalized world*. London and New York: Routledge.

Mudde, C. (2019). SYRIZA. *The failure of the populist promise*. New York: Palgrave MacMillan.

Pantazopoulos, A. (2013). *Leftish National Populism 2008–2013* (in Greek). Thessaloniki: Epikentro.

Pantazopoulos, A.(2017). "The National-Populist Illusion as a "Pathology" of Politics: The Greek Case and Beyond". *Telos* 11.

Salminen, J., lmerekhi, A., Milenković, M., Jung, S., An, J., Kwak, H. and Jansen, B. (2018). "Anatomy of Online Hate: Developing a Taxonomy and Machine Learning Models for Identifying and Classifying Hate in *Online News Media*". *Proceedings of the Twelfth International AAAI Conference on Web and Social Media*, San Francisco.

Skoulariki, A. (2018). "Conspiracy theories before and after the Greek crisis: Discursive patterns and political use of the "enemy" theme". *Επιστήμη και κοινωνία* vol. 37: 73–108.

Stafylakis, K. (2013). "Fragile Overidentifications: Emerging Alternatives in Greece's Cultural Activist Scenes". *Left Curve* 31 (Spring): 72–80.

Vamvakas, V. (2014). *The Crisis Discourse. Polarization, Violence and Reflection in Political and Popular Culture* (in Greek). Thessaloniki: Epikentro.

Vamvakas, V. and Dimitrakopoulou, D. (2018). "The online element in the intermedia agenda-setting: The case of the Greek indignant citizens movement". In: Juliet, D. (ed.). *From Tahrir Square to Ferguson: Social networks as facilitators of social movements*. New York: Peter Lang, pp. 331–353.

Zompetti, J.P. (2019). "Rhetorical Incivility in the Twittersphere: A Comparative Thematic Analysis of Clinton and Trump's Tweets During and After the 2016 Presidential Election". *Journal of Contemporary Rhetoric* vol. 9: 29–54.

CHAPTER 4

Transnational Soap Operas and Cultural Identity in Times of Change

Dimitra Laurence Larochelle

In the beginning of the last decade of the twentieth century, Stuart Hall (1992), remarked that the "old entities which stabilized the social world for so long are in decline, giving rise to new identities and fragmenting the modern individual as a unified subject. This so-called crisis is seen as part of a wider process of change which is dislocating the central structures and processes of modern societies and undermining the frameworks which gave individuals stable anchorage in the social world" (Hall 1992: 274). Hall's argument explains why the question of identity constituted one of the most frequent subjects of intellectual debates during the 1990s (Jenkins 1996). However, during the decades that followed, identity remained one of the main concerns of academic research. More precisely, the globalization of cultural products as well as the development of information and communication technologies resulted to the increase of studies focusing on the question of identity in a globalized environment (Hall 1991a; Miller 1992; Thompson 1995; Morley and Robins 1995; Hannerz 1996; Lemish et al. 1998; Kraidy 1999; Barker 1999; Strelitz 2004; Berglez and Olausson 2011; Gentz and Kramer 2012; Aronczyk 2013).

Identity as a societal phenomenon is formed by interaction with the "other". More precisely, social subjects tend to identify themselves with a social group with which they consider sharing similar characteristics[1] which are by definition considered as opposed to those of *different* social groups. The consciousness of belonging to the same collectivity emerges only face to other collectivities that are perceived as "different". Thus, *alterity* constitutes integral part of one's identity (Todorov 1989). It is alterity that defines who *belongs* to one particular group and who is *excluded* from it (Constantopoulou 1999).

National identity refers to the feeling of difference one individual experiences in relation to another. This difference is based on the conceptualization of the fact that these two individuals belong to different nations or to distinct national groups within a multicultural environment (Smith 1995). According

---

1   These characteristics may be objective or subjective. As objective characteristics we define differentiating features such as language, religion, history, etc. Subjective characteristics refer to the self-consciousness of a social group (Smith 1990).

to Jacques Derrida (1978), there is no culture or cultural identity which does not have its 'other' of the 'self'. In other terms, an identity can never be defined in isolation. In contrast, as Denis-Constant Martin (1995) pointed out, the only way to circumscribe an identity is by contrasting it against other identities. As a result of the identity formation process described above, the distinctive features between different social groups tend to be over-emphasized (İnaç and Ünal 2013). Consequently, in order to valorize their own identity, social groups tend to conduct a process described by the term *othering*. More precisely, individuals tend to construct positive stereotypes for their own social group while at the same time they create negative stereotypes for the individuals who are excluded from it (Constantopoulou 1999). Edward Said (1978), described this process through his book entitled *Orientalism*. As he explained, the Western world used othering as a pretext in order to legitimize the colonization of faraway countries.

However, according to Stuart Hall (1990) the concept of identity is neither transparent nor unproblematic. Instead of considering identity as an accomplished fact, Hall suggests to perceive identity as "a 'production' which is never complete, always in process, and always constituted, within, not outside, representation" (Hall 1990: 222). More precisely, for Hall, identity is an invention which is formed at the instable point where "untold" stories of subjectivity meet historical narrations, the narrations of a culture. Consequently, identity, is a phrase that is told in a specific moment (*I want to say something now*). What is told at this moment is not told forever, it is not a universal truth. Therefore, identity is always caught in a process of formation (Hall 1996). As a result, cultural identity is in constant negotiation.

Identity is a social phenomenon which is determined by historical and social factors. For instance, while in "pre-modern" European societies, religious identities where more influential, with the modernization process, national identity became one of the most influential elements of one's cultural identity (Martin 1995). For Benedict Anderson (1991), *nation* is a socially constructed imagined community. He refers to an "imagined" community because "the members of even the smallest nation will never know most of their fellow members, meet them, or even hear of them, yet in the minds of each lives the image of their communion" (Anderson 1983: 49). Within this context, television narratives—and particularly television dramas[2]—play a significant role

---

2   According to Alexander Dhoest (2004) television drama is a particularly important genre not only because it occupies an important position within the prime-time zone but also because "it is often considered as an important storyteller and myth-former for contemporary society" (Dhoest 2004).

as they provide common images that shape this "imagined community" described by Anderson (Dhoest 2004).

As cultural object, television is the main field of the production, the exchange and the consumption of goods and of symbols (Souza 2002). From a dramatological perspective (Goffman 1959), media narratives play a significant role in the performance of national identity contributing to the making of collective memory and to the construction of the "imagined community" described by Anderson. Therefore, media narratives can be analyzed as texts conveying the shared values of a society and which constitute explicitly or implicitly part of the society's national identity. Similarly, the study of the consumption practices of transnational media texts can inform us on the negotiation of meanings related to identification issues.

The relation between popular culture and national identity is not new. The policies of the public broadcasting sector regarding the promotion of national identities, the representations of national identities, as well as the reception of products of popular culture by national audiences, are some of the themes that have been largely discussed by several social researchers in different geographical areas (Burke 1992; Blain et al. 1994; Price 1995; Newvomb 1997; Mankekar 1999; Van Den Bulck 2001; Dhoest 2001a, 2001b, 2004; Edenson 2002; Castello 2007; Porto 2011; Feischmidt and Pulay 2016).

The aim of this chapter is to present the results of my empirical research on the reception by audiences in Greece, of Turkish culture and society projected by Turkish soap operas. More precisely, my study revealed that the viewing of the products in question corresponds to the need of redefinition of the Greek identity operated by a part of the Greek audience during the period of economic crisis. First, I will present the specificities of Turkish soap operas, the social and political context in which they are produced as well as its impact on the representations projected through them. Second, I will analyze the particularity of the Greek national identity and finally in the last part of my chapter I will present the results of my research focusing on the identity negotiation process operated by a part of the Greek audience during the period of economic crisis.

1   Methodology

To understand how representations of Turkish culture and society in Turkish soap operas affect communities of fans in Greece, I conducted an empirical study drawing upon both qualitative and quantitative methods. To generate qualitative data, in 2016 and in 2018, I conducted fifty semi-structured in-depth interviews with individuals of different socioeconomic groups[3] and ages,[4] who also live in different regions across Greece.[5] During both periods, the recruitment of participants followed a convenience sampling and snowball logic.

In order to study the representations of Turkish culture and society, I chose the soap operas that have been designed by my interviewees as the most remarkable ones. Consequently, my sample consists of the following six soap operas: *Fatmagül'ün Suçu Ne?*,[6] *Aşk-ı Memnu*,[7] *Muhteşem Yüzyıl*,[8] *Kara Sevda*,[9] *Sila*,[10] and *Ezel*.[11]

An online survey from September 2018 to October 2018, with the aim of mapping larger audiences' tastes and practices, followed the qualitative study.[12] More particularly, it concerned several aspects that had been discussed during interviews but needed to measure key variables at a larger scale in order to have a more representative idea about how Greek fan communities work.

2   *Diziler*:[13] an International Brand

Since 2000, the production of Turkish soap operas is in constant development. These soap operas are not only consumed in Turkey but they are also exported abroad. More precisely, they were first diffused in countries that were in the

---

3   Individuals who participated in my research are divided in the following professional categories: salaried or independent profession: 44%, at home: 20%, students: 20%, retired: 12%, unemployed: 4%.

4   Individuals who participated in my research are between 17 and 89 years old. However, my sample is characterized by an over-representation of individuals from 35 to 45 years old.

5   The interviews took place in the following cities: Athens, Thessaloniki, Komotini, Chalcis.

6   Soap opera aired in Turkey by the channel *Kanal D* between 2010 and 2012. The soap opera in question have been diffused in Greece by MEGA CHANNEL between 2012 and 2014.

7   Soap opera aired in Turkey by the channel *Kanal D* between 2008 and 2010. The soap opera in question have been diffused in Greece by ANTENNA TV between 2011 and 2012.

8   Soap opera aired from 2011 to 2014 in Turkey by the channel *Star TV*. The soap opera in question was diffused from 2012 to 2013 in Greece by ANTENNA TV.

9   Soap opera aired from 2015 to 2017 in Turkey by the channel *Star TV*. The soap opera in question was diffused from 2016 to 2018 in Greece by MEGA CHANNEL and SKAI TV.

10   Soap opera aired from 2007 to 2009 in Turkey by the channel ATV. The soap opera in question was diffused from 2012 to 2013 in Greece by MEGA CHANNEL.

11   Soap opera aired from 2009 to 2011 in Turkey by the channel ATV. The soap opera in question was diffused from 2011 to 2012 in Greece by ANTENNA TV.

12   1900 individuals from Greece replied to the online survey.

13   The term *dizi* in Turkish signifies "serial". *Diziler* is the term in plural.

sphere of cultural influence of the ancient Ottoman Empire (which means the Balkans and the Middle East). Later they were also exported even far, in Latin America, in China, in Pakistan, in India, in Bangladesh, in U.S.A., etc.

According to Hülya Ugur Tanriöver (2011), since the beginning of the first television channel in Turkey, soap operas had a privileged position among other media products. This happens, because as she explains, Turkish audience had already a cinematographic tradition which was established in the "golden age" of Turkish cinema (1960–1970). Thus, Turkish audience always had a particular interest for fiction. The crisis in the cinema industry (that occurred during the 1980s) as well as Turkey's financial situation during the same period are some of the reasons that stimulated Turks to massively adopt the entertainment offered by television at home. In the early years of television, when the number of local productions were still very limited, TRT[14] bought series from abroad that were highly appreciated by the public. Their success was so considerable that in social history, certain periods were named in reference to the series in question, such as the "Love Boat Years" or the "Dallas Years". This is one of the reasons why TRT insisted on producing local soap operas. During the nineties, private channels appeared in Turkish television and this caused augmented competitiveness in the sector. Hence, audience abandoned foreign series in the favor of local products. Today, local soap operas are the most popular television genre in Turkey (Tanriöver 2011).

As mentioned above, Turkish soap operas are also (particularly since 2000) exported abroad. For many specialists on the subject this exportation coincides with a change of paradigm concerning the exercise of foreign policy by the Turkish government. More precisely, Turkish soap operas seem to be considered by the Turkish government as a tool in order to enhance a positive image for Turkey and thus, augment its "soft power".[15]

Since the Party of Justice and Development (AKP) took the power in Turkey in 2002, new cultural and media strategies have been adopted, especially towards the countries of Balkans, of Caucasia, of the Middle-East and of North Africa. These new strategies aim notably in promoting the image of the country in order to enhance its political and economic influence to an important number of countries that were in the influence of the ancient Ottoman Empire (especially Arab and Muslim countries). As Nilgün Tutal-Cheviron and Aydin Çam (2017), explain, many strategies of the Turkish government have been

---

14   Turkish Radio and Television Corporation.
15   "Soft power" is a notion that has been developed by Joseph Nye in the late 1980s. Soft power is defined as the ability to attract (and therefore influence) through appeal and attraction (Joseph Nye 1990).

established in order to assist the production of Turkish soap operas. The public press agency (Anadolu Ajansi) and the financial aid that is provided to private television channels and to production companies for the creation of soap operas are two of the instruments of this policy. Consequently, the diffusion of Turkish soap operas outside Turkey's boarders seems to contribute to the effort of turning Turkey into a "model country". Thereby, the representatives of Turkish government have several times stated in public the importance of Turkish soap operas for the government. For instance, Egemen Bağış, while he was the minister of the European affairs (2009–2013) had declared: "Turkish series are a perfect tool for us to reflect Turkey's image and Turkish lifestyle. This, not only for our economic but also for our diplomatic and sociological interests. Turkish series have become one of the most effective means of our soft power" (Tutal-Cheviron and Çam 2017: 133).

Turkish soap operas are now exported in more than 140 countries. One of the most popular soap operas is *Muhtesem Yuzyil* (Magnificent century)[16] that has been watched by almost 400 millions of viewers worldwide.

The exportation of Turkish soap operas abroad initiated in 1999 with the soap opera entitled *Deli Yürek* in Caucasus (Matthews 2011). However, it was the success of the serial *Gümüş* in 2005 which turned Turkish soap operas popular outside Turkey's frontiers. The cast, the quality of production, the storylines as well as the colloquial use of the Arabic are elements that contributed to the great success of the soap opera in question in the Middle East (Buccianti 2010; Salamandra 2012). Since this first success of *Gümüş* which led to the expansion of the exportation of Turkish soap operas, much has been written on the impact of Turkish soap operas on local audiences. Salamandra (2012) argues that the romantic storylines presented through Turkish soap operas have a great appeal on women of the Arab Middle East.

Many researchers focus on the importance of Turkish productions from a geopolitical perspective (Yanık 2009a, 2009b; Anaz and Purcell 2010). Others, examine the exportation of Turkish soap operas as a tool aiming to enhance Turkey's soft power (Kaynak 2015; Yoruk and Vatıkıotis 2013; Anaz and Özcan 2016). For instance, Ghazzi and Kaidy (2013) argue that Turkish soap operas are tools for the Turkish state which aim to enhance business cooperation between Egypt and Turkey.

---

16   Historical soap opera based on the life of Ottoman Sultan Suleyman the Magnificent. It was originally broadcast on Show TV (2011) and then was transferred to Star TV (2012–2014). It is a production of the company TIM's Productions (source: website of the company, http://tims.tv/serie/muhtesem-yuzyil).

Today, Turkish soap operas constitute a global phenomenon. Some scholars prefer to do not label these products as "soap operas" but instead as "diziler"[17] in order to point out the particularities of these series in terms of production which distinguish them from telenovelas or American daytime and prime-time soap operas (Garapon and Villez 2018). However, according to Robert C. Allen, "each country's experience with the range of text to which the term 'soap opera' has been applied is different. It is a bit like ornithologists, taxidermists, and bird watchers from a dozen different countries all talking about birds, but in one country there are only eagles; in another pigeons and chickens but no eagles; in another macaws and pigeons but no eagles or chickens; and so on" (Allen 1989: 45). Consequently, as soap opera is a transnational (and transcultural) phenomenon, its interpretation may differ from one national culture to another. Many of the features of Turkish television products—e.g. centrality of the female characters, slow rhythm, emphasis on issues related to the private sphere, etc.—suggest that we can classify them to the soap opera genre. However, we have to take under consideration that Turkish soap operas can be classified in several different subgenres such as the melodrama or the *töre dizi*[18] (Tanriöver 2011).

3   Turkish Culture and Society through Turkish Soap Operas

According to Edgar Morin (1975), mass culture products do not reflect *reality*. Instead, they project the historically situated and provisional compromises of self-representation of each national society. Consequently, the study of media representations should always be accompanied by the study of the social and political context in which media texts are produced. Through this part of our chapter we aim to present the social and political context in which Turkish soap operas are produced as well as its impact on the representations of Turkish culture and society conveyed by the series in question.

3.1   *Turkish Cultural Identity: between Ottoman Tradition and Kemalist Modernity*

As indicated above, together with nation-state as a dominant socio-political structure, national identity is central as one of the most important forms of collective identity in modernity (Van Den Bulck 2001). According to Ernest Gellner (1983), industrialization in western societies coincided with the

---

17   *Dizi* in Turkish means "serial". *Diziler* is the term used in plural.
18   Soap opera genre featuring families of land owners in Anatolia.

modernization process and with nationalism. More precisely, the emergence of nationalism during the 18th and the 19th centuries, resulted to the demolition of different entities that where dominant since then and to the appearance of nation-states. However, the emergence of nation-states has not always been anodyne. According to Kevin Robins (1996), modernity is dynamic. It is affirmed constantly through denial and reject. Only if certain things change and are being replaced by others, modernity can maintain its identity. Within this context, the juxtaposition of the "Other" (the pre-modern) is the essential condition of self-understanding. This phenomenon has been translated to a remarkable geographical polarization: West has always been self-defined as dynamic while on the other hand, the Orient has been considered as static. Consequently, Orient represents the Other of occidental modernity and of its development project (Robins 1996).

As Kevin Robins (1996) argues, the success of the European project provoked the admiration of other cultures that wanted to integrate this "universal" modernity. However, as he explains, imitation efforts have been rarely translated to an authentic modernization. The exposition of these cultures to the modern (occidental) culture had as a result the enforced conformism of the "pre-modern" cultures. Within this context, Turks always wanted to be accepted as members of the occidental culture. However, even if they succeeded in several aspects to assimilate the European standards, they are still not considered as authentically occidentals. In contrast, the are being accorded the role of the outsider of the European Union. Turkey has long before operated an occidental turn by embracing unconditionally the occidental modernization. The Tanzimat period, the Young Ottomans movement and finally the foundation of the Turkish republic are part of this occidental turn (Robins 1996).

The Republic of Turkey was based on Kemalist ideology which was named after Mustafa Kemal who is also known as Atatürk (the father of Turks). Kemalism, introduced a new conception of Turkish identity that was defined by various political, social, cultural and religious reforms that intended to separate the Turkish state from the Ottoman Empire. Kemalist ideology was inspired by a "modern"/westernized model of regulation of the political and social affairs that included among other social reforms the establishment of democracy and secularism (Makdisi 2002).

Kemalist elites have been attracted from the modern "universal" culture, science, technology, rationalism and progress. They recognized that Turkey's modernization presupposed a fundamental social transformation of the people. Thus, the adoption of occidental institutions, of nationalism and of the nation state was imperative and had to be total. More precisely, modern Turkish culture is imitative and derivative from the European model. For Kemalist elites, the principles of the occidental modernity could be adopted only after the massive interdiction of the historical and traditional culture. In order to become a "civilized" country, Turkey had to abolish everything that was particular and inherent to the local culture. In other terms, everything that was considered "premodern". However, this ideology was imposed from "above". This will of "purification" of the Turkish society conducted to the denial and the suppression of the reality of the Turkish culture and society (Robins 1996).

Kemalist ideology was a reaction to different nationalist movements which fragmented the Ottoman Empire between the end of the 19th century and the post-World War I period (Makdisi 2002). For Fisher Onar (2009), Turkish Republic was based on the Kemalist interpretation of the Ottoman collapse which defined the nation-building project during the 1920s. According to this interpretation, the cultural, religious and linguistic heterogeneity that characterized the Ottoman Empire had turned it vulnerable to ethnic and religious minority secessionism. Thus, the Kemalist vision of the Turkish identity was based on principles that aimed to prevent such development in the future. One of these principles, was the adoption of a unitary, secular character of the nation-state influenced by western countries and the rejection of the theocratic basis of the Ottoman authority. Religion was then considered as a threat to Turkey's modernization and nationalization process and the new Republic opposed to the pluralism of identity that characterized the Ottoman Empire (Robins 1996). Therefore, during the nation-building process, Turkey— influenced by the French anticlerical tradition of laïcité, a form of state-enforced secularism—left behind the traditional and religious principles as elements that belonged to the ancient regime in order to embrace a "westernized" modernity (Ahmad 2003).

Within this context, "real" Turkey became the "Other" of the "official culture". The state undertook the responsibility of protecting the ideal nation against the "barbarians" that represented the values and the habits of the past. As far as media production is concerned, TRT always promoted the "official" cultural identity. On this point, we have to take under consideration that in modern industrial societies, public broadcasting sectors contribute at the creation of an "imagined community" for the modern nation-state (Van Den Bulck 2001).

However, the introduction of commercial television at the beginning of the 1990s put under question this secular, unified and coherent identity. Private channels were not subjected of the state's direct control and were constantly seeking new audiences. As a result, in contrast to the public television that reflected the "official" Turkish culture, private channels projected the real aspirations and habits of popular classes (Aksoy and Robins 2000). Consequently, the productions of commercial channels in Turkey do not only represent the ideal of modern Turkey but also the habits and the values that are influenced by tradition and thus constitute integral part of the "authentic" Turkish identity.

Moreover, private channels in Turkey accorded visibility to Islam (Aksoy and Robins 2000). During the last decades, Islam emerged again as a dynamic element of Turkish culture. However, particularly since 2002, revisionist politics concerning the republican Turkish identity which included neo-ottoman elements have been implemented (Onar 2002).

3.2   *Morality and Neo-Ottomanism in Contemporary Turkey*

During the last decades, we observe in Turkey a more intense convergence between religion and the Turkish Republic, making Sunnism the only legitimate basis for defining the republican moral norms (Paris 2017). More precisely, AKP wants to promote a modern Islamic identity by emulating successful European ideas and values (Yanik 2009). For AKP, Turkey's Islamic and European identities are complementary and it tends to consider Turkey as bringing the West and Islam (Yanik 2009).

To be more accurate, since 2002, the year that Justice and Development Party (Adalet ve Kalkınma Partisi/AKP) took the power in Turkey, a new vision concerning the exercise of Turkey's foreign policy has been adopted. This policy is based on the notion of "strategic depth" developed by Ahmet Davutoglu.[19] According to Davutoglu, the emphasis accorded to the relation of Turkey with Western countries since the creation of the Turkish Republic has conducted to the neglect of Turkey's interests to other countries that belonged to the ancient Ottoman Empire and particularly with the countries of the North Africa and the Middle East (Taspinar 2008).

The rediscovery of Turkey's imperial heritage presupposes "a more moderate version of secularism at home, and a more activist policy in foreign affairs" (Taspinar 2008: 15). This conception of Turkish foreign policy aims to the augmentation of Turkey's "soft power"[20] in countries that belonged to the former Ottoman Empire as well as in regions where Turkey has strategic interests. As Taspinar pointed out, "this broad vision for Turkish foreign policy requires an embrace of Ottoman "great power" legacy and a redefinition of Turkey's strategic and national identity" (Taspinar 2008: 15). Within this context, Islam plays a significant role "in terms of building a sense of shared identity" (Taspinar

---

19   Former academic and diplomat. Minister of Turkey's Foreign Affairs (2009–2014) and Turkey's Prime-Minister (2014–2016).

20   Soft power is a concept in international affairs, developed by Joseph Nye, and refers to the ability to influence through cultural attraction.

2008: 15) between Turkey and the Ottoman Empire's former provinces (particularly in North Africa and the Middle East).

While AKP's ideology is not explicitly Islamist but it is rather defined as "conservative" (Taspinar 2008), there are two elements pointing out the importance accorded by Erdogan's government to religion which is implicitly the base upon which morality is evaluated in modern Turkey: (1) the fact that there are many references to religion by AKP's representatives and (2) a number of reforms adopted during the last two decades strengthening the influence of religion on state institutions and social life in Turkey[21] (Shukri and Hossain 2017). Consequently, social conservatism in Turkey became synonymous to Islamic values.

The Arab Uprising has been considered as a chance for Turkey in order to accomplish a role of model country in the region as a Muslim but democratic Republic. Additionally, we have to take under consideration that even if Turkey is constitutionally a secular country, AKP's representatives are aware of the sentiments of their supporters, which are that a significant number of Turks want a "more conservative and Islamic government" (Shukri and Hossain 2017: 171). As a consequence, Islamist principles and values are not only necessary for Turkey's foreign policy but they are also of crucial importance as far as the establishment of AKP's power within Turkish borders is concerned.

Over the years, many scholars have noticed that the AKP has used its power in order to direct and reshape state institutions in order to reflect and promote its own political interests and ideology (Öztürk 2016). Consequently, educational, media or religious institutions, even if they are not under formal state control, they still serve as instruments that impose a certain vision of morality which is in accordance to the governments' interests.

Within this context, as I will further explain in the next section of my chapter, it seems that the representations of Turkish society projected by Turkish soap operas are conform to a certain type of morality which is prescribed by Recep Tayyip Erdoğan's government. On this point, we have to take under consideration that it is not hazardous if Kıvanç Tatlıtuğ—a well-known actor of Turkish soap operas—is named by his Arab fans "halal Brad Pitt". This expression emphasizes the "occidental" physical characteristics of the actor as well as the fact that the characters he impersonates are "halal" (in accordance with the Muslim principles and values) (Tutal-Cheviron and Çam 2017).

---

21   Such examples are the introduction in 2013 of laws restricting the sale and consumption of alcohol, the lift of the headscarf ban or even the proposal of criminalization of adultery and the promise of revising the current law on abortion after equating abortion with murder (Shukri and Hossain 2017).

3.3   *Representations of Turkish Culture and Society Projected through Turkish Soap Operas: between Globalized Imaginary and the "Turkish Touch"*[22]

Turkish soap operas contain ingredients that bring the viewer into a fantastic world of globalized consumerism and romantic love which defies national borders (Olson 2000). However, at the same time they project traditional family structures and gender roles. This is what distinguishes Turkish soap operas from the American prototype and what Alexandra Buccianti (2010) described as the "Turkish touch".

The audiovisual law in Turkey defines what is appropriate to be broadcasted by public and commercial channels according to several principles that should respect national traditions, spiritual values and morality. This law has been used many times from the Radio and Television Supreme Council in order to censor contents that have been considered as "inappropriate" as they didn't respect these three important principles: family, morality and nation (Berfin 2016).

The social and political context described above and in which Turkish soap operas are produced has a determinant impact on the representations projected through Turkish soap operas. The importance accorded to religion and to the institution of the family and to its patriarchic organization, the non-representation of members of the LGBTQI community, the taboo of sexuality and the importance accorded to maternity, the under-representation (or the negative representation) of non-Muslims as well as the respect of dominant hierarchies, are some of the main elements that characterize Turkish soap operas (Larochelle 2017a; 2017b; 2019).

Meanings are prescribed in relations of power which define who is included and who is excluded. Within this context, meanings are often organized in binary oppositions (Hall 1997). Though my analysis of representations of Turkish society through Turkish soap operas, I located the following binary oppositions: Muslims/non-Muslims, Turks/non-Turks, men/women, rich/poor, traditional/modern, center/periphery.

More precisely, Muslimness seems to be considered as inherent of Turkishness (Altunay and Altunay, n.d.). Within this context, the division between *Turks* and *non-Turks* is translated to the division between *Muslims* and *Non-Muslims*. Negative behaviors (or behaviors that are not in accordance with the

---

22   I borrow this expression from Alexandra Buccianti (2010). Buccianti used this expression in order to better describe the particularity of the representations projected from Turkish soap operas which distinguishes them from the American prototype.

dominant religious principles in Turkey—e.g. sexuality) are often attributed to *non-Muslims/non-Turks*.

Furthermore, traditional patriarchic stereotypes characterize the relations between *men* and *women*. Men are represented most of the times as being rational and responsible while women as being irrational and trouble-makers. As a result, the relationship between men and women could be assimilated to the relationship between a father and its child.

It is worth mentioning, that one of the main characteristics of the Turkish society as it is represented through Turkish soap operas is the division between *rich* and *poor* which is translated as a division *modern* and *traditional*. Rich families are represented as being "modern" and as having adopted a "westernized" lifestyle. In contrast, poor families maintain a traditional lifestyle which is characterized by habits and attitudes that are completely absent from the daily lives of rich families (e.g. importance accorded to religion, respect of the institution of the family[23] and of traditional ethics in general, etc.). Consequently, the opposition between rich/poor and modern/traditional could also be translated to the opposition non-authentic/authentic. On this point, we have to take under consideration that very often negative behaviors are attributed to rich persons while positive ones to individuals with poor or middle-class origin. Within this context the duality poor/rich is not only translated to the duality traditional/modern and authentic/non-authentic but also to the duality good/bad.

Finally, very often (mostly through *töre diziler*) the opposition modernity/tradition is also translated to the opposition between *center* and *periphery*. Istanbul, represents the center where "modern"/westernized lifestyle dominates while periphery represents a site where traditional attitudes and habits still persist.

As indicated through this section of my chapter, Turkish soap operas are characterized not only by ingredients that bring the viewer into a fantastic world of globalized consumerism and romantic love but also by traditional family structures and gender roles. Moreover, the opposition between ottoman tradition and Kemalist modernity as well as the convergence between religion and the Turkish Republic described in the previous section of the present chapter seems to influence the representations projected through Turkish soap operas.

---

23   This is one characteristic that exists for both types of families but it seems to be more important for the traditional/poor families.

4   Economic Crisis and Identity Negotiation

As mentioned above, identity is not static but in contrast it is always caught in a process of formation (Hall 1996). Stuart Hall refers to what he calls *historical nostalgia* which can be found in the discourse of certain individuals who often refer to a past society where everything is more "authentic" and "cohesive". He refers to this process of organic community "a community that always belongs to that childhood that has left us" (Cervulle 2013: 58). Thus, at a moment of crisis, where individuals fail to identify with the dominant society, they tend to reconstruct their identity by discovering *who they were before*. This is a crucial moment: it is the moment of the rediscovery of the roots, the moment of reinventing who we are by looking back.

During the period of economic crisis, media narratives played a significant role in presenting the European society. The narrative (the way in which a society describes itself in a symbolical way) is an extremely important element for this society's self-consciousness (Constantopoulou 2017). Symbols humiliating Greece, used by other European countries' media during the period of economic crisis, are of crucial importance in order to understand the sentiment of exclusion from the European "family" developed by a part of the Greek society. The image of the Venus de Milo—a symbol of Greece—featuring in the coverage of the German magazine *Focus* giving a middle finger to Europe, accompanied by the caption "Scammers in the Euro-family"[24] in 2010, or even the term "p.i.g.s." used to describe in a negative way the countries of the south of Europe—an acronym of the names of Portugal, Italy, Greece, Spain—from Anglo-Saxon financial analyzers and western media are some characteristic examples of such narratives. Within this context, it seems that Greece became the "Other" of the European West. Greece has been represented as being a "burden" for European countries. Thus, during this period European society has been characterized by the polarization between the West and the South. Within this context, the West has been self-represented as being the "authentic"/civilized/modern/hard-working Europe while the South (including Greece) has been represented as being the *Other:* non-authentic/non-civilized/backward/pariahs....

As a result, a part of Greeks felt *excluded* from the European family. Being unable to identify themselves with the European West, Greeks had to redefine their identity. If this one identity that a person is supposed to share since long-time is has been refused, this person has to look back in order to rediscover who he/she was before and what he/she has become. If this "universal

---

24   "Betrüger in der Euro-Familie".

occidental modernity" described by Kevin Robins (1996) is not an option any more then another option must be found. My results showed that the viewing of Turkish soap operas is a symptom of the need of redefinition of modern-Greek identity. For this reason, analyzing briefly the particularity of the modern-Greek identity seems to be of great importance in order to seize the identity negotiation process within the Greek society during the period of economic crisis.

4.1   *The National Greek Identity: between Hellene and Romios*
The Greek national identity is ambivalent (Couroucli 2002). This ambivalence is due at the co-existence of two different cultural heritages which determined the Greek identity during different historical periods. At the moment of its creation (1830) the Greek state was named *Hellas*. This name refers to the heritage of the ancient Greece and its claim by the Greeks who have been self-defined as *Hellenes*. We should explain that during the Ottoman Empire, Greeks were named *Romioi* (Romains) and formed the Rum-millet[25] of the Ottoman Empire having as religious and communitarian leader the Patriarch of Constantinople. The transit from Romios to Hellene symbolizes the transit to the official modern-Greek identity. During this moment, Greeks who were submitted to the Ottoman Empire became free. So, the term Romios refers to the descendants of the Byzantine Empire who became slaves of the Sultan and at the opposite side the term Hellene refers to the cultivated citizen of a modern democratic western nation-state.

Nevertheless, the link between modern Greece and antiquity was not the essential part of the popular identity. A significant part of Greeks was literate and residing in urban centers. The demand of an identity in continuity with ancient Greece took shape within this group with the support of philhellenes who were literate people with a classical education and militant for the return of Greece among the free and Christian nations.

On the other hand, the fighters of the war of Greek Independence (1821–1830) did not have the same origin. Many of them were speaking diverse popular dialects (sometimes with Albanese influence) and they knew neither ancient Greek language nor ancient Greek history not being thus involved in the national project from the beginning. In this way, the opposition between the culture of fighting people living mostly in southern Greece and that of literate and cultivated urban civils and scholars has been expressed through the opposition between a low, vernacular culture (the culture of "Romios") and a

---

25   The community of the Romains.

high, scholarly culture (the culture of Hellene). Popular culture was not then detached from the identity of Romios. Consequently, Greek identity is marked by this ambivalence between these two different traditions. While being European, the Greek cultural identity is also determined by oriental traditions, customs and ethics.

As a result, we observe in the modern Greek society, a perpetual movement between Orient and Occident. More precisely, there is a continuous back and forth between the past of the Greece under the Ottoman Empire and the demand of an identity referring to a European and modern country. Many ethnological researches on Greece revealed this movement between these two sociopolitical models and the identity representations that accompany them.

This duality of modern-Greek identity was highlighted by several researchers. For instance, Michael Herzfeld (1997) proposed the term of "cultural intimacy" in order to describe this phenomenon. By proposing this term, Herzfeld, explains that the official cultural affiliation (in the case of Greeks the heritage of ancient Greece) does not always correspond to the cultural affiliation affirmed at an intimate level (traditions and ethics inherited by the Ottoman Empire).

As Greeks claimed the glorious past of ancient Greece, they became its "hostages". Having been considered the successors of antiquity, they had to prove that they deserve to be considered as such. However, as we demonstrated above, modern Greece is also influenced by Orient habits. The cultural intimacy is precisely the recognition of aspects of the cultural identity that are an external source of embarrassment—as they do not coincide with the "official" cultural affiliation—but who at the same time allow to the members of the community to maintain a certitude as far as the application of a number of explicit and implicit rules that facilitate the regulation of social life is concerned.

This intimate, implicit or shared knowledge is acquired during the socialization process. It is a knowledge that permits to the members of a community to seize the eventual differences between norms and realities, between discourses and facts.... In other terms, it is the "common sense" of a society. Herzfeld demonstrated that in Greece, the official cultural affiliation differs from the cultural intimacy which is influenced by Orient traditions and ethics.

Nikiforos Diamantouros (2000), explained this cultural dualism of the Greek identity and its impact to politics in modern Greece. As he suggests, In Greece, there are two cultures which govern alternatively according to political circumstances. On one hand, there is the "underdog culture" which is marked by a xenophobia, anti-westernism and pre-democratic mentality highly influenced by the orientalist past of Greece and on the other hand, there is a more progressive culture which has its intellectual roots in the Enlightenment and in liberalism.

Diamantouros' dualist approach underlies the opposition between East (Romeic/"underdog" culture) and West (Hellenic/"progressive" culture) which is observed in modern Greece. As he explains, this back and forth between these two traditions, can be observed in every political or social crisis of modern Greece.

There are two examples of this cultural dualism from Greece's recent history. The first, is the dictatorship of colonels from 1967 to 1974. During this period, the colonels that took the power in Greece, used as main slogan for their project the phrase "Greece of Greek Christians".[26] Thus, they positioned themselves from the side of "Romios", which means within the tradition of the Greek Christian community under the Ottoman Empire. Through their populist discourse they denounced the political class and the intellectual elite of the country, which they considered to be submitted to the European countries. As a result, the colonels found a willing support from the ecclesiastical hierarchy who aspired to an augmentation of its influence to the political life of the country (Couroucli 2003).

Another example of this duality, is the public debate on the new identity cards during the Europeanization of the country (early 2000s). More precisely, between 1999 and 2004, the late Archbishop of Athens, Christodoulos, who was anti-European, pushed the Orthodox Church of Greece to campaign against the "Europeanized" government of Greece. This act, was mainly motivated by the decision of the government in power to do not indicate on citizens' identity cards their religious faith as it was considered to be sensitive personal data. During this public confrontation, the division of the society between these two traditions (Romeic/conservative–Hellenic/progressive) became more and more intense. Though the economy was not in crisis then, Christodoulos contributed to bring to power an opposition party whose views were subservient to his (Lindermayer 2018).

According to Dimitris Tziovas (2017), this cultural hybridity in modern Greece led to an ambiguous attitude of Greeks towards the state that is treated as a source of secure employment (a survival of the ottoman influenced clientelist mentality) and as an adversary (a result of the increasingly anti-systemic discourse of the underdog culture). As he suggests, "during the crisis this ambivalent attitude towards the state has been extended to the EU, leading to its being considered as both savior and enemy, and thus suggesting that the crisis

---

26   Ελλάς Ελλήνων Χριστιανών.

has simultaneously strengthened and profoundly undermined the authority of the modernizing discourse" (Tziovas 2017: 289).

As a consequence of the hybridity of the modern Greek identity, we can observe more intensely during crises, this back and forth between these two traditions. One example of this was the referendum of 2015 where "no" signified the reject of the EU and of its institutions. Moreover, the rise, during the economic crisis, of the right-wing party *Golden Down*, an anti-European, ultraconservative and pro-religious party, is another example of this intense cultural duality in modern Greece which was intensified during the period of financial and social crisis.

As far as media production is concerned, we can distinguish essentially two periods of media production in Greece: the period of the monopoly of public broadcasting (1970–1989) and the period of the commercial television (1989–today), (Koukoutsaki-Monnier 2003). During the first period of the state monopoly, local productions were perceived by the government as a means of stimulating the collective memory of the nation by evoking the Hellenic cultural heritage. Television series of the second period were characterized by increased materialism as well as by a consumer-oriented lifestyle. Soap opera as a televisual genre appeared during this period in Greek television (Koukoutsaki-Monnier 2003). Consequently, apart from the importation of successful American soap operas and Latin American telenovelas, since the 1990s, local soap operas are indispensable elements for the survival of private channels in Greece.

During the period of the economic crisis, due to the financial situation, local productions have been practically diminished. Thus, private channels turned to productions from the neighbor country.

4.2 Turkish Soap Operas in Greek Television

Among the countries that consume Turkish soap operas, Greece has become a great consumer of these products. This consumption has considerably augmented since the economic crisis. During this period, the local production has been practically diminished. It is worth mentioning that the production of a single episode of a Greek drama costs 70,000 to 80,000 euros, while buying an episode of a Turkish soap opera cost 7,000 to 8,000 euros (Moore 2013). Thus, it becomes evident that for the Greek channels, importing Turkish soap operas is much more profitable than producing local series.

Furthermore, according to the European Bank, Greek households were forced to adopt a certain number of strategies in order to affront the new financial situation. These strategies included reducing the consumption of specific goods, discontinuing subscriptions to services, postponing payments, obtaining an additional job or increasing the number of working hours, etc. Consequently, the consumption of "non-necessities" (theatre, cinema, museum, etc.) was dramatically reduced. Therefore, Turkish soap operas had an ideal context of diffusion, in this country in a state of lack.

Turkish soap operas had tempted long before the financial crisis to conquer the Greek media market. The first attempt was with the soap opera entitled *Yabanci Damat* back in 2005.[27] This particular soap opera narrates the love story between a Greek man and a Turkish woman. The soap opera in question was well received by the Greek audience as it marked particularly satisfying audience rates.[28] At this point, it is worth mentioning, that the success of this first Turkish soap opera in Greece, is based basically upon two major factors. First, this cultural product was diffused during a summertime. More often, during this period Greek channels suffer from a severe lack of fictions having as a result to diffuse again and again episodes from cult series. Thus, this soap opera was one of the few "new" products in the Greek market during that summer. Moreover, the storyline of this particular soap opera seemed to interest particularly the Greek audience as, as mentioned above, it treats the "forbidden" love between a Greek man and a Turkish woman. Images of both Athens and Istanbul, funny stereotypes for both populations (especially their oldest generations representants' attitudes), common cultural traits and of course the archetype of Romeo and Juliet were some of the elements that drew the attention of the audience.

Despite the huge success of this first Turkish soap opera in Greece, the Greek market seemed to be more resistant in adopting cultural products from the neighboring country. It is worth mentioning that at the same year (2005) another Turkish soap opera made its appearance on the Greek television, this time through the antenna of *Alpha TV*. This soap opera was entitled *Asmalı Konak*[29] and did not have the same success. Consequently, its diffusion was interrupted few months later.

It was five years later, in 2010, that the Greek market begun to import systematically soap operas from the neighboring country. More precisely, in June 2010, the soap opera entitled *Binbir Gece*[30] was the first big success that established the leading role of Turkish soap operas in Greece. The serial in question

---

27   This soap opera was aired in Turkey by *Kanal D* from 2004 to 2007. In Greece, the soap opera in question has been diffused by *MEGA Channel* in 2005.

28   From the first to the last episode this soap opera marked more than 30% of the television rate while the episode projected on the 25th of August 2005 marked a rate of 58.4%. Source: AGB Hellas (www.arianna.gr).

29   This soap opera was aired in Turkey from 2002 to 2003 by the channel *ATV*.

30   Soap opera aired from 2006 to 2009 in Turkey by the channel *Kanal D*.

that was diffused by *ANTENNA TV,* marked very high audience rates and thus was the top program in the prime-time zone during several weeks competing other Greek products of the same genre that were particularly successful until this moment. After this first successful attempt, the same channel also diffused in 2010 the soap operas *Dudaktan Kalbe*[31] and *Gümüş.*[32] The following year, the two other leading Greek channels (*Alpha TV* and *MEGA Channel*) followed the example of *ANTENNA TV* and begun to diffuse systematically Turkish soap operas. *Ezel* (*ANTENNA TV*),[33] Aşk-ı Memnu (*ANTENNA TV*),[34] *Aşk ve Ceza* (*MEGA Channel*),[35] *Acı Hayat* (*Alpha TV*),[36] *Unutulmaz* (*MEGA channel*),[37] *Sıla* (*MEGA channel*),[38] *Asi* (*ANTENNA TV*),[39] *Muhteşem Yüzyıl* (*ANTENNA TV*),[40] *Fatmagül'ün Suçu Ne?* (*MEGA channel*),[41] *Bir Çocuk Sevdim* (*MEGA channel*),[42] *Karadayı* (*ANTENNA TV*),[43] *Eve Düşen Yıldırım* (*MEGA channel*),[44] *Anne*

31   Soap opera aired from 2007 to 2009 in Turkey by the channel *Show TV*. The soap opera in question was diffused from 2010 to 2011 in Greece.
32   Soap opera aired from 2005 to 2007 in Turkey by the channel *Kanal D*. The soap opera in question was diffused from 2010 to 2011 in Greece.
33   Soap opera aired from 2009 to 2011 in Turkey by the channel *ATV*. The soap opera in question was diffused from 2011 to 2012 in Greece.
34   Soap opera aired from 2008 to 2010 in Turkey by the channel *Kanal D*. The soap opera in question was diffused from 2011 to 2012 in Greece.
35   Soap opera aired from 2010 to 2011 in Turkey by the channel *ATV*. The soap opera in question was diffused from 2011 to 2012 in Greece.
36   Soap opera aired from 2005 to 2007 in Turkey by the channel *Show TV*. The soap opera in question was diffused from 2010 to 2011 in Greece.
37   Soap opera aired from 2009 to 2011 in Turkey by the channel *ATV*. The soap opera in question was diffused from 2012 to 2013 in Greece.
38   Soap opera aired from 2007 to 2009 in Turkey by the channel *ATV*. The soap opera in question was diffused from 2012 to 2013 in Greece.
39   Soap opera aired from 2006 to 2008 in Turkey by the channel *ATV*. The soap opera in question was diffused from 2012 to 2013 in Greece.
40   Soap opera aired from 2011 to 2014 in Turkey by the channel *Star TV*. The soap opera in question was diffused from 2012 to 2013 in Greece.
41   Soap opera aired from 2010 to 2012 in Turkey by the channel *Kanal D*. The soap opera in question was diffused from 2012 to 2014 in Greece.
42   Soap opera aired from 2011 to 2012 in Turkey by the channels *Kanal D/Show TV*. The soap opera in question was diffused from 2013 to 2014 in Greece.
43   Soap opera aired from 2012 to 2015 in Turkey by the channel *ATV*. The soap opera in question was diffused from 2013 to 2014 in Greece.
44   Soap opera aired during 2012 in Turkey by the channel *Show TV*. The soap opera in question was diffused during 2013 in Greece.

(*ANTENNA TV*),[45] *Kiralık Aşk* (*Star channel*),[46] *Elif* (*Star channel*),[47] and *Kadın* (*ANTENNA TV*)[48] are some of the soap operas diffused between 2005 and 2020 in Greece.

4.3   The Consumption of Turkish Soap Operas and the Negotiation of the Modern Greek National Identity

As mentioned above, the identity in continuity with the ancient cultural heritage was a revendication of the urban elites and not of the popular classes. As Greek elites wanted to integrate the European family, they imitated the "universal westernized modernity". During the twentieth century, the adoption of this westernized modernity was translated not only to the rejection of traditional ethics and of the conservative lifestyle that characterized the Greek society since then, but also to the consumption of goods that were inherent to a "modern" way of life (Constantopoulou and Larochelle 2013).

More precisely, Greek traditions and local ethics have been considered as "backward" in comparison to the lifestyle that was (or at least was considered by Greeks to be) dominant in other European countries. The abandon of this "backwardness" was considered to be vital if Greeks wanted to consider themselves as "true" Europeans. This hybridity of the Greek society during the twentieth century has been represented through the Greek movies of the "golden age" of the Greek cinema (1950–1970). During this period, Greek society seemed to have left behind the traumas of numerous national disasters (two World Wars, a Civil War, exchange of populations with Turkey and the Nazi occupation) and struggled to adapt to a "westernized" modernity. Thus, the representations projected through Greek films of this period expressed this hybridity. Some of the characteristics of this period are the ideological conservatism, the great importance accorded to the institution of the family and to its patriarchic organization, the poverty that concerned a big part of the population and the continuous struggle for survival. The representation of popular Greece during this period presents the country as an amalgam of agricultural residues and western dreams where the choice of a new lifestyle which could be

---

45   Soap opera aired from 2016 to 2017 in Turkey by the channel *Star TV*. The soap opera in
       question was diffused from 2017 to 2018 in Greece.
46   Soap opera aired from 2015 to 2017 in Turkey by the channel *Star TV*. The soap opera in
       question was diffused from 2016 to 2017 in Greece.
47   Soap opera aired from 2014 to 2019 in Turkey by the channel *Kanal 7*. The soap opera in
       question is being diffused from 2018 until today in Greece.
48   Soap opera aired from 2017 to 2019 in Turkey by the channel *Fox*. The soap opera in question was diffused from 2018 to 2019 in Greece.

characterized as "modern" or "western" is the "moral lesson" (Constantopoulou and Larochelle 2013).

As far as Greece is concerned, the "westernization" of the country was accompanied by the consumption of goods as indicators of a "modern" lifestyle. Fast cars, comfortable apartments equipped with modern electronic devices, etc., became part of Greeks' life and their acquisition was frequently discussed in numerous Greek films[49] as a passage from the misery of the "old world" to the promising "euphoria" of the "new world".

As explained above, during the period of economic crisis, it seems that a considerable part of Greeks cannot any longer identify themselves as European citizens. Since the beginning of the economic crisis, a part of the Greek society, felt to have been marginalized by the European community and treated as citizens of a "second category". Consequently, cultural re-stratifications seem to be in process during this period in Greece by rejecting the modern/"western-influenced" lifestyle that Greeks had adopted before the economic crisis and by looking back to who they were before the "westernization" of the country. The viewing of Turkish soap operas seems to be a symptom of this trend. During the interviews conducted in the frame of my research 36 out of 50 persons pointed out this element.

Within the context of economic crisis, "westernized" modernity is being rejected. Consumerism which accompanied the "modernization" of the nation seems to be rejected and ethics and traditions that characterized the culture of popular classes are now embraced again.

The viewing of Turkish soap operas is perceived by the subjects interviewed as a reject of the occidental cultural products that represent, according to the individuals who participated in my research, a modern lifestyle far from tradition and ethics such as, for example, the respect of the institution of the family. For instance, many subjects mobilized a comparison between Turkish soaps and other similar cultural products they have viewed in the past and which represent a "westernized" lifestyle.

FEMALE (49 years old): "American serials represent the American lifestyle. Turkish series represent a lifestyle, mentalities and human relations that are closer to us. In American serials one girl will have sex with all the members of the family (...) I don't like that kind of serials. It is an ethical derailment".

---

49   E.g.: *Ah Auti I Gunaika Mou* (translation: *Oh! That wife of mine*, 1967), *I De Gyni na Fovitai ton Andra* (translation: *And the wife shall reserve the husband*, 1965), *I Kuria Tou Kuriou* (translation: *The lady of the gentleman*, 1962), etc.

FEMALE (53 years old): "What I like the most in these serials is that they don't project anything vulgar. I have enough with Greek serials that show all the time who had an affair with whom and that at the end they don't even know each other. They have (*Turkish serials*) beautiful stories even if sometimes they are sad or they have a tragic end ... I don't mind. I prefer watching a Turkish serial rather than a Greek who shows all the time how they kiss, how they ... whatever! I also like that they respect the institution of the family, they eat all together ... they respect each other, kids respect elders ... there are some values".

The rediscovery of the values left behind by embracing "modernity" is of crucial importance for the audience of these particular soap operas. This rediscovery in many cases was a motivation for the subjects who participated to our research in order to redefine who they are and how they place themselves in the contemporary complex geopolitical and sociocultural reality.

FEMALE (33 years old): "These serials help me to better understand myself as a Balkan. (...) I am a Balkan not a European".

At this point, it is worth mentioning that Greeks seem to identify themselves more easily to the characters of Turkish soap operas.[50] This identification of individuals to the characters, to the situations and to the social environments represented in Turkish soaps enhance their emotional attachment to the storylines. Furthermore, Turkish soap operas do not surprise them as they are capable of understanding the interpretations, the intentions, the attitudes, the roles and the social and cultural situations they watch and that they consider as being part of their own lives. This identification with the audiovisual contents dedicated to everyday life and culture creates a sense of proximity to the audiences which not only intensifies their interest for the program but also their emotional implication to them. As far as soap operas are concerned, their appreciation and their quality is evaluated in terms of identification and of representativity. One of the main characteristics of soap operas is their focus on everyday problems of the private sphere (And 1985; Geraghty 1991; Brown

---

50   On this point we have to take under consideration that among the 1900 individuals who participated in my online survey, 664 individuals (34.9%), are from families that came to Greece as refuges during the twentieth century. These families came to Greece either with the exchange of populations with Turkey in 1923, either later because of the persecutions that Greeks suffered by Turks until 1964.

1994; Modleski 1994; Harrington and Bielby 1995; Blumenthal 1997; Hobson 2003). Thus, their perception in terms of quality depends in an important level from their ability to identify themselves with the narratives projected through them. The more these narratives describe realities closer to their lives, the more their qualitative perception is raised.

> FEMALE (45 years old): "Turks have many similarities with Greeks. I recognize myself through these serials. I recognize my values. Values that have been lost today and that we don't see any more in Greek television. They look like us. The appearance, the customs, the foods, the hospitality, the importance accorded to God...".

Furthermore, the notion of *nostalgia* is of great importance for our study. As mentioned before, the representations projected by Turkish soap operas remind traditional Greek ethics and values that have been abandoned during the "modernization" process of the country. Thus, the representations projected through Turkish soap operas remind traditional Greece that now is considered to be lost and forgotten and which was better as "everything was better before" (Serres 2017). Taking under consideration that the past is something known, something through which we have survived, then the future is always something that hides potential dangers. This becomes obvious if we pay attention to the critiques of older generations towards the habits of the youngsters. Thus, the evasion towards the idealized past is a common trait of all societies. However, this nostalgic reference to past times makes sense if we consider that this period of financial crisis is a period full of uncertainty.

Svetlana Boym (2001), explained that nostalgia appears as a mechanism in a time of accelerated rhythms and historical upheavals. She makes a distinction between two kinds of nostalgia: the restorative and the reflective. The restorative nostalgia is defined as someone's desire to restore the past as if he was about to "rebuild the lost home and patch up the memory gaps" (Boym 2001: 41). This type of nostalgia emphasizes on "nostos" (the desire to return back home where we belong). Reflective nostalgia on the other hand, is the acceptance that time passes and that there is nothing to return to. In this definition of nostalgia, the emphasis is put on the notion of "algia" (the pain for the lost past). At this point, it is worth mentioning that "cultural nostalgia, can take the form of longing for a certain period of time, but also for a time that has never been experienced by one's society" (Primorac 2015: 37). Thus, the consumption of products referring to another period seems to correspond to the need of revival of this period and of the stability of well-established traditional habits and ideas that accompanied it. In a continuously changing and unstable world the revisit of a period that is perceived as emblematic of social certainties through cultural products is of crucial importance.

> MALE (57 years old): "What is projected in these serials is my life. This is how I grew up. Nobody loves something randomly. This is everything I have lived, the customs, the values, everything... (...) when I see these serials, I see a part of me that I have lost ... it's like a déjà vu".

Furthermore, apart from the rediscovery of who we were before, it seems that for individuals who participated in my research, Turkish soap operas represent the *authentic popular Greek cultural identity*. To be more accurate, for the Greek audience of Turkish soap operas, the "westernized" narratives are rejected as "constructed" or non-authentic. As narratives imported and thus referring to a far reality. In contrast, the representations of Turkish soap operas are considered to be closer to the Greek traditional mentality and society.

> FEMALE (40 years old): "We (*the Greeks*) had adopted the American lifestyle. In a certain way we were living like Americans. We were watching The Young and the Restless and we copied that kind of lifestyle. With the Turkish serials there is a balance that is restored".

Thus, the "modernization/westernization" of the country and the abandon of certain values and habits that were in a great level influenced by Ottoman traditions is now perceived from a part of the Greek audience as an "alienation". In contrast, Turkish soap operas are considered to be a "tool" that enhance cultural authenticity and through which subjects can find identification references.

> FEMALE (42 years old): "Through Turkish serials I find again the values we lost while we became Europeans".

Through the statements exposed above, we can understand the need of the subjects interviewed for rediscovering their roots as they find again what they've lost during the process of "modernization" of the country. The consumerism that accompanied the "modernization" of the country as well as the "progressive" values that had been adopted (at least at a superficial level) are now questioned. The "false" Europeanization that is considered to be the heart of the current financial crisis is now rejected and the accent that has been put on the consumption of goods during the previous years is now recalled in favor of the rediscovery of the lost values.

For the fans of these cultural products the ethical order of things is restored through these soap operas. Values that represent a more conservative lifestyle and thus more "authentic" as closer to Greek mentality, are now embraced while at the same time "westernized modernity" is rejected. Modernity, which as we explained has been accompanied by consumerism, is being rejected as it is now considered as one of the reasons of the current economic crisis. In contrast, values, ethics and traditions inherent to the culture of popular classes are embraced again. At this moment of crisis, the Hellene, who felt rejected by the European community, seems to become Romios again. "Constructed modernity" is now questioned and "traditional authenticity" is embraced.

5   Conclusion

Through this Chapter 1 tempted to present a brief analysis of the identity negotiation phenomenon that emerged during my empirical research on the reception of Turkish soap operas by a part of the Greek audience.

First, I briefly analyzed the social and political context in which Turkish soap operas are produced. Second, I examined the storylines projected through Turkish soap operas as texts conveying the shared values of a society. Thus, I demonstrated that the representations projected through Turkish soap operas are characterized not only by ingredients that bring the viewer into a fantastic world of globalized consumerism and romantic love but also by traditional family structures and gender roles. Moreover, the opposition between ottoman tradition and Kemalist modernity as well as the convergence between religion and the Turkish Republic described in the present chapter influence in an important level the representations projected through Turkish soap operas. Moreover, these representations are highly influenced by a certain vision of morality which is imposed by the Turkish censure and determined by religious values and principles. Additionally, these storylines remind the representations projected through Greek movies of the "golden" period of the Greek cinema where the established hierarchy and traditional habits were confronted with modernity.

As I discussed through this chapter, the Greek national identity is an ambivalent identity as it is determined by two different traditions and two different conceptions of Greekness. The official/"progressive"/European culture of the Hellene and the "conservative"/underdog culture of Romios. During the period of the state monopoly of the broadcasting sector, local productions were perceived by the government as a means of stimulating the collective memory of the nation by evoking the Hellenic cultural heritage. However, after

the commercialization of the audiovisual sector in Greece, Television series
were characterized by increased materialism as well as by a consumer-oriented
lifestyle. During the period of the economic crisis, due to the financial situation,
local productions have been practically diminished. Thus, private channels
turned to productions from the neighbor country.

During the period of economic crisis, an important part of the Greek population felt rejected by the European community and western media narratives
played a crucial role in this process. More precisely, European society has being
characterized by the polarization between the West and the South. Within this
context, the West has been self-represented as being the "authentic"/civilized/
modern/hard-working Europe while the South (including Greece) has been
represented as being the other: non-authentic/non-civilized/backward/pari-
ahs. As a result, a part of Greeks felt excluded from the European family. Being
unable to identify themselves with the European West, Greeks had to redefine
their identity. If this one identity that we are supposed to share since longtime
is now being refused to us, we have to look back in order to rediscover who we
were and what we have become.

Within this context, the viewing of Turkish soap operas is a symptom of
the identity negotiation operated by a part of the Greek audience during this
period of financial crisis. The "westernization" of the country was accompanied by the consumption of "modern" goods as indicators of the adoption of
a more European lifestyle giving the illusion to Greeks that they had left behind the past and that they had embraced once and for all the modern lifestyle having taken a European aspect. In this sense, modernity and the value
accorded to materiality are rejected while lost values such as the importance
of the family, of the religion, of traditional habits and values are re-embraced.
The nostalgia expressed by subjects who participated in our research during the interviews and the love for the past prove once more the reject of the
"alienating modernity" which is considered to have led the country to the existing financial crisis. Consequently, at this moment of crisis, the Hellene, who
felt rejected by the European community, seems to become Romios again.
"Constructed modernity" is now questioned and "traditional authenticity" is
embraced.

Bibliography

Ahmad, F. (2003). *Turkey: The Quest for Identity*. Oneworld.
Aksoy, A., and Robins, K. (2000). "Thinking across spaces: Transnational television
from Turkey". *European Journal of Cultural Studies* 3(3): 343–365.

Al-Ghazzi, O., and Kraidy, M. (2013). "Neo-Ottoman Cool 2: Turkish Nation Branding and Arabic-Language Transnational Broadcasting". *International Journal of Communication* 7: 2341–2360.

Allen, R.C. (1989). "Bursting Bubbles: 'Soap opera', Audiences, and the Limits of Genre". In: E. Seiter, H. Borchers, G. Kreutzner, and E.-M. Warth. *Remote Control: Television, Audiences, and Cultural Power*. Routledge.

Anaz, N., and Özcan, C.C. (2016). "Geography of Turkish Soap Operas: Tourism, Soft Power, and Alternative Narratives". In: I. Egresi (ed.). *Alternative Tourism in Turkey. Role, Potential Development and Sustainability*, vol. 121, pp. 247–258. Springer International Publishing.

Anaz, N., and Purcell, D.E. (2010). "Geopolitics of film: Valley of the wolves—Iraq and its reception in Turkey and beyond". *Arab World Geographer* 13(1): 34–49.

Anderson, B. (1991). *Imagined Communities: Reflections on the Origin and Spread of Nationalism*. Verso.

Ang, I. (1985). *Watching Dallas: Soap Opera and the Melodramatic Imagination*. Methuen.

Aronczyk, M. (2013). *Branding the Nation: The Global Business of National Identity*. Oxford University Press.

Berfin, K.E.C. (2016). "Pushing the limits of the family on Turkish television: Lost City, an alternative voice?" *European Journal of Communication* 31(6): 694–706.

Berglez, P., and Olausson, U. (2011). "Intentional and unintentional transnationalism: Two political identities repressed by national identity in the news media". *National Identities* 13(1): 35–49.

Blain, N., and O'Donnell, H. (1994). "The stars and the flags: Individuality, collective identities and the national dimension in Italia '90 and Wimbledon '91 and '92". In: R. Giulianotti and J. Williams. *Games Without Frontiers: Football, Identity and Modernity*. Arena.

Blumenthal, D. (1997). *Women and Soap Opera: A Cultural Feminist Perspective*. Praeger.

Boym, S. (2001). *The future of Nostalgia*. Basic Books.

Brown, M.E. (1994). *Soap Opera and Women's Talk. The Pleasure of Resistance*. Sage Publications.

Brunsdon, C. (2000). *The Feminist, the Housewife, and the Soap Opera*. Clarendon Press.

Buccianti, A. (2010). "Dubbed Turkish soap operas conquering the Arab world: Social liberation or cultural alienation?" *Arab Media & Society* 7: 1–7.

Burke, P. (1992). "We, the People: Popular Culture and Popular Identity in Modern Europe". In: S. Lash and J. Friedman. *Modernity and Identity*. Blackwell.

Castello, E. (2007). "The Production of Television Fiction and Nation Building. The Catalan Case". *European Journal of Communication* 22(1): 49–68.

Cemiloglu Altunay, M., and Altunay, A. (n.d.). *The Representation of Non-Muslims in the TV Series "Muhteşem Yüzyıl" (Magnificent Century)*. https://www.academia

.edu/30817968/The_Representation_of_Non-Muslims_in_the_TV_Series_Muhtes_ em_Yu_zy%C4%B1l_Magnificent_Century_.docx.

Cervulle, M. (2013). *Identités et Cultures 2. Politiques des Différences*. Éditions Amsterdam.

Constantinou, C.M., and Tziarras, Z. (2018). "TV Series in Turkish Foreign Policy: Aspects of Hegemony and Resistance". *New Middle Eastern Studies* 8(1): 23–41.

Constantopoulou, C. (ed.). (1999). *Altérité, Mythes et Réalités*. Paris: L'Harmattan.

Constantopoulou, C. (2010). *Leisure time: Myths and realities*. Athens: Papazisis.

Constantopoulou, C. (2017). *Récits de la crise. Mythes et réalités de la société contemporaine*. Paris: L'Harmattan.

Constantopoulou, C., and Larochelle, D.L. (2013). "Cultural re-stratifications and Turkish series in Greece during the economic crisis". *Koinonias Dromena* 1(1): 34–44.

Constantopoulou, C., Maratou, L., Oikonomou, Th., and Germanos, D. (1991). *We and the Others*. Athens: Tupothito.

Couroucli, M. (2002). "Le nationalisme de l'Etat en Grèce". In: A. Dieckhoff and R. Kastoriano. *Nationalismes en mutation en Méditerranée Orientale*. CNRS Éditions.

Couroucli, M. (2003). "Génos, ethnos. Nation et Etat-nation". *Identités, Nations, Globalisation*. Colloque Franco-Mexicain.

Derrida, J. (1978). *Writing and Difference*. University of Chicago.

Dhoest, A. (2001a). "National Identity as Normality: Representation and Typing in Flemish Television Fiction". *InterSections: The Journal of Global Communications and Culture* 1(2): 15–26.

Dhoest, A. (2001b). "Peasants in Clogs: Imagining Flanders in Television Fiction". *Studies in Popular Culture* 23(3): 11–24.

Dhoest, A. (2004). "Negotiating Images of the Nation: The Production of Flemish TV Drama, 1953–89". *Media Culture & Society* 26(3): 393–408.

Diamantouros, N. (2000). *Cultural dualism and political change in Greece after the end of the dictatorship*. Alexandria.

Edensor, T. (2002). *National Identity, Popular Culture and Everyday Life*. Berg.

Feischmidt, M., and Pulay, G. (n.d.). "Rocking the nation': The popular culture of neo-nationalism". *Nations and Nationalism 23*.

Fisher Onar, N. (2009). *Neo Ottomanism, Historical Legacies and Turkish Foreign Policy*. *2009*(3): 1–16.

Garapon, B., and Villez, B. (2018). "Diziler: Les séries télévisées turques". *TV/SERIES* 13: 1–10.

Gellner, E. (1983). *Nations and Nationalism*. Cornell University Press.

Gentz, N., and Kramer, S. (2012). *Globalization, Cultural Identities, and Media Representations*. State University of New York Press.

Geraghty, C. (1991). *Women and Soap Opera: A Study of Prime Time Soaps*. Polity Press.

Goffman, E. (1959). *The Presentation of Self in Everyday Life.* Doubleday.

Hall, S. (1990). "Cultural Identity and Diaspora". In: J. Rutherford. *Identity: Community, Culture, Difference.* Lawrence & Wishart.

Hall, S. (1991a). "Old and New Identities, Old and New Ethnicities". In: A.D. King. *Culture, Globalization and the World System.* Macmillan.

Hall, S. (1991b). "The Local and the Global: Globalization and Ethnicity". In A.D. King. *Culture, Globalization and the World System.* Macmillan.

Hall, S. (1992). "The Question of Cultural Identity". In: S. Hall, D. Held, and T. McGrew. *Modernity and its futures.* Polity Press.

Hall, S. (1996). "Introduction". In: Hall, S. and Gay, P. du. *Questions of Cultural Identity.* Sage Publications.

Hall, S. (1997). *Representation. Cultural Representations and Signifying Practices.* Sage Publications.

Hannerz, U. (1996). *Transnational Connections: Culture, People, Places.* Routledge.

Harrington, C.L., and Bielby, D.D. (1995). *Soap Fans: Pursuing Pleasure and Making Meaning in Everyday Life.* Temple University Press.

Herzfeld, M. (1997). *Cultural Intimacy. Social Poetics of the Nation State.* Routledge.

Hobson, D. (2003). *Soap Opera.* Polity Press.

İnaç, H., and Ünal, F. (2013). "The Construction of National Identity in Modern Times: Theoretical Perspective". *International Journal of Humanities and Social Science* 3(11).

Jenkins, R. (1996). *Social Identity.* Routledge.

Karanfil, G., and Kaptan, Y. (2013). "Turkey, the Middle East and the Media Special Section". *International Journal of Communication* 2013(7): 2419–2423.

Kaynak, S. (2015). "Noor and Friends: Turkish Culture in the World". In: B.S. Cevik and P. Seib. *Turkey's Public Diplomacy.* Palgrave Macmillan.

Kraidy, M.M. (1999). "The Global, the Local and the Hybrid: A Native Ethnography of Glocalization". *Critical Studies in Mass Communication* 16: 456–476.

Larochelle, D.L. (2017a). "La mise en scène du pouvoir à travers les séries télévisées turques difusées en Grèce: Création artistique ou propagande nationaliste? L'exemple de la série Soliman le Magnifique". *Mises En Scène Du Politique Contemporain* 2017(7): 1–11.

Larochelle, D.L. (2017b). "Theatricalization of Patriarchate's Power through Television Serials: Legitimation of Rape". *Open Journal for Sociological Studies* 1(2): 65–72.

Larochelle, D.L. (2019). "'Brad Pitt Halal' and the Hybrid Woman: Gender Representations and Religion through Turkish Soap Operas". *ESSACHESS* 12(2 (24)): 61–78.

Lemish, D., Drotner, K., Liebes, T., Maigret, É., and Stald, G. (1998). "Global Culture in Practice: A Look at Children and Adolescents in Denmark, France and Israel". *European Journal of Communication* 13(4): 539–556.

Lindermayer, O. (2018). *"Better the Turkish turban than the Pope's tiara": The conspiracy theory and the anti-Western attitude of Eastern Orthodox Christians in modern*

Greece. Staying—Moving—Settling, 15th EASA Biennial Conference, Stockholm University.

Macé, É. (2001). "QU'EST-CE QU'UNE SOCIOLOGIE DE LA TELEVISION? Esquisse d'une théorie des rapports sociaux médiatisés les trois moments de la configuration médiatique de la réalité: Production, usages, representations". *Réseaux* *105*: 199–242.

Macé, É. (2006). *La société et son double. Une journée ordinaire de télévision*. Paris: Armand Colin.

Makdisi, U. (2002). "Ottoman Orientalism". *The American Historical Review* 107(3): 768–796.

Mankekar, P. (1999). *Screening Culture, Viewing Politics. An Ethnography of Television, Womanhood, and Nation in Postcolonial India*. Duke University Press.

Martin, D.-C. (1995). "The choices of identity". *Social Identities. Journal for the Study of Race, Nation and Culture* 1(1).

Matthews, O. (2011). "Turkish soap operas are sweeping the Middle East". *Newsweek*. https://www.newsweek.com/turkish-soap-operas-are-sweeping-middle-east-67403.

Miller, D. (1992). "The Young and the Restless in Trinidad". In: E. Hirsch and R. Silverstone. *Consuming Technologies: Media Information and Domestic Space*. Routledge.

Modleski, T. (1994). *Loving with a Vengeance: Mass-produced fantasies for women*. Routledge.

Morin, E. (1975). *L'esprit du temps*. Grasset.

Morley, D., and Robins, K. (1995). *Spaces of Identity: Global Media, Electronic Landscapes, and Cultural Boundaries*. Routledge.

Newcomb, H. (1997). "National Identity/National Industry: Television in the New Media Contexts". In: G. Bechelloni and M. Buonanno. *Television Fiction and Identities: America, Europe, Nations*. Ipermedium.

Olson, S.R. (2000). "THE GLOBALIZATION OF HOLLYWOOD". *International Journal on World Peace* 17(4): 3–17.

O'Neil, M.L. (2013). "Selfish, Vengeful, and Full of Spite: The representations of women who have abortions on Turkish television". *Feminist Media Studies* 13(5): 810–818.

Öztürk, A.E. (2016). "Turkey's Diyanet under AKP rule: From protector to imposer of state ideology?" *Southeast European and Black Sea Studies* 16(4): 619–635.

Papadimitriou, L., and Tzioumakis, Y. (2012). *Greek Cinema. Texts, Histories, Identities*. The University of Chicago Press.

Paris, J. (2017). "La morale nationale et internationale des histoires. L'impératif moral dans la production et la circulation des séries télévisées turques". In: D. Marchetti (ed.). *La circulation des productions culturelles. Cinémas, informations et séries télévisées dans les mondes arabes et musulmans*, pp. 148–167. Centre Jacques-Berque.

Porto, M. (2011). "Telenovelas and representations of national identity in Brazil". *Media Culture & Society* 33(1): 53–69.

Price, M.E. (1995). *Television, the Public Sphere and National Identity.* Clarendon Press.

Primorac, A. (2015). "Cultural Nostalgia, Orientalist Ideology, and Heritage Film". In: D. Hassler-Forest and P. Nicklas. *The Politics of Adaptation. Media Convergence and Ideology.* Palgrave.

Robins, K. (1996). "Interrupting Identities: Turkey/Europe". In S. Hall and P. Du Gay (eds.). *Questions of Cultural Identity*, pp. 61–86. Sage Publications.

Said, E. (1978). *Orientalism.* Pantheon Books.

Salamandra, C. (2012). "The Muhannad Effect: Media Panic, Melodrama, and the Arab Female Gaze". *Anthropological Quarterly* 85(1): 45–77.

Serres, M. (2017). *C'était mieux avant!* Éditions Le Pommier.

Shukri, S.F.M., and Hossain, I. (2017). "Political Discourse and Islam: Role of Rhetoric in Turkey". *The Journal of Social, Political and Economic Studies* 42(2): 157–179.

Smith, A.D. (1990). *National Identity.* Penguin Books.

Smith, A.D. (1995). *Nations and Nationalism in a Global Era.* Polity Press.

Souza, M.D. (2002). "Télévision et identité culturelle". In *Télévision, mémoire et identités nationales.* L'Harmattan.

Strelitz, L. (2004). "Against cultural essentialism: Media reception among South African youth". *Media, Culture & Society* 26(5): 625–641.

Tanriöver, H.U. (2011). *Turkish Television Broadcasting.* Istanbul Ticaret Odasi.

Taspinar, Ö. (2008). "Turkey's Middle East Policies: Between Neo-Ottomanism and Kemalism". *Carnegie Middle East Center* 2008(10): 1–36.

The impact of the crisis on households in Greece. (n.d.). European Bank for Reconstruction and Development. http://litsonline-ebrd.com/the-crisis-impact-in-greece/.

Thompson, J.B. (1995). *The Media and Modernity: A Social Theory of the Media.* Polity Press.

"Turkey's TV drama exports exceed $250 million". (2016, Juin). *Hürriyet Daily News.* http:// www.hurriyetdailynews.com/turkeys-tv-drama-exports-exceed-250-million-93801.

Tutal-Cheviron, N., and Çam, A. (2017). "La vision turque du « soft-power » et l'instrumentalisation de la culture". In: D. Marcetti (ed.). *La circulation des productions culturelles. Cinémas, informations et séries télévisées dans les mondes arabes et musulmans*, pp. 125–147. Centre Jacques-Berque.

Todorov, T. (1989). *Nous et les Autres. La réflexion française sur la diversité humaine.* Éditions du Seuil.

Tziovas, D. (2001). "Beyond the Acropolis: Rethinking Neohellenism". *Journal of Modern Greek Studies* 19: 189–220.

Tziovas, D. (2017). "From junta to crisis: Modernization, consumerism and cultural dualisms in Greece". *Byzantine and Modern Greek Studies* 41(2): 278–299.

Van den Bulck, H. (2001). "Public Service Television and National Identity as a Project of Modernity: The Example of Flemish Television". *Media, Culture & Society* 23(1): 53–69.

Yanık, L.K. (2009a). "The Metamorphosis of 'Metaphors of Vision': "Bridging" Turkey's Location, Role and Identity After the End of Cold War". *Geopolitics* 14(3): 531–549.

Yanık, L.K. (2009b). "Valley of the Wolves-Iraq: Anti-geopolitics Alla Turca". *Middle East Journal of Culture and Communication* 2(1): 2–18.

Yörük, Z., and Vatikiotis, P. (2013). "Soft Power or Illusion of Hegemony: The Case of the Turkish Soap Opera 'Colonialism'". *International Journal of Communication* 7: 2361–2385.

CHAPTER 5

Narrative Structures and the Export of Meaning: the Case of South Korean Popular Culture's Reception in Central and Eastern Europe

Valentina Marinescu

The ability of South Korean culture and media industry to translate Western or American culture to fit Asian tastes is considered as a key-factor that explained the success of Hallyu and it is considered as a possible "effective bridge or buffer functioning between the West and Asia" (Ryoo 2008).

According to the studies devoted to Hallyu phenomenon (Tada-amnuaychai 2007), the expansion of South Korean popular culture had two distinctive stages: the period before the year 2000 and after this date (what it is called now "Hallyu"). If in the case of the first stage, South Korea exported especially movies and television series in various countries, the untimely success of Hallyu is based on the combination between "the cultural mix" and the use of the newly emerged economic opportunities—mainly the access to the digital scope, the Internet (Cho 2005).

If Asian "family-friendly" values were considered as the main reason for the success of Korean television series exported abroad, the interest in South Korean popular music seems to be due to its increasingly transnational and hybrid aspects (Jung 2011). At the same time, the strategic cultural hybridization on which Hallyu is based has as the main reason the need to meet the complex desires of various consumer groups, which maximizes capitalist profit (Jung 2011).

Scholars in cultural and audience studies have long examined the interrelationships between audience participation and mass media in fan and fandom studies (Baym 2000). The relation of the fan and their object of fandom is considered to be rooted in emotional consumption (Sandvoss 2005). The objects of fandom are defined as "fans' extension of self in which no meaningful distinction between the fan and the object of fandom is maintained" (Sandvoss 2005).

If we center our analysis on "identity" (or the "self" from the above-mentioned text), we can notice that we have to discuss an extremely complex concept (De Fina 2004). Many sociologists and psychologists still assume that identities are stable structures, built in a more sophisticated way, from a variety of "building blocks" (Cohen 2008). However, writers such as Bourdieu (1994) talk of the "biographical illusion" that describes life as a coherent path according to culturally available interpretive patterns and images. In the same vein, Bhabha challenge this assumption and states that the articulation of the difference between "spaces" is where we need to focus our attention (Bhabha 2012). This is important in the case of Hallyu's fans, which are located in other countries but act also as "online/ virtual communities" (Kim 2008).

The centrality of fans for popular culture was stressed by Baym (2007) who noticed a double movement. On the one hand fans have increasing influence in shaping the phenomena around which they organize themselves and, on the other hand, the modern popular culture industry relies on online communities to publicize and provide testimonials for their products (Baym 2007).

This chapter presents the results of a research project made between 2011 and 2017 with the help of Academy of Korean Studies Grant (AKS-2013-R71) (see also Marinescu 2014a; Marinescu 2015). The following research questions have guided the empirical approach:

RQ1. What are the main characteristics of the consumers (public/audiences) of South Korea popular culture in the case of the countries from Central and Eastern Europe?

RQ2. What are the ways in which members of groups of fans from the countries from Central and Eastern Europe build their (online and offline) communities of fans of the Korean popular culture?

RQ3. What are the means through which fans granted the passage between the "real" existences of local groups of Korean-fans their membership to the "imagined communities" (Anderson 2006) of Hallyu consumers?

The principal research methodology used is a sociological one, based on online questionnaires (Marinescu 2014a; Marinescu 2015). The research universe of the project covers four countries: Czech Republic, Slovakia, Poland and Hungary—and four distinctive, national samples of South Korean fans are analyzed: nineteen (19) respondents were from the Czech Republic, thirteen (13) from Hungary, fifty-one (51) from Poland and fifteen (15) from Slovakia. The samples were made mainly from young women (aged 13–30 years). In the case of the Czech respondents, all the interviewees were women, and 83% were aged 13–19 years old. 90% of the Hungarian sample was made of women (only 10% were men)—42.90% of them are 13–19 years old while 46.40% were 20–30 years old. The Polish sample comprised 96.1% women—52% of them were 13–19 years old, and 44% were 20–30 years old. In the Slovak sample's case, 86.7% of the respondents were women, 66.7% aged 13–19 years old and 26.7% aged 20–30 years (see also Marinescu 2014a; Marinescu 2015).

1   Analysis of the Results

"Amazing", "colorful", "fascinating", "beautiful", "exotic", "interesting", "special" and "unique" were the main words used by the Hallyu fans from the four countries when they characterized the Korean culture in brief. One can notice in the case of this question the existence of local (national) variations among a group of fans. Thus, the Slovak respondents used in a higher degree—13.3%— the word "amazing" when they referred to South Korea, while 16.7% of the Hungarian fans had assessed South Korea as "unique" and 11.8% of the Polish interviewees defined it as "interesting". 10.5% of the Czech fans briefly described South Korea using the word "pride", and another 10.5% of them had referred to it as "beautiful". Only the Polish fans had associated South Korea with a specific cultural product—7.8% of them defining it through the word "K-pop".

As the majority of the respondents were young (13–30 years old), we were interested to see how they started to be interested and attracted by the South Korean cultural products. One can notice some interesting differences among the countries analyzed. Thus, 53.3% of the Slovak respondents had become interested in Hallyu because they listen to K-pop while only 21.1% of the Czech interviewees were at the beginning attracted by K-pop. In the same vein, while 23.3% of the Hungarian respondents had declared that Hallyu attracted them after they had watched K-dramas, only 17.6% of the Polish respondents became Hallyu-fans after they watched South Korean TV series.

In the meantime, 10.5% of the Czech respondents started to be interested in South Korea after they played Korean PC games while 3.9% of the Polish interviewees were at the beginning attracted by the Japanese popular culture (manga, anime and Japanese TV dramas) and, after that, had shifted their interest towards South Korean popular culture. Also, 10% of the Hungarian sample and 7.8% of the Polish respondents had become attracted by the South Korean culture while they learn the Korean language and literature at the University (see Figure 5.1).

As regards the main positive traits of South Korea, as our data showed, "respect" was the main characteristic mentioned by fans from Hungary, Poland and Slovakia (see Figure 5.2). Thus, 6.7% of Hungarian fans and Slovak respondents, and 2% for the Polish interviewees had used this word when they pointed out the main traits of South Korea's popular culture. At the same time, local variations were recorded among our groups of fans: the Czech fans differentiated themselves by naming "Confucianism" (10.5%) and "The importance of family" (10.5%) as the main positive characteristics and "Hardwork" (3.9%)

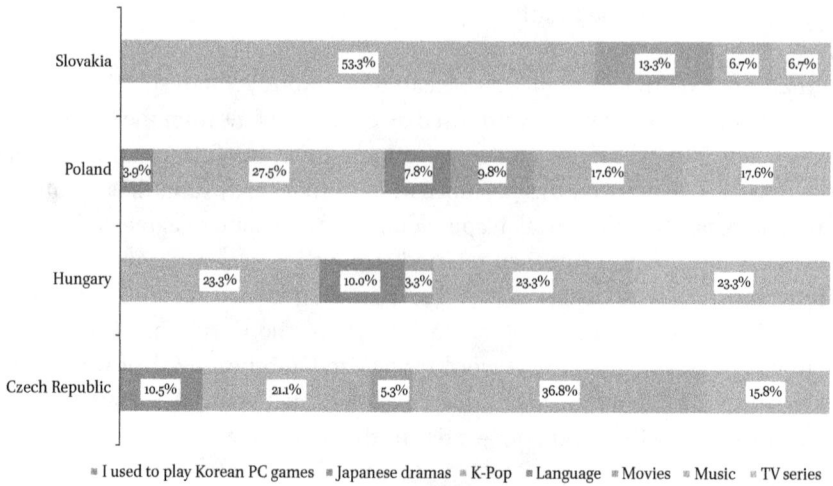

FIGURE 5.1 The beginning of the respondents' interest in South Korean culture

Legend: I used to play Korean PC games · Japanese dramas · K-Pop · Language · Movies · Music · TV series

Slovakia: 53.3% | 13.3% | 6.7% | 6.7%
Poland: 3.9% | 27.5% | 7.8% | 9.8% | 17.6% | 17.6%
Hungary: 23.3% | 10.0% | 3.3% | 23.3% | 23.3%
Czech Republic: 10.5% | 21.1% | 5.3% | 36.8% | 15.8%

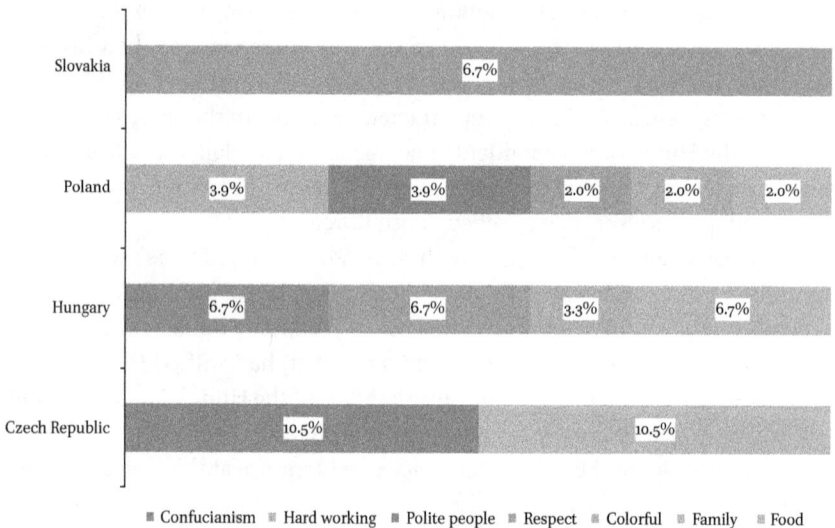

FIGURE 5.2 Main positive characteristics of South Korean popular culture

Legend: Confucianism · Hard working · Polite people · Respect · Colorful · Family · Food

Slovakia: 6.7%
Poland: 3.9% | 3.9% | 2.0% | 2.0% | 2.0%
Hungary: 6.7% | 6.7% | 3.3% | 6.7%
Czech Republic: 10.5% | 10.5%

plus "Politeness" (3.9%) were used only by the Polish respondents concerning positive aspects of South Korean culture and society (see Figure 5.2).

As regards the standard set of group and individual involvement our data pointed out that fan meetings, the activity of listening to K-pop music, the watching of Korean TV dramas, learning Korean language and involvement in the activities of the internet-based communities of fans were common activities in all four countries (see Table 5.1).

TABLE 5.1   Main individual and group activities related to South Korea in which the
respondents were involved

	Czech Republic	Hungary	Poland	Slovakia
Fan meetings	31.6%	24.0%	11.9%	6.7%
Watching K-dramas	31.0%	10.0%	23.6%	2%
Listening to K-pop	47.4%	45.4%	45.2%	33.4%
Learning Korean language	21.0%	30.1%	15.7%	46.7%
Watching Korean movies	21.0%	10.0%	9.9%	6.7%
Writing and translating articles related to K-culture for the Internet	15.8%	13.2%	2%	6.7%

The Polish fans were the only ones who mentioned "reading Korean literature" (5.9%) among their South Korea-related activities, and some of them also had declared that they attended "Korean concerts" (2%) and "Korean cultural events" (2%). The Hungarian fans mentioned among their activities related to South Korea "playing Korean PC games" (6.7%), "enjoying Korean food" (11%) and "performing traditional Korean dance and music" (6.6%). It was obvious that, once again, local-national variations and differences among the four groups of South Korea-fans were evident.

"The online activities of South Korea's fans groups" were mentioned by almost half of each national sample (47.4% in the case of Czech fans; 46.7% by the Hungarian respondents; 39.2% by the Polish interviewees and 40% in the case of Slovak fans). Other activities mentioned by our respondents were "activities of the fan clubs of K-pop" (with a peak for the Slovak respondents—40%), "activities on the Facebook" (in this case the maximum was recorded by the Hungarian interviewees—40%) and "offline meetings of fans", this being mentioned mainly by the Czech fans (57.9%) and Slovak respondents (40%) (see Table 5.2).

But, as the results showed, only the Czech fans had mentioned "meetings in common with Japanese culture's fans" (5.3%), and the Polish fans differentiated themselves by naming "making translations from Korean language into Polish language" (2%) as known activity of Hallyu's fans.

Because South Korea exports also other types of materials goods, being one of the leading world economic powers, one question included in the questionnaire has intended to measure the degree of information about this topic among the respondents. In this case the differences were obvious among

TABLE 5.2   Activities of the Hallyu fan groups known by the interviewees

	Czech Republic	Hungary	Poland	Slovakia
Activities of the fan clubs of K-pop	21.1%	26.7%	30.8%	47.8%
Activities of the Facebook pages of South Korea's fan groups	26.8%	40.0%	27.2%	20.0%
Online activities of the fan groups (forums, blogs, etc.)	47.4%	46.7%	39.2%	40.0%
Events and flashmobs related to Korean culture	10.6%	20.0%	15.7%	13.4%
Offline meetings of South Korea's fan groups	57.9%	32.4%	35.3%	40.0%

TABLE 5.3   South Korean goods present on the national markets as they were identified by the respondents

	Czech Republic	Hungary	Poland	Slovakia
The advertisements of different South Korean products and goods		3.3%	6.0%	
South Korean cars				6.7%
South Korean cosmetics	15.8%	3.3%	2.0%	
South Korean electronics	5.3%		3.9%	6.7%
South Korean technology	5.3%		9.8%	6.7%

national samples included in analysis: "cars" (mentioned by 6.7% of the Slovakian respondents), "electronics" (mentioned by 5.3% of Czech fans, 3.9% of Polish fans and 6.7% of Slovak respondents) and "cosmetics" (mentioned by 15.8% of the Czech interviewees, 3.3% of the Hungarian respondents and 2% of the Polish fans) (see Table 5.3).

The South Korean "key-features" which could be successful borrowed and used in their own country, according to our respondents, "the importance of education", "love of the country" and "the importance of respect". Once again,

TABLE 5.4   National variations regarding the things that the respondents' country can "learn" from South Korea

	Czech Republic	Hungary	Poland	Slovakia
Ethics	5.3%		5.9%	
Politeness	10.5%	3.3%		
The way in which Korean men treat Korean women			3.9%	
Balance in attitudes and values			3.9%	
Culture	5.3%	3.3%		
Search of the progress		3.3%	2.0%	

the data shows that national groups of fans assessed in different ways the main characteristics that their country can "borrow" or learn from South Korea. According to the opinions of the Czech fans "politeness" was the main traits which can be learnt from South Korean society and culture, while the Polish respondents declared that "ethics" was the key-characteristic which can be borrowed by the Polish society from the South Korean one (see Table 5.4).

2   Conclusions

Referring to the impact of South Korea's popular products worldwide, Shin (2006) stressed the fact that the paradox of globalization in South Korea is the existence of two (seemingly) contradictory trends: the co-existence between "nationalist appropriation of globalization" and "the intensification of ethnic/ national identity in reaction to globalization". Shin's (2006) conceptualization of globalization and the South Korean response to it can be extended to the globalization of culture, in which South Korea finds both the forces of homogenization and heterogenization in play.

If Hallyu should be understood as an alternative to the U.S. or West-dominated cultural globalization (Kim and Ryoo 2007) its new hybrid forms of popular culture enclosed elements of both the West and the East (Jenkins 2004).

At the end of this analysis, we can offer some general assessments of the main characteristics of the consumers of South Korea popular culture in the case of the countries from Central and Eastern Europe. Thus, as our results have showed, in the case of Central and Eastern European audiences for Hallyu products (TV series and/or K-pop music) we have witnessed the validation of two sets of theories. On the one hand, the data showed the validation of the theories emphasizing globalism and the hybridity of these cultural products (Chan and Ma 1996; Cho 2005; Dator and Seo 2004). On the other, our results have validated Liebes and Katz theories (Katz and Liebes 1984; Katz and Liebes 1986a; Katz and Liebes 1986b) regarding the cultural motivations involved in media consumption.

The fact that Internet plays a major role K-pop success, as "avenue for organization of transnational consumption of pop culture" (Kim 2008) is widely accepted, many Hallyu fan-groups from other countries being, in fact, "mirror-images" of the Korean-based ones (Kim 2008). This "manufactured" character of Hallyu fan groups is considered to be the main peculiarity of them. As the existing studies point out (Kim 2008; Bergen 2011) the Hallyu fan groups are often established by the artist or the production companies as "means of sustaining consumer interest to extend the longevity of what would otherwise be an essentially ephemeral phenomenon" (Kim 2008).

Related to this "manufactured" nature of fan groups, our analysis showed that the groups of fans from Czech Republic, Hungary, Poland and Slovakia lived a "double-life": a real one, strong related to national identity and a virtual one, close connected to Hallyu's ideals. Our results also confirm Boyd's (2007a; 2007b) thesis according to which for computer-mediated communication, a series of "imagined communities" emerged through the articulation of networked virtual friends.

Referring to modern cultural identity as an essential element in the construction of social identity (for individuals and groups), Hall shows that (1990) it passes through constant transformation. In direct connection to Hallyu this "constant transformation" could be further assessed with reference to East-Asian cultures as embodying a "double inscription" in which the global culture is always and already present in national and regional cultures (Hall 1996).

At present, as stated in other analysis of South Korea's export of cultural products (Marinescu and Balica 2013; Marinescu 2014b), one can assess that the hybrid cultural products consumption (as is the case with South Korean exported cultural products) is brought along not only by new consumption motivations (polyvalent) but also by new abilities to decode them (derived especially from the mix of media "genres" made possible through the technological and digital process). From here, in our opinion, the analysis of Hallyu' spread in Central and Eastern Europe could open the way towards new questions related to the appearance of a new "cultural identity" in the case of postmodern public for various cultural products (Jung 2011).

Bibliography

Anderson, Benedict. (2006). *Imagined communities: Reflections on the origin and spread of nationalism.* Verso Books.

Baym, Nancy K. (2000). *Tune in, log on: Soaps, fandom, and online community.* Vol. 3. Sage.

Bhabha, Homi K. (2012). *The location of culture.* London & New York: Routledge.

Bourdieu, Pierre. (1994). *Raisons pratiques : Sur la théorie de l'action.* Editions du Seuil, Paris.

Boyd, Danah. (2007). "Incantations for muggles: The role of ubiquitous web 2.0 technologies in everyday life". *O'Reilly Emerging Technology Conference* March 28, 2007. 2007a. Available at: http://www.danah.org/papers/talks/Etech2007.html (accessed on March 12, 2020).

Boyd, Danah. (2007). "Choose your own ethnography: In search of (un)mediated life". *The Society for Social Studies of Science (4S) Annual Conference,* October 13, 2007. 2007b. Available at: http://www.danah.org/papers/talks/4S2007.html (accessed on March 11, 2020).

Chan, Joseph Man, and Eric K.W. Ma. (1986). "Asian television: Global trends and local processes". *Gazette* (Leiden, Netherlands) 58, no. 1: 45–60.

Cho, Hae-Joang. (2005). "Reading the 'Korean wave' as a sign of global shift". *Korea Journal* 45, no. 4: 147–182.

Cohen, Robin. (2008). *Global diasporas: An introduction.* London & New York: Routledge.

Dator, Jim, and Seo Yongseok. (2008). "Korea as the wave of a future: the emerging dream society of icons and aesthetic experience". In: *Korea: The Past and the Present* (2 vols.), edited by Susan Pares and Jim Hoare, pp. 490–506. Global Oriental.

De Fina, Anna, (2006). Deborah Schiffrin, and Michael Bamberg. *Discursive Construction of Identities.* Cambridge: Cambridge University Press.

Hall, Stuart. (1990). "Cultural identity and diaspora". In: *Identity: Community, culture, difference,* edited by Jonathan Rutherford, pp. 222–237. London: Lawrence and Wishart.

Hall, Stuart. (1996). "When was 'The Post-Colonial'? Thinking at the limit". In: *The Post-Colonial Question: Common Skies, Divided Horizons,* edited by Iain Chamers, and Lidia Curti, pp. 242–260. London: Routledge.

Jenkins, Henri. (2004). "Pop Cosmopolitanism: Mapping Cultural Flows in an Age of Media Convergence". In: *Globalization: Culture and Education in the New Millennium,* edited by Marcelo Suarez-Orozco and Desiree B. Qin-Hilliard, pp.114–140. Berkeley and Los Angeles: University of California Press.

Jung, Sun. (2011). *Korean Masculinities and Transcultural Consumption: Yonsama, Rain, Oldboy, K-Pop Idols.* Hong Kong: Hong Kong University Press.

Katz, Elihu, and Tamar Liebes. (1984). "Once upon a time, in Dallas". *Intermedia* 12, no. 3: 28–32.

Katz, Elihu, and Tamar Liebes. (1986). "Mutual aid in the decoding of Dallas: Preliminary notes from a cross-cultural study". In *Television in Transition,* edited by Phillip Drummond and Richard Patterson, pp. 187–198. London: British Film Institute.

Kim Eun Mee, and Jiwon Ryoo. (2007). "South Korean Culture Goes Global: K-Pop and the Korean Wave". *Korean Social Science Journal* 34, no. 1: 117–152.

Kim, Youna, ed. (2008). *Media consumption and everyday life in Asia.* Routledge.

Liebes, Tamar, and Elihu Katz. (1986). "Patterns of involvement in television fiction: A comparative analysis". *European Journal of Communication* 1, no. 2 : 151–171.

Marinescu, Valentina, and Ecaterina Balica. (2013). "Korean Cultural Products in Eastern Europe: A Case Study of the K-Pop Impact in Romania". *REGION: Regional Studies of Russia, Eastern Europe, and Central Asia* 2, no.1: 113–135.

Marinescu, Valentina. (2014a). "Reconstructing Social Identities in the Balkans and Central Europe through Popular Culture". *Anthropological Research and Studies* 3: 22–23.

Marinescu, Valentina. (2014b). "Many faces of Hallyu in the Global World". In: *The Global Impact of South Korean Popular Culture: Hallyu Unbound,* edited by Valentina Marinescu, pp. 1–5. Lexington Books.

Marinescu, Valentina. (2015). "Searching the Sameness and Otherness through Hallyu in the Balkans and Central Europe". *Wiener Beiträge zur Koreaforschung* VII: 83–98.

Ryoo, Woongjae. (2008). "The political economy of the global mediascape: the case of the South Korean film industry". *Media, Culture & Society* 30, no. 6: 873–889.

Sandvoss, Cornel. (2005). *Fans: The mirror of consumption.* Polity.

Shin, Gi-Wook. (2006). *Ethnic Nationalism in Korea: Genealogy, Politics, and Legacy.* Palo Alto, CA: Stanford University Press.

Tada-amnuaychai, Montira. (2007). "K-Pop, Korean entertainment industry and its cultural marketing strategy in Thailand". *Journal of Communi cation Arts* 25: 12–24.

CHAPTER 6

What Can Be Seen by Breaking "Bad"?

Amalia Frangiskou

1   Introduction

This famous television series (2008–2013), which offered a unique TV experience, is approached by two different readings, according to its ambiguous title: the deeper analysis of what "bad" is considered to be is the first reading, and the second being the choice of individual transformation, which overcomes any moral constrains. The multi-dimensional world of Breaking Bad creates ethical and political issues in a specific socio-political and cultural context. A fallen society that does not provide real protection, but one, however that can host fragmented and deeply divided identities. Struggle for survival and search of concept on a non-solid ground that allows the invention of the self, being related via imitation of human relationships. Nothing is as it may seem, failure can lead to a constant fall and survival often requires unbridled activity.

2   Excitement and Fear: an Ambivalent TV Watching

First of all, I would like to say a few words about this TV series, especially for those who haven't seen or heard of it. I was one of them too, till recently when I discovered this television series that has been an over-time reference, a real genre characterized by a highly addictive way of viewing. "Breaking Bad is masterfully designed: from the 60-hour narrative and character arc to developing visual metonymies, synecdoches, and metaphors, from narratological experimentation to defamiliarization and color symbolism. It is beautiful. Breaking Bad represents the finest achievement in a genre that we have just watched reach maturity" (Wood 2015: 23).

After that finding that I had never heard of, seen or read anything about, another big surprise came: a plethora of academic articles, journalistic, blogs, devoted fans discussions and in general a great debate and dialogue around this series.

It has already been stated, that this phenomenon, having been unlike anything seen in television before, "has changed the way television is approached.

'Breaking Bad' is not just a great television show; it is a cultural landmark"
(Blevins and Wood 2015: 8). In addition, "Breaking Bad is a work that facilitates,
perhaps even makes possible, a dialogue about aesthetic, philosophical, psychological, and ethical elements in our culture in a way we have yet to see in
television. For each of those elements, it is a work that centers itself on fric-
tion, fragmentation, conflict and discord, but it seeks to structure such discord
in a way that draws the audience into the dialogue itself" (Blevins and Wood
2015: 7).

As an empirical researcher, I have to convey the unique experience I have
had of watching 62 episodes, a fact that at the time it was happening and according to my self-critique I considered a waste of time and a lack of will to
stop doing. What was happening to me? While I was in that certain situation,
without being able to explain why and without being able to talk about what I
had been watching, at the same time thousands of thoughts flooded my mind.
Also, in my daily life in a country under a severe crisis, I often caught myself
recalling scenes from this series, which seemed not related at first place, associations to events and observations of every-day real life that often upset me.
I was feeling fear and admiration simultaneously. I was looking for explanations about how strange and incredible situations had become familiar, in order to share with others my experience of viewing. This was mainly the reason
why I tried to find out anything I could, related to Breaking Bad.

Some analytical approaches found, was a relief and stimulants for more research, such as the argument that "the magical realism of the series is ground-
ed in our suspension of disbelief that this is possible" (Di Leo 2015: 27). Moreover, "the ambivalence of identification processes in Breaking Bad implies that
liquidity is not just an option but a condition that viewers have to negotiate
throughout the series. This is because we realize that there is no higher morality justifying Walt's efforts to defend his drug empire, just as there is no grand
narrative to make sense of his initial impasse. Instead, viewers are faced with
the deterioration of social bonds as a structural condition of late modernity—
viewers share this condition with Walt, who experiences it on screen, and
around this similarity, identification, albeit unsteadily, is built" (Pribram 2014:
163).

An investigation of audience offered additional support. "Breaking Bad
presents a potent object lesson instructing the viewer as to how the actions of
the show's protagonists ... mirror the imperfect condition of humanity, the seductive nature of power, and the vulnerabilities of the "common man" to break
bad. These roles are significant due to the viewers' projective identification
with their characters who present something shared but unacknowledged by

all of us. It presents us with our flawed humanity" (Keown, Thomas, Rhoads and Sundblad 2015: 151).

This award-winning television series has opened up multi-dimensional discussion topics. As it has been written, "to experience and closely study a television serial like Breaking Bad ... is a persisting struggle with the enormity and depth of the world that unfolds across the work over a considerable span of time" (Logan 2016: 9).

Academically, this "cinematic"—as it has been characterized—has been approached in many ways of analysis: genre, scenario, morals, ethics, gender, politics, psychology, literature, philosophy and so on.

The TV series was telecasted from 2008 to 2013, via a subscription channel. The transmission mode, the time, the serial duration and the concept are components of the final result. "Breaking Bad's expressiveness and meaning, largely rest on its self-conscious handling of serial television form" (Logan 2016: 2). In addition, "the 2008 financial crisis, which formed the basis of new themes in quality television series, especially in the United States, and is rapidly gaining an international audience due to the internet ... with a particularly cynical approach to reality, offering back the cynicism of the international political and economic system to a partial television audience" (Apostolidis 2015: 12).

Stat Rosa Pristina Nomine, Nomina Nuda Tenemus
UMBERTO ECO (*"The name of the rose"*)

The protagonist is a high school chemistry teacher, underpaid and unappreciated. He ineffectively tries to inspire his students. "Chemistry is the study of matter, but I prefer to see it as the study of change", says Walter White to his students.

Although he has the qualifications, he lost the opportunity to the American corporate dream. He is married, having a son with disabilities and his wife is pregnant. He has a mortgage to pay. He gets a second job in a car wash in order to meet his obligations. And feeling a failure, he systematically ignores some signs of his illness, avoiding to get examined. Finally he is diagnosed with lung cancer and little time ahead to live. There is a treatment which might save him, but he cannot afford it. He also cannot provide anything for his family after his death.

He is an inadequate husband, father, teacher. He is alone. The only relationship he develops is with a delinquent ex-student "a tainted father-son relationship, a reflection and complement of the relationship with his paraplegic son" (Apostolidis 2015: 42).

No human relationships. Just a *simulacrum* of them! There is a family but there are no real bonds. With typical or awkward greetings—they say "Hi" to each other—when they have breakfast, the only concern being a healthy diet. Even when they meet the broader family, that means five persons in total, in order to discuss they have to follow a "ritual" apparently transferred from group-therapy, according to which the person who has the pillow takes the floor.

The concept of "family" that runs the whole series as an ultimate value, whose protection justifies Walter's criminal activity, is a spiteful, lying, indifferent, alienating framework.

No social protection is in place. There is access to health structures but not to the expensive treatment which might cure him, revealing the failure of the American health care system.

Everything is there but looks like a wrapper without any substantial content. Nothing is as it may seem, just idols the existence of which makes the fate of the people who fall even more tragic. Failure is unacceptable and survival often requires a constant evaluation of identities, institutions and discredited values.

3   *O Tempora O Mores!*

Walt White is one of the working people, called "the middle class" in U.S. rhetoric as Chomsky indicates in an interview. He says that the "state-corporate programs of the past 35 or so years have had devastating effects on the majority of the population, with stagnation, decline and sharply enhanced inequality being the most direct outcomes. This has created fear and has left people feeling isolated, helpless, victims of powerful forces they can neither understand or influence" (Chomsky's interview, 2016). These are the feelings of Walt, a well-educated chemist, high school teacher, who works two jobs to provide for his family. He is frustrated, discredited, humiliated. He has to live with a bad prognosis for lung cancer. He feels a failure: he lacks masculinity, enough material resources, dignity.

He is in danger!

He lives in a fallen society that does not provide any protection, but it can host fragmented and deeply divided identities, the case of "liquid modernity" Bauman has introduced. Likewise, an era of seemingly "ever-accelerating industrialised modernity" as identified by Logan. "A characteristic of this period that helps cast light on Breaking Bad is its increasing complexity of social and commercial and technological organisation, such that an intensified degree of specialisation is required of individuals whose lives take shape within these structures. ...Such a condition can be thought to undermine any stable sense of personal coherence..." (Logan 2016: 148).

His life becomes a struggle for survival and search of concept of a nonsolid ground which allows the reconstruction of his identity through cooking meth and turning gradually from a teacher into a drug Kingpin "Heisenberg", the name of the German physicist who discovered the uncertainty principle in quantum mechanics. This nickname is well supported during many episodes by the uncertainty in Walt's fragmented identity.

According to Blevins, he "functions as the new manifestation of the tragic hero ... a hero that emerges from the 21st-century contexts of health care concerns, a fallen economy, indefinite gender roles, gun violence, and the confrontation with the ethnic other (primarily in the immigration issues arising from Mexican border violence). Walter White must be a different kind of hero, one whose presence is located in a very different cultural context, but a context that is undeniably ours" (Blevins 2015: 2). In addition, Breaking Bad must "more properly understood as a story of, and about, the theatrical desire for superheroics. Inherent to such a desire is a personality fragmented along the line separating one's ordinary life from its more extraordinary, fanciful projections" (Logan 2016: 6).

Walt White lives a schizophrenic life. So he can comfortably, tenderly embrace his newborn baby relaxing at the end of the day, after having caused several deaths directly or indirectly through drug production.

In the name of love "Heisenberg" delivers "poison" and death. In the name of family, he moves away and destroys his family, even though he knows he doesn't have much time left. And it is only at the end that he confesses that all of his actions were about him, not about his family's care.

As he admits: "I did it for me. I liked it. I was good at it. And ... I was ... really ... I was alive". He no longer needs to justify his actions by invoking reasons for his monstrous activity, remaining connected, albeit perverted, with human ones.

He does no longer need excuses, but he can also express his satisfaction. Beyond any limit, just an enormous ego that breaks bad. And he is allowed to do so. Not only because he is not arrested but also because the whole context in which he is acting is deeply illegal. "Lawlessness is a cancer that can feed upon the fabric of a society ... dissolving the bonds of society until it decomposes into something that can no longer be considered a civilization ... immorality, absence of principles beliefs leads to ignore the common, mutually beneficial purpose" (Darbeau 2015: 165).

As David Pierson argues in his analysis "The central idea underscoring the neoliberal ideology is that the market should be the organizing agent for nearly all social, political, economic, and personal decisions ... the TV series Breaking Bad intersects with neoliberal policies and discourses, and exemplifies several of its detrimental social and political effects" (Pierson 2014: 18). Also Di Leo sees the series from a political point of view. "The promise, of neo-liberalism was that it would allow everyone the opportunity to be a shareholder, an owner, and an entrepreneur. ...Walt participated in the promise; however, the promise was lost. But in this way, Walt's fate was not unusual because for many in America the new economy quickly faded away and was replaced by a much more vicious one: the debt economy". As Di Leo comments, "the power of the neoliberal vision of Breaking Bad is that it provides a commentary on both the fortunes of the "indebted man" (Walter White) and the "entrepreneurial man" (Heisenberg)" (Di Leo 2015: 42). Furthermore, "Walt's transformation from a dying, emasculated public school teacher to a self-confident, aggressive drug lord attests both to the seductive power and the dangers of a neoliberal life-style where there can only be winners and losers. Even when Walt's cancer goes into remission and he has amassed plenty of capital, he still wants to continue to cook meth" (Pierson 2014: 30).

The TV series is fiction, but many contents of the series are not fiction. Actually, the series highlights the huge problem that parts of the U.S. have with this particular drug (crystal methamphetamine). It's an established drug of misuse in countries like the Czech Republic, where it is manufactured in "meth labs" similar to the one portrayed in Breaking Bad (Owen 2013). The cartels and the brutal narco war is real, so many people are killed as a result of drug violence (Torres 2017). Offshore companies and money laundering businesses do exist. People who want to gain no matter the cost, do exist as well.

From one point of view the story is a "critical reflection of contemporary society. Granted there may be plot holes in some of the narrative devices used and the show can, at times, seem hyper-realistic but the context and the character arcs and behaviors are realistic. The symbolism and the overall message aim to illustrate how morally unrestricted an individual can be if presented with alluring incentives following a set of psycho-social strains" (Wondemaghen 2015: 128).

Indeed, the protagonist drowning in debt, in disrepute, in a meaningless life and shallow relationships or absence of them, faces the prospect of his natural death by choosing a perverted identity and diving into "bad".

He became a monster; "Evil" without any moral hesitation or restriction. According to the scenario instead of being in danger he becomes "the danger". He says to his wife:

Walter/Heisenberg: I am not in danger, Skyler. I am the danger! A guy opens his door and gets shot and you think that of me? No. I am the one who knocks!

I am constantly amazed by man's inhumanity to man.
PRIMO LEVI

He chose the least vulnerable position offered "The ghost of vulnerability is hovering over the "negatively globalized" planet. We are all in danger and each of us is dangerous to the other. There are only three available roles—perpetrators, victims and collateral losses" (Bauman 2007: 131).

The whole range of these roles unfolded in the series in a context of moral decline, lack of consciousness and a self-referential science detached from morality and ethics. "Scientific hubris has become criminal hubris" (Brodesco 2014: 55). But there is no hint of Nemesis. Neither is there a Catharsis after so many deaths and fear. On the contrary, even the lyrics of the song—Baby blue, Badfinger—at the spectacular finale, emphasize the impenitence and complacent dominance of evil. "Fear and evil are Siamese twins ... What we fear is evil. Whatever is bad, we are afraid of. But what is evil? ... Evil is what defies and explodes this intelligibility that makes the world viable ... We resort to the idea of 'evil' when we cannot determine which rule has been violated or circumvented by the appearance of the act for which we seek the proper name" (Bauman 2007: 77). Moreover "evil can be hidden everywhere ... anyone can be in his service ... Of course, such a view is a gross exaggeration: of course, not everyone is fit and willing to serve evil. Of course, there are innumerable people who are insufficiently immune to evil, sufficiently hostile to resisting ... The bottom line is that we don't know who they are and how to distinguish them from those who are most vulnerable to the intrigues of evil" (Bauman 2007: 94).

The only clue to the discovery of the elusive protagonist came from a poetry book which was found—in a semiotic approach of scenario—in the bathroom. The initials of the protagonist's name were the same with the initials of the poet Walt Whitman and this led to the investigation of the criminal action. This, in my opinion, can also be read as a "spicy" connotation that poetry has been exiled from our materialistic world, but it is poetry that can offer inspiration to the world. What prognosis can be there for the future, if we are indeed at the borderline, human beings are about to cross by acting as villains without values, in an obscure era of realities and illusions, persons and avatars?

As a professor of philosophy put it "Walter White came to us just when we needed him. Breaking Bad offered a world reeling from the effects of lengthy recession some glimmer of hope, but more importantly it now offers us a potential lesson in values and about ourselves. The cultural impact of the show will be more meaningfully assessed 10 years from now, when we will know if, as it seems, this is an era drawing to a close, or whether the story of the rise and fall of Heisenberg—to give White his alias—is just a blip in our popular consciousness" (Koepsell 2013).

4   Conclusion

From this perspective, in the era of modernity, the above legendary television series was analyzed in relation to the scandalous revelations of immorality and greed.

The global economic crisis has been attributed—even in technical terms—to the totally uncontrolled financial system and to a speculative market driven by the "world money leaders" who have crossed the line regarding the regulated rules of the game.

It could be argued that they, themselves have broken bad!

Market sovereignty, indolent wealth, unbridled stockbrokers, ineffective politics, fragmented identities, meet together in a "liquid world"; this is an attack of wild instincts, which did not meet any resistance by any legal order with timely and strong reflexes. Neither did it meet any sufficient resistance by the political system, nor any restrain deriving from a disordered and fragmented society.

Bibliography

Apostolidis, A. (2015). *The black frame: The Police Series and the Television Spring after 2000*. Athens: Agra Publications.

Bauman, Z. (2007). *Liquid Fear*. Athens: Polytropon. [first edition 2006].

Blevins, J. and Wood, D. (2015). *The methods of Breaking Bad, Essays on Narrative, Character and Ethics*. Jefferson, NC: McFarland & Company, Inc., Publishers.

Chomsky, N. (2016). Breakdown of American Society and a World in Transition, Interview *Truthout*. Available at: https://truthout.org/authors/c-j-polychroniou/.

Darbeau, W.R. (2015). "Scientific Ethics and Breaking Bad". In: Blevins, J. and Wood, D. (eds.). *The methods of Breaking Bad, Essays on Narrative, Character and Ethics*. Jefferson, NC: McFarland & Company, Inc., Publishers, pp. 165–182.

Di Leo, R.J. (2015). "Flies in the Marketplace: Nietzsche and Neoliberalism in Breaking Bad". In: Blevins, J. and Wood, D. (eds.). *The methods of Breaking Bad, Essays on Narrative, Character and Ethics*. Jefferson, NC: McFarland & Company, Inc., Publishers, pp. 26–46.

Brodesco, A. (2014). "Heisenberg: Epistemological Implications of a Criminal Pseud-
onym". In: Pierson, P.D. (ed.). *Breaking Bad: Critical Essays on the Contexts, Politics, Style, and Reception of the Television Series*. Plymouth, UK: Lexington Books,
pp. 50–65.

Keown, McB, Thomas, B.D., Rhoads, C.J. and Sundblad, D. (2015). "Falling hard for
Breaking Bad: An investigation of audience response to a popular television series".
Participations: Journal of audience and reception studies 12(2): 147–167. Available at:
https://doc.uments.com/s-falling-hard-for-breaking-bad-an-investigation-of-audi
ence-response.pdf.

Koepsell, D. (2013). "Why the time was right for Breaking Bad guy Walter White". Available
at: https://theconversation.com/why-the-time-was-right-for-breaking-bad-guy-wal
ter-white-18715.

Logan, E. (2016). *Breaking Bad and Dignity: Unity and Fragmentation in the Serial Television Drama*. UK: Palgrave Macmillan.

Owen, B.J. (2013). *Why meth hasn't broken bad in the* UK. The Conversation, UK. Available at: https://theconversation.com/why-meth-hasnt-broken-bad-in-the-uk-18708.

Pierson, P.D. (2014). "Breaking Neoliberal? Contemporary Neoliberal Discourses and
Policies in AMC's Breaking Bad". In: Pierson, P.D. (ed.). *Breaking Bad: Critical Essays
on the Contexts, Politics, Style, and Reception of the Television Series*. Plymouth, UK:
Lexington Books, pp. 18–32. [first edition 2013].

Pribram, E.D. (2014). "Feeling Bad: Emotions and narrativity in Breaking Bad". In:
Pierson, P.D. (ed.). *Breaking Bad: Critical Essays on the Contexts, Politics, Style, and
Reception of the Television Series*. Plymouth, UK: Lexington Books, pp. 168–204. [first
edition 2013].

Torres, C.A. (2017). "Why glamorising narco culture, on screen and in Sydney's pop-
up shop, is wrong". *The Conversation*, UK. Available at: https://theconversation.
com/why-glamorising-narco-culture-on-screen-and-in-sydneys-pop-up-shop-is-
wrong-75851.

Wondemaghen, M. (2015). "The psychopath to whom we can all relate?" In: Blevins, J.
and Wood, D. (eds.). *The methods of Breaking Bad, Essays on Narrative Character and
Ethics*. Jefferson, NC: McFarland & Company, Inc., Publishers, pp. 122 131.

Wood, D. (2015). "Flies and One- Eyed Bears: The maturation of a genre". In: Blevins, J.
and Wood, D. (eds.). *The methods of Breaking Bad, Essays on Narrative, Character
and Ethics*. Jefferson, NC: McFarland & Company, Inc., Publishers, pp. 11–25.

CHAPTER 7

The Representation of the Current Crisis in the Greek Cinema: Investigating Mnemonic Itineraries and Flashbacks

Maria Thanopoulou

Cinema, an art having the possibility to create and impose representations (Constantopoulou 2010: 160), reminds us of the interconnection between representations and memory (Mantoglou 2012: 51–55). Drawing inspiration from political events and social phenomena (Hadouchi 2010) cinema has created fiction stories and contributed to the preservation of memory (Maazouzi 2008; Villareal 2010; Eid 2010; Kornetis 2014). It is proved to be an efficient tool for stocking and using images of the past (Lemonidou 2017). There are numerous cinematic representations of history that can be classified by types according to the relationships they entertain with history (Ferro in Bartholeyns 2000); they refer to various historical periods over time, like Antiquity (Collognat 1994), Middle Age (Barrio 2008), the Second World War (Lindeperg 1997).

Crucial political events and social phenomena in Modern Greece have inspired Greek filmmakers in different ways. The Second World War and the Civil War (Tomai 2006), the post war migration of Greeks to foreign countries (Lemonidou 2017), the Colonels' dictatorship (Roussos 2014) are treated in a great part of the filmic production nourishing the plot and the symbolism of the films. The last decade the Greek financial crisis gave birth to the cinema of "crisis". This cinema can be considered as one important cultural effect provoked by this crisis, as well as an exportable cultural product abroad (Mademli 2016; Basea 2016; Lykidis 2015b). Greek filmmakers have produced a great variety of films referring to different aspects (Pfeifer 2016) and social effects of this crisis; they give emphasis on "isolated or alienated characters, dysfunctional family relationships, desperate or anti-social behavior and breakdowns in communication" (Lykidis 2015a).

At the same time the Greek financial crisis has inspired filmmakers to produce also a great number of documentaries.[1] Capturing traces of the past these documentaries are related to memory (Decarie-Daigneault 2016: 27); they

---

1 As Papadimitriou states until then "the documentary filmmaking in Greece remained a highly insular and, indeed, marginal affair" (Papadimitriou 2015: 31).

constitute outcomes of selections made within various mnemonic processes, such as the selection of the subject, the space, the people participating, the duration of the filming, the scenes to film or to omit (Wiseman 1994; Olick 1999: 346). More specifically, as they consider different aspects of this crisis, sometimes expressed even in their titles (like "Debtocracy", "Freedom besieged", "Catastroika"), these documentaries constitute transcriptions and representations of the economic and social processes experienced in Greece the last decade. In doing so the filmmakers of these documentaries use fragments of individual and collective memory and manage them accordingly in order to build their own vision on Greek crisis.

Among the numerous visions produced by filmmakers on Greek financial crisis we have chosen the documentary film of Yorgos Avgeropoulos titled *Agora. From democracy to the Market* (2015) as a good example illustrating the management of individual and collective memory in documentaries. With this documentary as a starting point our text aims at pointing out that the crisis representation addressed to the spectator is a product of ana-synthesis made in the present time—time of the documentary film's creation—an ana-synthesis of various fragments of collective memory. So, what the spectator sees on screen is the result of different montages: the result of the film director's montage based on previous montages, the ones made by the documentary's interviewees while interviewed.

Our analysis lies on two loans. The first comes from Maurice Halbwachs, the well-known sociologist of memory. It has to do with the selective character of the recall process, because Halbwachs considers memories as reconstructions made at the present time—time of the recall—in order to respond to present needs (Halbwachs 1967: 57–58; Olick and Robbins 1998: 129; Olick 1999: 341). So recalling refers to a selective use of the past implying, at the same time, silence or forgetting (Olick 1999: 335), a selective use that is socially conditioned (Kansteiner 2002: 184). The second loan comes from the well-known filmmaker Sergei Eisenstein. It has to do with the definition of montage as related to a conflict of sequences and aiming at producing ideas that could influence the spectator (Eisenstein 1967: 8, 12, 24). In his relative book on montage, whilst speaking about this conflict, Eisenstein implies that the montage process is based on a continuous selection of appropriate sequences serving the director's main idea (Eisenstein 1967: 54) and excluding the non-appropriate ones. In that way every piece of the montage is a particular representation of the film's general subject (Eisenstein 1967: 27–28).

Other filmmakers, whilst defining or describing the montage, give also emphasis on the selectivity of the process. Manthoulis considers that the montage process begins when choosing the sequences to film, as well as the shooting angle to do it according to the filmmaker's objective (Manthoulis 2015: 16, 32). This process continues when cutting some sequences in order to ensure connections of images and meanings (Manthoulis 2015: 65). Pinel's definition of montage refers to a selection of images and an organization of the narration based on flashbacks and flashes forward (Pinel 2013). Wiseman describes the montage as a sequence of choices related to the material transcribed and representing also the memory of filming (Wiseman 1994). Comolli, considering the montage as a process of deconstruction leading to a reconstruction and a metamorphosis (Comolli 1994), implies that this process contains successive choices. And, of course, the interior representation of the filmmaker orients the choices made and the associations of ideas adopted during the montage process, as Baudry states (Baudry 1994).

These loans of ideas helped us to formulate the argument that the recall process of the documentary's interviewees, as a selective process, resembles the montage process of the film. To support this argument, we have carried out research in order to study the selective management of collective memory in the documentary. It is to note that our investigation focuses mainly on the oral discourse transcribed in the documentary film, leaving out of our analysis other forms of memory, visual (sequences) and acoustic (sounds and music) ones. It is not by chance that we have made this choice. We feel a professional affinity to the interview process, though used in the documentary in a journalistic way. Moreover, we feel familiar with the analysis of oral and written memory contained in testimonies and documents.

Focusing on the selective management of the collective memory evoked in this documentary we tried to investigate some mnemonic itineraries and flashbacks guiding the recall process. This selective management of the collective memory is considered on two levels. The *first level* of our investigation is related to the interviews presented in the documentary and has to do with the montage made by the interviewees while recalling the past and speaking of their life. The *second level* of this investigation refers to the filmmaker himself and concerns the montage process of the film *Agora* as presented in the final filmic product.

1   The Filmmaker and the Documentary

Avgeropoulos is a journalist and a filmmaker who has produced many interesting documentary films among which the documentary *Agora,* a film dealing with the Greek financial crisis. He records the development of the crisis from its early beginning and traces its impact. That is why he transcribes crucial

political events and collective phenomena having to do with it: popular protests and demonstrations against austerity measures, protests in the public
spaces, especially the movement at the Constitution Square, violent conflicts
with the police, the rise of unemployment, as well as the rise of the extreme
right and Fascism, the development of solidarity movements, etc.

2   The Montage Made by the Interviewees While Recalling the Past

The documentary *Agora* contains many interviews. Avgeropoulos' interviewees come from a large social spectrum as he organizes the interview part of
the filmmaking using a complex logic. According to this logic actors of the
crisis—and of his documentary—are not only the protagonists of the crucial
events, but also the everyday people experiencing the various crisis impacts.
These are people designated in the documentary to remember, to interpret the
situation and to speak for others (Crane 1997: 1382). Avgeropoulos seems to
guide the interviews not only as a journalist, but also as a filmmaker using oral
discourse in a complementary way, in order to underline the images already
shown to the spectator. This may be the reason why interviewees seem to answer questions that are not asked by the filmmaker but could be asked by the
spectator.

Searching the reasons for this crisis he seeks answers from significant Greek
and foreign personalities: politicians, analysts, bankers, ministers, key decision
makers from the national and international scene, academics and experts.
While interviewing them he gives emphasis on the facts related to the beginning of the economic crisis in Greece, as well on interpretations and assessments of the new situation. More specifically when addressing political actors,
Avgeropoulos guides their recall process towards a reconstruction of the recent past, i.e. the time period 2010–2014, by invoking their political memory. In
this process the mnemonic itineraries of the political actors seem to follow the
evolution of facts, as time passes, without making flashbacks in a more distant
past, the period before the crisis. The selective management of political memory made by them responds to the idea that the coming of crisis was
inevitable.

Interviewing looks different when the filmmaker turns his camera towards
simple people, as if influenced by the Oral History approach (Thompson 1978).
Avgeropoulos is interested in tracing the impact of economic crisis in the life
of everyday people and adopts a long-term observation method by participating and filming their lives for a period of five years (2010–2014). As his intention
is to give voice to people that cannot be heard, he chooses to observe people

suffering from pauperization, unemployment and homelessness from different social classes. Protagonists of the documentary are also workers that have
lost their jobs in the shipyards of Perama, unemployed that cannot find a job,
living in the street and experiencing insecurity for the future, old people retired with low pensions going to public markets in search of low prices. Moreover, in the film are "acting" people belonging to the middle strata: people having had before crisis a normal life that have become homeless in the center of
Athens, entrepreneurs whose enterprises have closed, personnel of private
companies that have been dismissed. With his camera Avgeropoulos observes
them over time and interviews them on the effects of the crisis. He invokes
their autobiographical memory, the memory of events that they themselves
experience (Olick 1999: 335). He then presents in his documentary their small
individual stories using them as impacts typical of the crisis. In doing so he il-
lustrates the painful situation of people experiencing injustice because of the
financial crisis as transcribed in the collective memory of middle and low social strata. Moreover, he creates life documents (Plummer 2000: 65–68) that
witness how people experience the financial crisis in Greece.

As our research has shown, the recall made by these everyday people is
based on a main flashback corresponding to a break of time in two pieces: a
dichotomy into before and after, that is before and after crisis. Before is related
to the years of prosperity and after to the years of deprivation. This flashback
refers, in most cases, to a rather recent past, to the period before the coming of
the crisis. It implies a comparison of their present situation to a past one: a
comparison reflecting the idea of an abrupt worsening of life conditions, a
painful transition from a regular status of life to an irregular one. It is a flashback underlining a sort of scission, of discontinuity, of unexpected change, of
upheaval. This flashback leads to a mnemonic itinerary that is short in terms of
time, but painful in terms of social and psychological cost.

More specifically it is interesting to note the case of an interviewee of older
age, unemployed in the shipyard zone of Piraeus. As he belongs to the generation that has experienced starvation during the Second World War, his recall
process is related to a flashback from the present to the past, even further back
in time. This flashback reaches a more distant past transcribed in the individual and collective memory, the war experience of nearly 70 years ago. Through
an association of ideas based on the experience of deprivation, a long mnemonic itinerary comes into surface: an itinerary having on one side the present
deprivation and on the other the deprivation during the war. It is a flashback
reminding the cyclic evolution of events and social situations, as the years of
prosperity experienced before the current crisis had been anticipated by the
years of high deprivation during and after the Second World War. It is a

mnemonic return underlining that the individual and collective memory of low social strata in crisis is directly connected to the collective memory of the Second World War.

The flashback corresponding to the dichotomy between before and after takes another meaning when the filmmaker brings onto the surface some other serious impacts of this crisis: suicides, as well as murders and injuries provoked by the rise of fascism in the period of crisis. Meeting members of families suffering from the loss of the husband, the father or the son, as well as a migrant-victim of a racist attack, the filmmaker presents on the screen witnesses of the current political events and social phenomena. These witnesses, when speaking of the tragic events that have shocked them, use flashbacks referring to a short period of time, the one just before these tragic events. They do so in order to describe how the situation of the persons was before their suicide or before their murder by the fascists. But there are also moments of long silence in the documentary, silence speaking on their behalf for the beginning of their personal tragedy. Their presence in the documentary signals the need not to forget these particular crisis victims. Moreover, this presence underlines the duty not to forget fascism as related to dictatorships, wars and occupations, but also as threatening democracy. Though the mnemonic itineraries mentioned above bridge the present with the past, in some interviews of everyday people one can also note another itinerary: a sort of projection of the present situation onto the future; as if the individual and collective memory of the crisis, as experienced for four years of total despair, could pre-announce what the future will be; as if there could be no return to the situation of prosperity before crisis and no way out.

The interviewees' answers prove to be the result of different mnemonic itineraries followed by various flashbacks which serve to bridge the present with the past, but also the present with the future. To a certain extent our analysis has shown that the interviewees, whilst being interviewed in front of the camera, make their own montage—i.e. a selective management of individual and collective memory. This montage-management of memory is made by them for various reasons: to respond to the filmmaker's expectations, to protest for their personal degradation, annihilation and tragedy, to indicate events that should not pass into silence or oblivion. So our investigation related to the documentary's interviews—first level—shows that the interviewees' narratives on the crisis are like a puzzle, a mosaic constructed of pieces detached from the individual and collective memory. As Crane states, "what remains has more to do with who is acting as a witness and who is remembering lived experience than it does with whether a narrative adequately sums up a historical event" (Crane 1997: 1378).

3   The Montage of the Film *Agora* as Presented in
        the Final Filmic Product

After the coming of the financial crisis Avgeropoulos refuses to ignore the
events related to this crisis. As if making his "duty of memory" (Gensburger
and Lavabre 2005) he works in order to restore a wholesome memory (Eid
2010) by constructing and organizing the remembering of these events. He
seems to make a montage aiming at reminding the spectator what he should
not forget while experiencing the impacts of crisis. Having transcribed for five
years what he considers as impacts of the financial crisis, the filmmaker has
collected a filmic material representing 1500 hours of initial filmmaking. A long
and difficult selective process has been needed in order to transform the initial
filmic material of so many hours into a documentary of 117 minutes. It is a selective process that has to do with the filmmaker's representation of the
crisis.

The montage of the documentary lies on rich material representing different forms of individual and collective memory and resulting from different
ways of transcribing and recalling collective memory: letters explaining the
reasons of suicide and the texts of memoranda signed by politicians coexist
with the voices of well-known actors and unknown victims of the crisis situation. This montage is an ana-synthesis of fragments of collective memory
based on some ideas and principles that inspired the filmmaker to create the
scenario and helped him select the appropriate fragments of memory, as well
as reorganize them in a new context.

The montage of this documentary is based on the adoption of some main
notions related to the ideas and beliefs of the film director. These notions constitute the vertebral column of the documentary. Such a main notion is the
notion of agora used in two senses. The first one is the sense given in ancient
Greek cities where Agora is the public space related to the function of Democracy, the gathering place of active citizens, the city center and center of political, economic, athletic, artistic and spiritual life. The second sense is the one
given in modern Greece where the word agora has lost its initial sense and
denotes only the place and act of commercial transactions. By using the word
agora throughout the documentary Avgeropoulos invites the spectator's memory to go back in time and remember the place of Agora as the cradle of Democracy. He makes a pun with the two senses in order to juxtapose them and
show that the word agora has lost its first sense in Modern Greece today, as, in
times of democracy, the country goes through a financial vortex.

Other main notions inspiring the montage made by the filmmaker are also
the notions of irregularity, submersion of human lives, injustice, pauperization

and obscenity of the country. These notions directing the montage of the film-ic material lead to associations of ideas and coherences of senses. They seem to dictate, during the montage process, the ways Avgeropoulos makes the man-agement of a great variety of material and, of course, the management of the interviewees' oral discourse. Step by step he seems to advance to a gradual se-lection of things that have to be remembered versus things that could be for-gotten. The montage of the documentary is also based on the adoption of symbols illustrating the fall of Europe. Greece, a symbol for the European civi-lization because of its ancient heritage, faces dramatic conditions of non-prosperity: homeless people, soup kitchens, unemployment, poverty, an un-settled social situation, violent conflicts and the rise of the extreme-right.

Avgeropoulos, while making the montage, prevails contradictions, opposi-tions and conflicts of sequences. The montage plays with the succession of sequences related to two different levels of social life: the unofficial versus the official one. So, sequences referring to everyday life of simple people suffering from the impact of crisis are succeeded by sequences projecting political ac-tors and decision makers' views and attitudes on crisis and vice-versa. The high political level in Brussels is opposed to the low level of the daily life of a home-less man; the official political discourse of Greek politicians is opposed to the simple discourse of everyday people. Everyday life made of "small and trivial" events concerning survival is compared to the political life connected to the "big and important" events. TV news, political speeches and expert interviews frame everyday men' s stories bringing into surface contradictions between speeches and impacts of austerity policies, conflicts between statements and deeds, all resulting in social conflicts. In that way the management of collec-tive memory made by the filmmaker underlines the differentiation of collective memory on crisis per social stratum and per level of public and private life.

The montage also plays with comparisons based on numbers concerning the country's debt and the relative indexes. Numbers of 2007—before the crisis—are compared to numbers of 2014—after the crisis. And numbers of 2009—at the beginning of the crisis—are compared to numbers of 2014—six years after. In this way the filmmaker introduces in the documentary another important category of collective memory, the memory of numbers, usually managed by economists and politicians. In the film this memory is managed by the filmmaker in different ways in order to remind the spectator of the pres-ence of the markets in the era of numbers.

The montage lies on a dominant flashback having as a starting point the time period of completion of the documentary—that is the year 2015—and going back to the beginning of the crisis in 2009. Through this flashback the filmmaker proposes to the spectator to reconsider the four years of crisis.

Having as a starting point a time period when the situation of crisis is taken for granted the filmmaker leads the spectator back to the beginning of this crisis and reminds the political events on the national and international scene that announced it. This mnemonic itinerary proposed in the documentary goes from the present back to the recent past. Then the filmmaker invites the spectator to follow the evolution of political events, social reactions and social impacts year after year. This second mnemonic itinerary proposed leads from the past back to the present. Both mnemonic itineraries related to this dominant flashback also organize the use of individual and collective memory made by the filmmaker so as to support his scenario. Nevertheless, Avgeropoulos also proposes another mnemonic itinerary back to a more distant past. Whilst a well-known centrist politician of the Socialist Party (PASOK) speaks on the crisis, a subtle association of ideas appears in front of the spectator connecting three different periods of time: the students' claims for "bread, education and liberty" during the dictatorship of 1967 (1967–1974), the "bread abundance" during the PASOK governance (1981–1989) and the lack of bread during the present period of hard austerity.

Avgeropoulos adopts the complementarity of mnemonic sources by using written memory in order to frame oral memory as it appears in the documentary. In fact, written memory takes mainly two forms. On the one hand it is the memory contained in letters and notes of persons that committed suicide because of the financial crisis. These written documents are used in a complementary way, when the relatives speak of these people in front of the camera. On the other it has the form of notes transcribing thoughts and feelings related to the crisis; these notes are written by simple people who have participated in the protests in public spaces and pinned on tree trunks. These notes are shown to the spectator when the camera is filming these protests and zooming in on "details" appearing on the tree trunks. By choosing to include these forms of written memory in his documentary, Avgeropoulos also makes a management of written collective memory serving his main idea on the Greek crisis. This idea implies that agora, in the sense of the place and act of commercial transactions, as experienced in Greece at the time of crisis, is leading to suicide not only the citizens of the country, but also Agora in the sense of Democracy.

So, our investigation on the filmmaker himself and, on a second level, on the montage of the documentary, shows that this montage lies on various mnemonic itineraries and flashbacks: those adopted by the interviewees, as already said, but also those followed by the film director. At this level our analysis highlights aspects of the selective management of collective memory made by Avgeropoulos. This management reflects the way he, a Greek filmmaker of international fame, conceives the representation of the financial crisis in Greece.

Our analysis also underlines that the documentary *Agora,* like a puzzle or a mosaic (da Silva Borges 2007) made of various pieces of individual and collective memory, unravels different facets of the Greek financial crisis. Additionally, our approach may have also shown that the representation of what really took place is "a complex exercise" for the filmmaker (Villareal 2010).

4   Concluding Remarks

The representation of the current financial crisis in the documentary *Agora* is connected to multiple ways of managing individual and collective memory; these ways, as shown, are all related to the selective character of recalling the past in order to face needs and answer questions of the present, mainly asked by the filmmaker. So, the film *Agora* is a document of what happened in front of the camera, as well as of the way this camera was used in order to represent it (Nichols 2001: 36). We could add to this that *Agora* is also a document of the way the collective memory is used in order to represent the Greek financial crisis. In fact, the representation of crisis in this documentary is related not only to the mechanism of recalling collective memory adopted by the interviewees, but also to the mechanism of recalling collective memory adopted by the filmmaker whilst filming images of crisis, as well as whilst editing the documentary. As shown in our investigation, the film itself is a fragment of collective memory related to the financial crisis in Greece, but also with all other levels of social and political elaboration of the collective memory of this crisis. Our attempt to analyze the documentary of Avgeropoulos on the above levels supports two statements. The first is that any representation of crisis is tightly related to the mechanism of selectivity implied in any mnemonic process of recalling and narrating the past, mechanism varying per social stratum and level. The second statement is that this is also valid for film directors when preparing documentary films as they also work selectively while collecting their material, but also while editing their films.

The filmic representation of crisis, in the case of documentaries, reflects quite clearly the film director's relationship to the collective memory all over the process of filmmaking: the different ways in which he stimulates this memory is recalled by his interviewees on various occasions and is transcribed for the sake of the filmmaking. That means that the documentary film can be analyzed not only on the level of facts invoked and situations described, which would lead to a historical approach of the filmic product. It can be also considered as a creation representing long and complex mnemonic itineraries of the film director, which would lead to a sociological approach of all mnemonic processes implied in the film making, as well transcribed in the film product. So, the documentary cinema is an appropriate medium for creating visual and audiovisual memory, preserving past events from oblivion, but also proposing a critical approach of the past (Villareal 2010).

This type of analysis could advance the research made on the crisis representations towards other directions. One research direction could be to consider the ways films and documentaries, as final filmic products, can contribute to the establishment and the typification of the collective memory on crisis, as well as lead to a crisis representation appearing objective and stereotyped. Another research direction could be to study the ways in which the filmic representation of historical events stimulates the spectator's memory (Eisenstein 1967: 33) and provoke "a memory flow" with emotions and souvenirs (Yasbek 2011).

By combining different levels of analyzing the filmic representation of historical events it is possible to better understand the dialectic between memory and history. Also by scrutinizing the tracks of memory (Eid 2010) it is important to observe the memory construction made by memory makers and study the receptivity of memory users (Kansteiner 2002: 197); it is crucial to investigate how societies work for the preservation and transmission of their memory on periods that are critical for their survival (Connerton 1989).

Bibliography

Barrio, J.A. (2008). "The Middle Ages in USA cinema". *Imago Temporis. Medium Aevum* II: 229–260. Available at: https://repositori.udl.cat/bitstream/handle/10459.1/47844/Imago_Temporis_2_2008.pdf?sequence=1&i.

Bartholeyns, G. (2000). "Representation of the past in the films: Between historicity and authenticity". *Article Information* 48(189): 31–47. Available at: https://doi.org/10.1177/039219210004818904.

Basea, E. (2016). "The 'Greek Crisis' through the Cinematic and Photographic Lens: From 'Weirdness' and Decay to Social Protest and Civic Responsibility". *Visual Anthropology Review* 32(1): 61–72. Available at: http://onlinelibrary.wiley.com/doi/10.1111/var.12093/full.

Baudry, A. (1994). "Montage comme interprétation". *Images documentaires* 17, 2ème trimestre. Available at: https://www.google.com/search?client=firefox-b-d&q=IMAGES+documentaires+17+2ème+trimestre.

Collognat, A. (1994). "L'Antiquité au cinéma". *Bulletin de l'Association Guillaume Budé* 3: 332–351. Available at: https://www.persee.fr/doc/bude_0004-5527_1994_num_1_3_1611.

Comolli, J.L. (1994). "Montage comme métamorphose". *Images documentaires* 17, 2ème trimestre. Available at: https://www.google.com/search?client=firefox-b-d&q=IMAGES+documentaires+17+2ème+trimestre.

Connerton, P. (1989). *How societies remember*. Cambridge: Cambridge University Press.

Constantopoulou Ch. (2010). *Free time: Myths and Realities*. Athens: Papazissis (in Greek).

Crane, S. (1997). "Writing the individual back into collective memory". *The American Historical Review* 102(5): 1372–1385. Available at: https://www.jstor.org/stable/2171068.

da Silva Borges, Ch. (2007). *Vers un cinéma en fuite: le puzzle, la mosaïque et le labyrinthe comme clefs de composition filmique*. Thèse de doctorat en Études cinématographiques et audiovisuelles, Paris: Université Paris 3. Available at: http://www.theses.fr/2007PA030149.

Decarie-Daigneault, N. (2016). *La mémoire tranquille: Enquête documentaire sur une mémoire familiale*. Mémoire de maitrise en Communication, Montréal: Université du Québec. Available at: https://archipel.uqam.ca/8935/1/M14484.pdf.

Eid, R. (2010). *Le cinéma libanais d'après guerre : Construction de mémoire et recomposition identitaire*. Thèse de doctorat en Centre des études arabes, Paris: Université Paris. Available at: http://www.theses.fr/2010PA030128.

Eisenstein S. (1967). *Problems of film direction. The dialectic of film. Montage*. Athens: Cinematographic Editions (in Greek).

Gensburger, S. and Lavabre, M.C. (2005). "Entre « devoir de mémoire » et « abus de mémoire » : La sociologie de la mémoire comme tierce position". In: Muller, B. (dir.). *Histoire, mémoire et épistémologie. A propos de Paul Ricoeur*. Lausanne: Payot, pp. 76–95.

Hadouchi, O. (2010). "Mémoire des luttes contre les dictatures du Cône Sud (Argentine, Chili et Uruguay) dans le cinéma documentaire contemporain". *L'Ordinaire des Amériques*. Available at: http://journals.openedition.org/orda/2412.

Halbwachs, M. (1967). *La mémoire collective*. 2eme edition. Paris: PUF.

Kansteiner, W. (2002). Finding meaning in memory: A methodological critique of collective memory studies. *History and Theory* 41: 179–197. Available at: https://www.jstor.org/stable/3590762.

Kornetis, K. (2014). "From Reconciliation to Vengeance: the Greek Civil War on Screen in Pantelis Voulgaris's A Soul so Deep and Kostas Charalambou's Tied Red Thread". *Filmicon; Journal of Greek Filmic Studies* 2, September. Available at: http://filmicon-journal.com/journal/article/2014/2/6.

Lemonidou E. (2017). *History on the big screen*. Athens: Taxideftis (in Greek).

Lindeperg, S. (1997). *Les Écrans de l'ombre. La Seconde Guerre mondiale dans le cinéma français (1944–1969)*. Paris: CNRS Éditions.

Lykidis, A. (2015a). *Greek cinema since the crisis*. Available at: https://www.academia.
edu/12277656/Greek_Cinema_since_the_Crisis.

Lykidis, A. (2015b). "Crisis of sovereignty in recent Greek cinema". *Journal of Greek Media and Culture* 1(1): 9–27. Available at: http://www.ingentaconnect.com/content/
intellect/jgmc/2015/00000001/00000001/art00002.

Maazouzi, D. (2008). "Rendre le passé colonial à la mémoire collective française / *Le cinéma post-colonial français* de Caroline Eades. Cerf-Corlet, « Septième Art »", 423p.
Spirale 223: 30–31. Available at: https://www.erudit.org/en/journals/spirale/1900-v1-n1-spirale1061713/16749ac.pdf.

Mademli, G. (2016). "From the crisis of cinema to the cinema of crisis: A "Weird" Label
for contemporary Greek cinema". *Frames Cinema Journal* 9. Available at: https://
framescinemajournal.com/article/from-the-crisis-of-cinema-to-the-cinema-of-cri
sis-a-weird-label-for-contemporary-greek-cinema/.

Manthoulis, R. (2015). *Montage*. Athens: Gavriilidis.

Mantoglou, A. (2012). *Memories. Individual—Social—Historical*. Athens: Papazissis.

Nichols, B. (2001). *Introduction to documentary*. Bloomington/Indianapolis: Indiana
University Press.

Olick, J. (1999). "Collective memory: the two cultures". *Sociological Theory* 17(3): 333–
348. Available at: https://journals.sagepub.com/doi/10.1111/0735-2751.00083.

Olick, J. and Robbins, J. (1998). "Social memory studies: From "Collective Memory" to
the Historical Sociology of mnemonic practices". *Annual Review of Sociology* 24:
105–140. Available at: https://www.jstor.org/stable/223476.

Papadimitriou, L. (2015). "The power of the local: Greek documentaries in the 2000s". In:
Giukin L., Desser, D. and Falkowska, J. (eds.). *Small Cinemas in Global Markets: Genres,
Identities, Narratives*. London: Lexington Books, pp. 31–47. Available at: https://
www.academia.edu/7212223/The_Power_of_the_Local_Greek_Documentaries
_in_the_2000s.

Pfeifer, M. (2016). "Cinema in the Age of Austerity: On the Representation of Debt in
Greek Cinema". *Filmicon: Journal of Greek Studies* 4. Available at: http://filmicon-
journal.com/blog/post/53/cinema-in-the-age-of-austerity.

Pinel, V. (2013). *The montage*. Athens: Patakis.

Plummer, K. (2000). *Documents of life. An introduction to the problems and literature of
a humanistic method*. Athens: Gutenberg (in Greek).

Roussos, G. (2014). *Greek cinema in the post-dictatorship years*. Available at: https://
tvxs.gr/news/sinema/o-ellinikos-kinimatografos-sta-xronia-tis-metapoliteysis.

Thompson, P. (1978). *The voice of the past: oral history*. Oxford: Oxford University Press.

Tomai, F. (2006). *Representations of the war. The testimony of cinematic image*. Athens:
Papazissis (in Greek).

Villareal, P. (2010). "Cinéma, Histoire et Mémoire, quelques problèmes théoriques
et méthodologiques pour son étude". *Quaina* 1. Available at: http://quaina.univ
-angers.fr/revues/numero-1-2010/article/cinema-histoire-et-memoire.

Wiseman, F. (1994). "Le montage, une conversation à quatre voix". *Images documentaires* 17, 2ème trimestre. Available at: https://www.google.com/search?client=firefox-b-d&q=IMAGES+documentaires+17+2ème+trimestre.

Yazbek, E. (2011). "Histoire, mémoire et fiction dans le cinéma américain contemporain". *Conserveries mémorielles*. Available at: http://journals.openedition.org/cm/832.

CHAPTER 8

Film Narratives on the Current Economic Crisis: the Case of the French Film "the Law of the Markets"

Joanna Tsiganou

1   Introduction

Since the advent of the current economic crisis in Europe and Greece multiple scientific works have been devoted to its study by numerous social scientists (indicatively, Petropoulos and Tsobanoglou 2014).[1] Within these works certain narratives have been formulated and advanced for the impacts of the current crisis to every aspect of social life. The crisis' influence on the persistence and/ or emergence of lawful and unlawful behavior has also been addressed (Tsiganou 2013).

In the present study film narrations are used, by means of decoding the narratives produced in the French film titled "the Law of the Markets",[2] within the broad domain of sociology in general and visual sociology in particular. The aim of the study is to attempt to decipher certain reflective stories of contemporary fears associated to the current crisis in the countries of Europe. The advent of the crisis is therefore treated as a reflective fabric upon which established value and control systems are questioned, characters and/or heroes of new as well as traditional types of perpetrators and victims are created, novel areas of insecurity in people's lives, are projected.

With the power of the "screen" and cinema "images" the structural consequences of the economic crisis upon sectors of social order are energizing social imagery in a way reflecting both abstract fears and concrete social situations. Thus, contemporary social phenomena in Greece and elsewhere become more ready to social science scrutiny and understanding.

---

1   Also, see the scientific journals, "Greece under crisis" the Greek Review of Social Research, Special Issue, vol. A–B, no. 133–4, 2011, Athens, EKKE. "The crisis", Social Sciences, no. 2–3, 2013.

2   The analysis is based on the French movie produced in 2015 and titled "the Law of the Markets", ("La Loi du Marche", in the original production), directed by Stephen Brize.

2   Epistemological and Methodological Scripts on the "Script"

Within a film, narratives are partly produced through the film's script. Addressing the specific movie's script some preliminary conceptual and methodological issues should be initially clarified. In order to decode film narratives on the
current economic crisis, the main question addressed is whether there is a distinction between the script and the underline story conveying social messages
to broader audiences.

Following distinct sociological traditions on film narratives, we are stum-
bling at a dualism introduced by Russian formalism and employed broadly in
narratology[3] which describes narrative construction, between the emplot-
ment of the narrative, in other words, the plot, the way a story is organized
throughout the movie, (the *"syuzhet"* in cinema terms) and the *raw material* of
a story, (the *"fabula"* in cinema terms), (Propp 1928/1968). This dualism, has
energized multiple critics of course: post-structuralists note a certain contradiction in assigning priority to either the plot or the story (Culler 1981). As Derrida has put it, narrative is both employment and a subjection of the stuff of
story, represented through narrative. Derrida views narrative "as having a terrible secret, in its way of oppressing story" (Derrida 1979: 94).

On the other hand, within the symbolic interactionist perspective the above
dualism between the plot and the story has also been raised. For Bruner there
is the plot of narrative and the story as a "timeless underlying theme" (Bruner
1986: 7, 17–21). Thus, the story becomes the "virtual text" (Bruner 1986: 32) to
the narrative grammars. In the domain of language studies, Bakhtin, like Derrida, remains suspicious of the hegemony of narrative over story. For Bakhtin
"narrative genres are always enclosed in a solid and unshakable monological
framework" (Bakhtin 1973: 12). Story, for Bakhtin, is decidedly more dialogue-
based in the "polyphonic manner of the story" (Bakhtin 1973: 60). On the other
hand, Whorf has contended that rather than past-present-future, as segregated
plot, life experiences may be seen as one of "eventing" (Whorf 1956: 256).

From the point of view of the sociology of narratives, since the 1980s, when
"the antistructuralist and antipositivist agenda has animated the "narrative
turn" in the social sciences ... a more uniquely sociological approach has studied stories in the interactional, institutional, and political contexts of their tell-
ing ... (A) cluster of approaches, rooted variously in conversational analysis,

---

3 Narratology is used in this text in the sense of the study of narrative and narrative structure
   and the ways that these affect human perception, as in the *General Introduction to Narratology*, College of Liberal Arts, Purdue University. Also in Gerald Prince, 1994, "Narratology",
   Johns Hopkins Guide to Literary Theory and Criticism.

symbolic interactionism, network analysis, and structuralist cultural sociologies, has both responded to problems associated with the narrative turn and
shed light on enduring sociological questions such as the bases of institutional
authority, how inequalities are maintained and reproduced, why political chal-
lengers are sometimes able to win support, and the cultural foundations of
self-interest and instrumental rationality" (Polletta et al. 2011: 109).

Polletta argues that narratives might be forms of discourse, vehicles of ideology, and elements of collective action frames, but unlike all three, they can
be identified in a chunk of text or speech by their formal features (Polletta
2006). Others consent that narratives also may be a distinctive mode of cogni-
tion (Bruner 1986).

Labov's definition of narratives in visual arts conceives narrative as an ac-
count of a sequence of events in the order in which they occurred to make a
point (Labov and Waletsky 1967). Most scholars of the field of fiction and film
see narratives as having characters (Chatman 1978; Jacobs 2002). Audiences
usually feel a sense of empathy with at least one character (Sarbin 1995). Only
relevant events are included in the story, and later events are assumed to explain earlier ones. The causal links between events, however, are based not on
formal logic or probability but on plot. Plot is the structure of the story. It is
the means by which what would otherwise be mere occurrences are made into
moments in the unfolding of the story. Plots are familiar to audiences from
stories they have heard before, although the relations between the underlying
plot structure and a particular story are complex (Brooks 1984). In addition,
"events in a story project a desirable or undesirable future. They make a normative point" (Polletta et al. 2011: 111). Storytellers rarely exhibit explicitly to
their audiences the moral undertones of the story. The story's larger meaning
seems to be given rather by the events themselves (White 1980), while requiring interpretation on the audience's part (Iser 1972; Polletta 2006). Insofar as
stories "draw on a cultural stock of plots, they communicate the normative
values that are associated with those plots ... Unlike an explanation, then,
a narrative represents cause and effect relations through its sequencing of
events rather than by appeal to standards of logic and proof" (Polletta et al.
2011: 111).

However, as it has been pointed out, we need to know much more about
what makes stories politically persuasive. Plot, for example, is thought to be
crucial to narrative's effects, but few studies have investigated whether plot
actually works to structure narrative interpretation in the way it is thought to.
Character, too, remains understudied, despite the fact that character may be
more important than plot and that character more than events seems important in policy debates. More challenging methodologically is the possibility

that the most effective stories are those that are not told explicitly but instead are simply alluded to, with the speaker treating the story as already known by the audience. The challenge is to get at those stories empirically. Framing theorists, for example, argue that frames must be both empirically credible and faithful to dominant cultural narratives to be effective (Benford and Snow 2000). But stories' empirical credibility may be a product of their narrative fidelity (White 1980). That is, they seem true because they accord with familiar stories. Expectations about the truth value of stories probably vary across story genres as well as settings and speakers. But as it has been pointed out "it is worth studying the circumstances in which narrative is pitted against other modes of representing reality" (Polletta et al. 2011: 123).

From another vein of thought "popular movies are stories, narratives" (Cutting 2016: 1713). The deciphering of narrative structure has occupied many disciplines across the humanities and social sciences. In this vein, story grammars (Mandler and Johnson 1977; Rumelhart 1975) and related concepts like discourse (Kintsch and Van Dijk 1978), scripts (Schank and Abelson 1977), and schemata (Brewer 1985; Brewer and Lichtenstein 1981), have been studied. In movies, the prototypic schema form is genre. As Bordwell noted, "in a Western, we expect to see gunfights, barroom brawls, and thundering hooves even if they are neither realistically introduced nor causally necessary" (Bordwell 1985: 36).

In this chapter, however, I wish to investigate the narrative structure of a single popular movie—as a case study—beyond genre schemata. My focus is on the story as it is physically told, not on the story as it is comprehended. Although I will explore how this story form has been designed, to engage spectators, I hesitate to make inferences about how the film's narrational form should affect the viewer. My goal is a standard one for the initial phases of any investigation in the cognitive sciences. As Bordwell suggested, "the syuzhet (plot) ... is the dramaturgy of the fiction film, the organized set of cues prompting us to infer and assemble story information" (Bordwell 1985: 52). Again, what is constructed in the mind of the spectator is not at issue here; it will vary with every individual. So I am interested in the plot and the narratives introduced at it to reflect "the raw material of the story". Also, I am not interested in the film style or filmmaker's choices of cinematic devices but only occasionally, and only when they offer an import to narratives. As Thompson (1999) suggested, movies as a story form they can be fine art, emotionally absorbing, thought provoking, educational, and entertaining, all at once (Thompson 1999; Brewer and Lichtenstein 1982). They can even be thought of as a kind of "mind candy" where we get to exercise our theory-of-mind faculties (Levin, Hymel and Baker 2013; Zunshine 2012).

That is to say that I will resist the appealing idea to follow in detail the initial formulation of narrative structure promoted by Aristotle who wrote 2,500 years ago that stories are wholes in three parts: the beginning of a play, the *protasis,* which introduces the characters and setting; the middle of the play, the *epitasis,* which contains the main action of the story building to a climax; and the end, the *catastrophe,* which presents the climax and final resolution (Aristotle 2008: ch. 7, 1447a–1447b, 1449b–1450b). I tend to include to my reading of the movie Bordwell's idea that "classical narration treats film technique as a vehicle for the syuzhet's (plot's) transmission of fabula (story) information" (Bordwell 1986: 26). As he notes elsewhere, "narration is more than an armory of devices; it becomes our access, moment by moment, to the unfolding story.... Narration in any medium can usefully be thought of as governing our trajectory through the narrative" (Bordwell 2008: 12).

More precisely, based to the above, I am interested in how information unfolds over a movie's narration. My major assumption is that the plot should reflect narrative states and I will attempt in my case study of the particular movie to pin them down.

3   The Plot of the Movie

As already mentioned, I shall refer to narratives of the current crisis as projected through the French movie produced in 2015 and titled "the Law of the Markets". The plot is developed upon the fabric of the structural turbulence of the labor markets globally brought about by the current economic crisis and the new working conditions that have dominated the markets ever since. The results of these transformations are projected as they are reflected in specific social situations, behaviors and moral dilemmas.

The plot of the movie is reflecting on the above issues with the help of a film character, that of a common person, a person of "the next door", Thierry Togourdo, who has been fired from the company that worked for 25 years and remains unemployed for 20 whole months. His daily life is devoted to strenuous efforts to find a job to support his family and take care of his son, a teenager with mental and physical health problems.

The plot follows the agonizing efforts of Thierry, in searching for a job. The protagonist at some point is hired as a supermarket security agent. Scene after scene, spectators are introduced into scenes of social reality that encircle and encapsulate the endless Thierry's tries. With exemplary storytelling accuracy, the film maintains consistently low narrative tones, underlying psychological tensions. With small episodes taken out of everyday life, the movie delicately reveals and restores the conceptual patterns of the pressures imposed upon the social subjects by the relentless laws of the contemporary neo-liberal labor market operating undisturbed under conditions of capitalist growth and flexible working relations. Obliged to live under the dominance of these laws, Thierry, personifies all unemployed or dismissed populations whose job losses occurred due to labor markets' restructuring to respond to globalization and the current economic crisis' new demands. Thus, in the unravelling of the plot, the consequences of losing a job in the contemporary socio-economic milieu are successfully visualized: people cannot maintain loans and are losing their homes. Families cannot support their disabled members since they are losing relevant social benefits. Under the new laws of the markets, work experience is devalued, followed by a paradox substitution of workers' de-skilling with programs of re-skilling. The unemployed are forced to transform themselves into flexible "personas" in job search, that is to accept orders on how to "fit in", to the new working conditions, that is orders on how to talk, how to set up, how to dress, how to write resumes, even orders on the specialty they should be trained in order to re-enter the labor market.

Through this specific medium of visual narratives, we recognize Cohn's structure of visual sequential narratives (Cohn 2013; 2015). The *establisher*, (loss of job), which indeed sets up an interaction but without any action. The *initial*, (agonizing repetitive efforts in searching for job) which initiates the tension in the narrative to follow. The *prolongation*, which continues the trajectory of the protagonist's path. The *peak*, which marks the height of the narrative tension. Pretty clearly, this is a climax. And finally, there is the *release*, very close to the functions of an epilog, which dissolves the tension of the interaction. In another vocabulary (Watts 1996), the above stages may be seen as the *stasis* (the prolog, setup, or exposition), the *trigger* (the inciting incident), the *quest* (the lock-in on a path toward achieving the goal), the *surprise* (one or a series of derailing events like those found in the complication), the *critical choice* (the transition at the end of the complication into the development where the protagonist doubles down to achieve the goal), the *climax*, the *reversal* (as in the epilog, where the new norm is established, often with characters' roles reversed), and the *resolution* (where loose ends of the plot are tied up, also as in the epilog).

Throughout the movie, spectators across the world, follow all the above steps made by the main character, the protagonist, of the movie, reflecting upon their own relevant life experiences. At the same time, they are introduced to the climate of the psychological tensions produced during Thierry's search of a new job. However, the film, resists exaggeration and emotion, under the clear look of its director Stephen Brize, and removes any melodramatic filter from Thierry's portrait. This way the succession of the hero's emotions are clearly projected reflecting upon the gradual building of contemporary psychological tensions: Thierry's glances, face expressions and body stance as anxiety is substituted by despair, as despair is substituted by passivity, as passivity is substituted by a growing sense of impatience and finally as all the above are substituted by the joy of freedom, are projected and reflect upon relevant spectators' agonizing fears. The presence of the protagonist in almost every shot, as the cinema frame includes him even though the "action" involves other persons, the fact also that he remains mostly silent and restrained in his reactions, thus becoming a participant and at the same time an observer, reflect exactly the work of the sociological researcher as a participant observer.

As noted, screenplay's brightest and darkest moments (Cutting 2016) where lighting shapes the reality in front of the lens, makes also light a co-partner to tell the story (Kiwan and Butler 2013). As also noted, the brighter the image, the better viewers generally feel, as brightness affects mood and modulates emotion in the real world as well as in movies (Valdez and Mehrabian 1994). Additionally, sizing up characters in visual narration (Cutting 2016; Cutting and Armstrong 2016), that is choices on how much of the frame should be filled by a character's face and body, as the close-up has inspired fascination, sentiments, emotions and it has been seen as the vehicle of the star, the privileged receptacle of affect, the guarantee of the cinema's status as a universal language (Doane 2003), indicates that the larger the character in the frame (ever-present in our case), the easier it is to judge the response of that character to the events in the narrative (Cutting 2016). Additionally, one can read the movies in general and the specific movie of our case study in particular, through action shots and "the pacing of scenes and narrative shifts" (Cutting 2016; Monaco 1977). As generally remarked not all shots in action films are action shots. Most "doing" in movies entails a moving character or a moving object. However, some "doings" are well beyond the norm (Cutting 2016). Also, continuity and discontinuity, the psychological impression in movies of ongoingness versus change, are not what they might first appear. Cuts do not always disrupt the continuity of the unfolding story. But discontinuities do occur and they occur with cuts and other transitions at scene boundaries, at what has been called narrative shifts (Zwaan et al. 1995; Zwaan and Radvansky 1998) which may be earmarked by changes in *location*, changes of *characters* and changes of *time* such as in a flashback, or a dream. All these are important in decoding the narratives behind the plot. As Cutting has put it, aspects of form and meaning in popular movies are not independent. That is, there are strong correlations between the progression of the narration and the narrative states of movies (Cutting 2016). According to Thompson "the intricate web of character, event, time, and space" in the story becomes "transparently obvious" through the style conventions in the plot (Thompson 1999: 11). In McNamara's and Magliano's terms, these films are high in the ease of processing and in this medium we viewers are high in our skill at extracting their information (McNamara and Magliano 2009: 301).

Followingly, the skillful way in which the hero is projected in the movie of our case study, internalizing his sentiments and externalizing his attempts to act methodically and effectively, renders him a three-dimensional cinematic character that underpins the ideological core sustaining modern aspects of alienation: the moral-economic-political dilemmas faced by contemporary social subjects, which are answered with cinematic immediacy and political clarity. Nevertheless, the film also connotes the means and ways collective conscience is unearthed and dictates not only social behavior but also "moral" and humane reactions against immoral and inhumane labor markets' de-regulation. Thus, the story is inclusive also of the offsets to the alienating forces of the contemporary social world which can be identified in the role and the function of traditional social structures and values of social belonging, such as the role and the operations of family, of culture, of social solidarity and of certain communal forms of social action and reaction. For example, dancing is projected as compensating for the obstacles, the misery and the unhappiness of contemporary social life. The resort to strong family ties is counter-balancing dissolution trends through the praised promotion of individualism and self-centeredness in contemporary societies. Most importantly social solidarity and traditional, more humane communal forms of reacting to various forms of disobedience and rule-breaking are unearthed to counteract the dominating power of the inhuman law of the market. Thus, the strict enforcement of surveillance mechanisms adopted for security policing (i.e. for the protection of supermarket goods) is receding in front of the projected "moral" obligation to feed those in need. This way the pensioner who due to cuts in pensions in the midst of the current crisis is steeling meat, otherwise inaccessible, the cashier who steels discount vouchers to support her nephew's drug-habit etc., are not reported, by the film hero. Nevertheless, rule-breaking under the surveillance mechanisms of the labor market rulemaking, cannot be tolerated and the power to punish is ultimately restored. However, for Thierry, and the spectators, "katharsis", in the sense of "exodus" eventually occurs, when the hero becomes intolerable of the cruelty of contemporary official controls that undermine social bonds and "walks away fully content". This way the moral foundations of the Law of the Market that currently and cruelty dominates social lives are questioned and collective conscience as the driving force of societies' regulation is restored.

4   Film Narratives of the Current Economic Crisis vis-à-vis
        Sociological Paradigms

The narratives produced throughout the movie's narration (plot) provide a
unique fabric in order to comprehend the consequences of the current economic crisis across Europe (and the world). These narratives constitute reflexive accounts not only of structural but also of cultural perspectives all well
imbedded in social actors' point of view.

    An initial narrative reflects the consequences of economic crises on peo-
ple's lives through job losses. In the area of salaried work, the uncertainty produced when losing one's job puts in question the satisfaction of basic needs
and human rights, such as access to housing, health, education and nutrition
(indicatively, Permetzidou and Papatheodorou 1998; Papadopoulou 2012; Panagiotopoulos 2013; Demertzis et al. 2017). These issues are visualized in the face
and the body of the protagonist as despair conquers the glance and the physical stance of the movie's hero. When confronting the "system", either in the
form of applying for a loan, or in the form for waiting for an opportunity for a
dissent job, the hero's speech and movement into the film dictate his feeling of
"powerlessness" in confronting structural constrains. Thus, the film produces
reflexive accounts on part of the viewer of the social subject's impotency
against the power of the State or the Laws governing the labor market in the
capitalist mode of production, concurring with neo-liberal politics under conditions of economic crises (Piketty 2015). Yet, this film narrative underlines the
concept of "powerlessness", as an aspect of alienation leading to social isolation and concurring marginalization (Seeman 1972; Nachmias 1976).

    A third narrative is helping the surfacing of the *paradox* marked in labor
recruitment in times of economic crisis under conditions of neo-liberalism
which underlines at the same time aspects of social hypocrisy. This *paradox* is
projected throughout the narration with "images" of the current crisis, which
on the one hand, leads people of the productive age to unemployment and de-
skilling while on the other hand leads them to re-skilling through "empower-
ment" and training mechanisms useful to the undergoing labor market's restructuring (indicatively, Roberts et al. 1994; Gallie 1991). Also, this *paradox*,
promoted by the movie's plot, becomes crystal-clear as the social actors' point
of view is disregarded as irrelevant, while individual talents, merits and
strengths have to be recruited if re-inclusion to the labor market is to be
affected.

    There are other important narratives, of course, imminently connected to
the progress of the film's story. Economic crises—the classical and neo-classical
schools of sociology of deviance have taught us—have a significant bearing to

the rise in criminal activity, especially in unlawful behaviors associated to crimes against property, violence and thefts. The movie clearly undermines the rational of these theoretical views, as it reminds us of the importance of the mediating variables of the value system in the occurrence of rule-breaking behavior. It also brings into the discussion the issue of law-obedience as connected to the morality of the laws to be obeyed. Therefore, it reminds us that when the moral foundations of laws and regulations are not in alignment with societies' collective conscience official controls and the power to punish are undermined and questioned (indicatively, Lilly et al. 1989; Box 1981; Halpern 2001; Downess and Rock 2016).

Some other, more latent, narratives are also promoting theoretical ideas on the consequences of economic crises to people's lives associated with uncertainties and fears. The handling of those anxieties and fears through official and unofficial exercise of controls are extremely obvious. In particular, the classical school of criminology idea that modern societies under crisis are more in need of the "panopticon", strict surveillance and the need to punish (Wilson 1975; Conklin 1975; Morgan 1978; Reiman 1979), is visualized virtually and symbolically. Throughout the plot of the movie a latent narrative is revealed in reflexive accounts of the connection among labor markets restructuring, the social production of policing, the handling of social anxieties, uncertainty and fears through the exercise of effective controls and the power to punish (Garland and Young 1983). Under the Law of the Market, in the dystopian city of the "panopticon" law-offenders and sympathizing security officers to them have no place (Reichman 1986; Ewald 1991; Box 1987). On the contrary, through visions of social control, certain forms of "social punishments" are reinvented and enforced in parallel to the system of official controls to obtain conformity (as in Cohen 1985).

Finally, another narrative is revealed through the protagonist's placement into the film. As he, himself carries the burden of the whole movie, either present, or absent, either, participating or simply observing, a narrative is built symbolizing and visualizing the triumph of individualism in the modern capitalistic societies of risk and uncertainty (Beck 1992; Garland 1996; Mazerolle and Roehl 1998). More importantly this narrative, as built upon the theoretical idea of transcending the criminal-civil law distinction and on using civil remedies and actuarial practices to achieve criminal law objectives in addition to strict penal regulation, is reflecting the reinforcement of social controls by the concomitant use of civil and penal sanctions upon individuals. This way, the classical school of criminology with its exclusive focus on individual responsibility and blame for law-offending is revived, intensifying controls upon individuals, especially those most impotent (Simon 1988; Lianos and Douglas 2000;

Cohen 1979). The conceptualization of crime idea that crime is a result of individual choice is reviving in introducing the role of civil sanctions in social control in contemporary societies. All these are exceptionally visualized in the film with reflecting their bearing upon the senses of loneliness and impotency which tend to dominate contemporary social life.

However, intrinsically to the above grim narratives, the movie is promoting a clearly optimistic narrative based on the theoretical idea that the contemporary cruelty of official controls may be counter-balanced by tolerance, a premodern facet of social control and an important dimension of social cohesion (Daskalakis 1986). Tolerance, advanced by empathy as well as social solidarity are symbolically and emphatically visualized provoking this way relevant reflexive reactions to spectators.

Also optimistic is the narrative underlined at the end of the movie, as an *exodus*, or as an *epilogue*, which serves at the same time as *catharsis* with a screen shot praising individual craving, will and desire not for law, offending but for freedom, a freedom away from the relentless chains of contemporary reinforcement of societal controls and merciless labor market's de-regulation.

5   Towards the "End": the Climax, the Reversal, the Resolution

Considering again literature, at this concluding section we are returning and turning to our major assumption that the plot of the movie in question did actually reflect narrative states relevant to its theme. Although we agree with the assertion that a full understanding of movies is not yet on the horizon (Polletta et al. 2011), I hope that the present case study may help our path towards this direction.

Through the theoretical preconditions exhibited to the above, an attempt was made to reveal the narrative structure of a film through a chain of events that linked causes and effects, that involved a single protagonist, who, however, exhibits universal desires and seeks a universal goal, who, as many others in real life, has the path to that goal blocked in multiple ways, and then tries to overcome it, and in achieving that goal establishes a new universal social order. These parts have film-style correlates in shot durations and transitions, that is, a word, a list, a sentence, an isolated decision, a glancing expression, a fleeting movement. They also acquire cinematographic characteristics, such as, motion, luminance, scale, contrasts between conversations and patterns of character, introduction and scene changes, all cues in the plot for the viewer to construct the story, all cues that emphasize patterned norms of story production, of narration.

The universality reflected in the protagonist's wants and acts, the striking sameness of the narration in the varied audiences' experiences seem to reinforce and even recall cultural values which help to justify a reaction against systems relatively innocuous and offensive to humanity. It is this universality of needs and deeds which seem to even subvert established societal values to resist labor markets' insolence and rude morality. In this way a new universal social order, freed from the chains of the labor market's neo-liberal regulation seems to be established. This way, for the moviegoer these narrative results, as reported here, help trigger dynamic changes not only in physiological states (motion and emotion) but also by reflecting schemas allow for more rapid processing of the story correlated with engagement and positive affect (Pronin 2013). As in other popular movies, the narrative form feeds into and fits deeply within our minds, full of meaning which projected in the larger scale found in movies may reveal a lot about what our minds like best and what do we prefer within given domain.

In our case, as we have learned from the narratives projected, the advent of the current economic crisis, is treated indeed as a reflexive fabric upon which established value and control systems are questioned, characters of new types of perpetrators and victims are created, novel areas of insecurity in people's lives, are projected. With the power of the screen the structural and cultural consequences of the economic crisis upon sectors of social order are energizing social imagery in a way reflecting both abstract fears and concrete social situations. Thus, contemporary social phenomena in Greece and elsewhere become more ready to social science scrutiny and understanding.

Bibliography

Aristotle. (2008). *Poetic.* Salonica: Zytros.

Bakhtin, M. (1981). *The Dialogic Imagination: Four Essays.* Austin: University of Texas Press.

Beck, U. (1992). *Risk society; Towards a New Modernity.* Newbury Park/London: Sage.

Benford, R.A. and Snow, D.A. (2000). "Framing processes and social movements: an overview and assessment". *Annual Review of Sociology* 26: 611–639.

Bordwell, D. (1986). "Classical Hollywood cinema: Narrational principles and procedures". In: Rosen, P. (ed.). *Narrative, apparatus, ideology.* New York, NY: Columbia University Press, pp. 17–34.

Bordwell, D. (1985). *Narration in the fiction film*. Madison: University of Wisconsin Press.

Bordwell, D. (2008). *The poetics of cinema*. New York, NY: Routledge.

Box, St. (1981). *Deviance Reality and Society*. London: Holt, Rinehart & Winston.

Box, St. (1987). *Recession, crime and Punishment*. London: Macmillan.

Brewer, W.F. and Lichtenstein, E.H. (1981). "Event schemas, story schemas, and story grammars". In: Long, J. and Baddeley, A.D. (eds.). *Attention and performance*. Hillsdale, NY: Erlbaum, pp. 363–379.

Brewer, W.F. (1985). "The story schema: Universal and culture-specific properties". In: Olson, D.R., Torrance, N. and Hildyard, A. (eds.). *Literacy, language, and learning*. Cambridge, UK: Cambridge University Press, pp. 167–194.

Brewer, W.F. and Lichtenstein, E.H. (1982). "Stories are to entertain: A structural-affect theory of stories". *Journal of Pragmatics* 6: 473–486.

Brooks, P. (1984). *Reading for the Plot: Design and Intention in Narrative*. New York: Knopf.

Bruner, J. (1986). *Actual Minds, Possible Worlds*. Cambridge, MA: Harvard University Press.

Chatman, S. (1978). *Story and Discourse: Narrative Structure in Fiction and Film*. Ithaca, NY: Cornell University Press.

Cohen, St. (1979). "The punitive city; notes on the dispersal of social control". *Contemporary Crises* 3: 339–363.

Cohen, St. (1985). *Visions of Social Control: Crime, Punishment and Classification*. Cambridge: Polity Press.

Cohn, N. (2013). "Visual narrative structure". *Cognitive Science* 34: 413–452.

Cohn, N. (2015). "Narrative conjunction's junction function: The interface of narrative grammar and semantics in sequential images". *Journal of Pragmatics* 88: 105–132.

Conklin, J.E. (1975). *The Impact of Crime*. New York: Macmillan.

Culler, J. (1981). *The Pursuit of Signs: Semiotics, Literature, Deconstruction*. Ithaca, NY: Cornell University Press.

Cutting, J.E. (2016). "Narrative theory and the dynamics of popular movies". *Psychonomic Bulletin and Review* 23(6): 1713–1743.

Cutting, J.E. and Armstrong, K.L. (2016). "Facial expression, size, and clutter: Inferences from movie structure to emotion judgments and back". In: *Attention, Perception & Psychophysics* 78(3): 891–901.

Daskalakis, E. (1986). *The Criminology of Social Reaction*. Athens: Panteion.

Demertzis, N., Balourdos, D., Kikilias, E., Spyropoulou, N. and Chrysakis, M. (2017). *The Social Portrait of Greece*. Athens: EKKE – ION.

Derrida, J. (1979). "Living on". In: Bloom, H., Derrida, J., De Man, P., Hartman, G. and Miller, J.H. (eds.). *Deconstruction and criticism*. New York, NY: Seabury Press, pp. 75–176.

Doane, M.A. (2003). "The close-up: Scale and detail in cinema. Differences". *A Journal of Feminist and Cultural Studies* 14(3): 89–111.

Downess, D. and Rock, P. (2016). *Understanding Deviance*. Oxford, UK: Oxford University Press.

Ewald, F. (1991). "Insurance and risk". In: Graham, B., Gordon, C. and Miller, P. (eds.). *The Foucault effect: studies in Governmentality*. London: Harvester Wheatsheaf, pp. 201–205.

Gallie, D. (1991). "Patterns of skill change. Upskilling, Deskilling or the Polarisation of skills?" *Work, Employment and Society* 5(3): 319–351.

Garland, D. (1996). "The Limits of the Sovereign state". *The British Journal of Criminology* 36(4): 445–471.

Garland, D. and Young, P. (1983). *The Power to Punish*. London: Macmillan.

Halpern, D. (2001). "Moral Values, Social Trust and Inequality—Can Values Explain Crime?" *The British Journal of Criminology* 41: 236–251.

Iser, W. (1972). "The reading process: a phenomenological approach". *New Literary Histories* 3: 279–299.

Jacobs, R.N. (2002). "The narrative integration of personal and collective identity in social movements". In: Green, M.C., Strange, J.J. and Brock T.C. (ed.). *Narrative Impact: Social and Cognitive Foundations*. Mahwah, NJ: Lawrence Erlbaum, pp. 205–228.

Kintsch W. and Van Dijk, T.A. (1978). "Toward a model of text comprehension and production". In: *Psychological Review* 85(5): 363–394.

Kiwan, S. and Butler, L. (2013). "The art of film and lighting: Understanding and manipulating light from an artistic standpoint". In: *E Magazine*. Retrieved from: http://magazine.sae.edu/2013/03/10/the-art-of-film-lightingintro-understanding-and-manipulating-light-from-an-artistic-standpoint/.

Labov, W. and Waletsky, J. (1967). "Narrative analysis: oral versions of personal experience". In: Helm, J. (ed.). *Essays on the Verbaland Visual Arts*. Seattle: University of Washington Press, pp. 12–44.

Levin, D.T., Hymel, A.M., Baker, L. (2013). "Belief, desire, action, and other stuff: Theory of mind in movies". In: Shimamura, A. (ed.). *Psychoncinematics*. New York, NY: Oxford University Press, pp. 244–266.

Lianos, M. and Douglas, M. (2000). "Dangerization and the end of deviance". *The British Journal of Criminology* 40(2): 261–278.

Lilly, J.R., Cullen, Fr.T., Ball, R.A. (1989). *Criminological Theory: Context and Consequences*. Sage.

Mandler, J.M. and Johnson, N.S. (1977). "Remembrance of things parsed: Story structure and recall". *Cognitive Psychology* 9(1): 111–151.

Mazerolle, L.G. and Roehl, I. (1998). *Civil Remedies*. New York: Criminal Justice Press.

McNamara, D.S. and Magliano, J. (2009). "Toward a comprehensive model of comprehension". *The Psychology of Learning and Motivation* 51: 297–384.

Monaco, J. (1977). *How to read a film*. New York, NY: Oxford University Press.

Morgan, P. (1978). *Delinquent Fantacies*. London: Temple Smith.

Nachmias, D. (1976). "Modes and Types of Political Alienation". *The British Journal of Sociology*: 478–493.

Panagiotopoulos, N. (2013). *The violence of unemployment.* Athens: Alexandria.

Papadopoulou, D. (2012). *The sociology of social exclusion in times of globalization.* Athens: Topos.

Permetzidou, M. and Papatheodorou, Ch. (1998). *Poverty and Social Exclusion*. Athens: Exandas.

Petropoulos, N. and Tsobanoglou, G. (2014). *The Debt Crisis in the Eurozone. Social Impacts.* Cambridge: Scholars Publishing.

Piketty, Th. (2015). *The Capital in the 21st Century*. Athens: Polis.

Polletta, F., Ching, P., Chen, B., Gharrity, G. and Motes, A. (2011). "The Sociology of Storytelling". *Annual Review of Sociology* 37: 109–130.

Polletta, F. (2006). *It Was Like a Fever: Storytelling in Protest and Politics*. Chicago: University of Chicago Press.

Polletta, F. (2009). "How to tell a new story about battering". *Journal of Violence Against Women* 15(12): 1490–1508.

Pronin, E. (2013). "When the mind races: Effects of thought speed on feeling and action". *Current Directions in Psychological Science* 22: 283–288.

Propp, Vl. (1928/1968). *Morphology of the Folk Tale*. University of Texas Press.

Reichman, N. (1986). "Managing crime risks; towards an insurance-based model of social control". *Research in Law, Deviance and Social Control* 8: 151–172.

Reiman, J.H. (1979). *The Rich Get Richer and The Poor Get Prison*. New York: Wiley.

Roberts, K. et al. (1994). "Flexibility and Individualisation: A comparison of transitions to into employment in England and Germany". *Sociology* 28(1): 32–54.

Rumelhart, D.E. (1975). "Notes on a schema for stories". In: Bobrow, D.G. and Collins, A. (eds.). *Representation and understanding: Studies in cognitive science*. New York, NY: Academic Press, pp. 211–236.

Sarbin, T.R. (1995). "Emotional life, rhetoric, and roles". *Journal of Narrative Life Histories* 5: 213–220.

Schank, R.C. and Abelson, R. (1977). *Scripts, plans, goals, and understanding*. Hillsdale, NJ: Erlbaum.

Seeman, M. (1972). "On the Meaning of Alienation". In: Lazarsfeld, P., Pasanella, A. and Rosenberg, M. (eds.). Continuities *in the Language of Social Research*. New York: Free Press, pp. 25–34.

Simon, J. (1988). "The Ideological effects of Actuarial practices". *Law and Society Review* 22: 771–800.

Thompson, K. (1999). *Storytelling In the new Hollywood.* Cambridge, MA: Harvard.

Tsiganou, J. (2013). "Economic crisis and crime". In: Zarafonitou, Ch. (ed.). *City, Criminality and Insecurity in times of Economic Crisis.* Athens, Dionikos, pp. 45–57.

Valdez, P. and Mehrabian, A. (1994). "Effects of color on emotions". *Journal of Experimental Psychology* 123(4): 394–409.

Watts, N. (1996). *Writing a novel: And getting it published.* Chicago, IL: NTC/Contemporary.

White, H. (1980). "The value of narrativity in the representation of reality". *Critical Inquiry* (7): 5–27.

Whorf, B.L. (1956). *Language, Thought and Reality—Selected Writings.* MIT Press.

Wilson, J.Q. (1975). *Thinking about crime.* Basic Books, New York.

Zacks, J.M. (2015). *Flicker: Your brain on movies.* New York, NY: Oxford University Press.

Zunshine, L. (2012). *Getting inside your head: What cognitive science can tell us about popular culture.* Baltimore, MD: Johns Hopkins University Press.

Zwaan, R.A. and Radvansky, G.A. (1998). "Situation models in language comprehension and memory". *Psychological Bulletin* 123(2): 162–185.

Zwaan, R.A., Langston, M.C., Graesser, A.C. (1995). "The construction of situation models in narrative comprehension: An event-indexing model". *Psychological Science* 6(5): 292–297.

CHAPTER 9

Representations of the Crisis within Five Greek Films

Eleni Zyga

1   Introduction: Greek Cinema since the Crisis

Since 2009, Greece has experienced an enduring economic crisis with enormous social and political consequences. Economic stagnation, rising poverty, high levels of unemployment, income inequality, increasing risk of social exclusion and mental health problems are some of them (Sotiropoulos 2014; Matsaganis 2013; Katsas 2011). Media were presenting a negative image of the country. Greeks have been characterized as either victims of worldwide neoliberalism or perpetrators of corruption and poor financial management (Papadimitriou 2014: 2).

On the contrary, domestic cinema was on the rise during the period of the economic downturn despite the lack of funding (Karalēs 2012: 278). At the same time, Contemporary Greek Cinema, labeled as the "weird wave", emerged. *Dogtooth* (2009), a Greek drama film directed by Yorgos Lanthimos about a married middle-aged couple who keeps their children ignorant of the world outside their property, was the landmark film for this label of "weird" cinema:

> New York Times called the film a conversation piece. "Though the conversation may ... be more along the lines of: 'What was that?'" 'I don't know. Weird'. 'Yeah'. [shudder] 'Weird'.
> SCOTT 2010

Greek filmmakers have been gaining international attention and their films have accomplished worldwide exposure via the festival circuits and met with great success as many of them premiered abroad, winning awards and critical recognition (Papadimitriou 2014: 3): Yorgos Lanthimos's *Dogtooth/Kinodontas* (2009, Cannes Film Festival), Panos Koutras's *Strella/A Woman's Way* (2009, Berlin), Filippos Tsitos's *Akadimia Platonos/Plato's Academy* (2009, Locarno), Athena Tsangari's *Attenberg* (2010, Venice), Syllas Tzoumerkas's *Hora Proelefsis/Homeland* (2010, Venice), Lanthimos's *Alpeis/Alps* (2011, Venice), Elina Psykou's *I Eonia Epistrofi tou Antoni Paraskeva/The Eternal Return of Antonis*

Paraskevas (2013, Berlin), Michalis Konstantatos's *Luton* (2013, San Sebastian), Alexandros Avranas's *Miss Violence* (2013, Venice), Yannis Economides's *Mikro Psari*, Stratos and Athanassios Karanikolas's *Sto Spiti/At Home* (both 2014, Berlin).

The so-called "Greek Weird Cinema" is considered to be a challenge to conventional interpretation, incorporating films dealing with the social consequences of the crisis. Furthermore, this is the cinematic trend that directs us to a "creative resistance" movement in the context of urban progress and sustainability (Nikolaidou 2020: 144). The Greek Weird Wave could be characterized as equivalent to other European Waves appearing after the millennium, which also expressed and reflected social anxiety and restlessness, such as the Romanian New Wave and the New French Extremity (Varmazi 2019: 48). It is about cinematic waves that reflected upon and expressed particular cultural, political, and economic circumstances during times of instability and austerity.

However, even some films that come from the weird cinema, and not explicitly mentioned in the crisis (*Kinodontas/Dogtooth* and *Alpeis/Alps* by Lanthimos), they do contain also some evidence that the violence observed among protagonists, actually stems from the fundamental systemic violence of capitalism (Lykidis 2015: 11). This happens through a narrative emphasis on isolated or alienated characters, problematic family relationships, anti-social behavior and poor communication. According to academics, these films enable also the audience to understand the crisis by highlighting the disappointment of the neo-liberal era (Lykidis 2015: 10).

According to Lykidis again (Papadimitriou 2015: 4), the cinematic representation of power structures in these movies also testifies to the lack of democratic representation in modern neoliberal societies. Thus, these films are mainly regarded as allegories of the socio-political upheavals that took place in that period (Basea 2016: 63).

Three years after the outbreak of the crisis, films coming from the commercially-orientated sector, referring to the Greek recession, were made to be shown on the movie theatre screen (Papadimitriou 2014: 7). The Greek crisis through them was represented in a particular way, mainly through love stories (*What If* / Papakaliatis 2012, *Worlds Apart* / Papakaliatis 2015).

The majority of them gained the public's preference and attracted sizeable audiences. And although there was an issue about these movies which had to do principally with their naturalization (covering of their history) (Nikolaidou 2020: 146), their representations and the depictions of the crisis were emerged through them, proved useful for film scholars in collecting rich material for analyzing and gaining an understanding of the other trend of weird-labeled cinema, which had already flourished during this period.

Since the "Golden Age" of Greek Cinema (the 1950s and 1960s), films have reflected the social reality and everyday life of city dwellers, influenced by Western culture (Constantopoulou 2009: 157). The Greek New Wave Cinema fluctuates between visibility and invisibility of the crisis concluding weird films and films whose narratives are connected directly to the hallmarks of crisis, reflecting the hard socio-economic and political conditions (Basea 2016: 63):

> A significant number of films use the financial crisis as a plot device, such as *The Daughter* (2012) by Panos Anastasopoulos, *Boy eating the bird's food* (2012) by Ektoras Lygizos, *Congratulations to the Optimists* (2012) by Constantina Voulgaris, *Runaway Day* (2013) by Dimitris Bavellas, *A Blast* (2014) by Syllas Tzoumerkas, *At Home* (2014) by Athanasios Karanikolas, *Spring Awakening* (2015) by Constantine Giannaris, *Wednesday 4:45* (2015) by Alexis Alexiou.

2   Theoretical Framework: Film and Society

Moscovici (1961) introduced the notion of social representations expanding their interconnection with mass communication. The author highlighted that mass communication is a distinct social reality, and diverse communicative strategies contribute to the formation and evolution of social knowledge within a social environment.

Social representations are dynamic ensembles, and their status is that of a producer of behaviors and relations with the environment, of actions that modify both, and not that of the reproducer of that behavior and those relations, of a reaction to a given external stimulus (Moscovici 2008: 10).

Moscovici (2007) also emphasized the role of the Media in the growth of new social representations. Cinema, one of the most powerful mass media, uses images, sound and editing. Through it, the directors communicate with their audiences and transfer their ideas, visions, and thoughts (Huda 2004: 3).

Film began at the end of the nineteenth century as a technological novelty. It transferred to a new means of presentation and distribution an older tradition of entertainment, offering stories, spectacles, music and drama for popular consumption. It was also instantly a true mass medium due to the fact that it quite quickly reached a very large proportion of populations, even in rural areas (McQuail 2005: 32).

Ferro (1988) argued that studying film and observing it, in relation to the world that produces it, is neediness: "That film, image or not of reality, document or fiction, true story or pure invention, is history" (Ferro 1988: 29).

Allen and Gomery (1985) stated that films are social representations, indirect or oblique. Their assertion was that films "derive their images and sounds, themes, and stories ultimately from their social environment", indicating that cinema is not only an instrument of influence but both the product and the motivator of matter (Fritsche 2013: 86).

> So, "*analyzing film is becoming increasingly important in a mediatized society. As a media of communication, films are embedded in the circumstances by which society communicates and interacts. Movies are part of discursive and social practices. They reflect the conditions and structures of society and of individual life*".
>
> MIKOS 2014: 409

3 Methodology

In the framework of the research, we used a qualitative research technique to analyze 5 films from contemporary Greek cinema of the years 2010–2017, which were related to the Greek financial crisis: 4 dramas and 1 comedy. The narrative medium (film) was selected for our analysis as a mediator of "visual communication".

Referring to Moscovici's theory of social representations[1] and our understanding of the dynamics and transformation of social knowledge, "communication" and "social interaction" are the active and dynamic processes through which social representations acquire and express their prescriptive power. They are also sustained through the same processes.

Our central question was how the Greek crisis was depicted in these films and more specifically, which factors were highlighted. The method used was *content analysis*: Analysis of films' action and speech and classification of the processed material into thematic categories.

The major criterion by which the films were selected was mainly their relevance to the subject of the financial crash. We chose three mainstream movies from the named "commercial" cinema (*What If, Worlds Apart* and *Success*

---

1 For Moscovici, social representations are dynamic because they both communicate and create knowledge ... These representations, which are shared by many, enter into and influence the mind of each, they are not thought by them; rather, to be more precise, they are re-thought, re-cited and re-presented (Moscovici 1984: 9). [...] from the dynamic point of view, social representations appear as a "network" of ideas, metaphors and images, more or less loosely tied together, and therefore more mobile and fluid than theories (Moscovici 2001: 153).

TABLE 9.1   List of films analyzed

	Title	Year	Director	Genre
1.	"45m^2"	2010	Stratos Tzitzis	(Social) Drama
2.	"What If"	2012	Christophoros Papakaliatis	Drama
3.	"A Blast"	2014	Syllas Tzoumerkas	Drama/Thriller
4.	"Worlds Apart"	2015	Christophoros Papakaliatis	Drama
5.	"Success Story"	2017	Nikos Perakis	(Black) Comedy

Story) and two art films (*45 Square Meters* and *A Blast*). (See the appendix at the end of this chapter for more information on these movies.) We examined 1 movie per almost 2 years (Table 9.1) in order to cover seven years of the economic downturn (2010–2017).

4   Results and Discussion

The main categories identified through the analysis of the narrative medium are: the *feelings* of the lead characters about the crisis and its consequences, the *family relationships* they experience, some *gender-related differences*, the effects of the recession on *employment* and *work sector*, and *the impact of the crisis in the wider social context*.

The *main feelings* in the first category are: sadness, anger, fear, insecurity, depression, loss of control, anxiety, and stress, mainly related to the changes in the main characters' lives. These are changes that affect them in a variety of areas, such as the work sector (which is directly related to the economic situation of the person), social life and mental health.

Central heroes of all five films (Christina in *45m^2*, Dimitris and Christina in *What...If*, Maria in *A Blast*, Giorgos in *Worlds Apart*, Tzortzina, Vasiliki and Panagis in *Success Story*) experience these unpleasant feelings due to the debt crisis. Some of them, however, seem to experience them more intensely due mainly to coexisting factors. Problematic family relationships result in them often turning to psychotropic medications (Giorgos in *Worlds Apart*) or completely losing the control (Maria in *Blast*).

Dimitris and Christina in *What If* (in the first version of the film where the couple is married), fight to create their own family in spite of the adverse conditions caused by the economic recession. These conditions have greatly affected their emotional state. Financial difficulties and the stress of finding a job, combined with the fact that they now have the extra responsibility of caring for their child, result in intense feelings of anxiety, sadness and resentment in their daily lives.

However, we observe the same feelings experienced by Dimitris, in the second version of the film where the protagonist is a bachelor, with a small difference perhaps—as presented by the director—that in the case the crisis finds someone engaged, maybe things are better, considering he is not fighting alone, has more reasons to set goals and most importantly, is not faced with the feeling of loneliness.

The main heroine of *A Blast*, Maria, is the only person who is able to support the paternal family in this difficult time. Her mother is no longer able to work as she is in a wheelchair, her sister is too immature to take on any responsibility, and her father is a weak character. In her quest to save her family's small business (a grocery) and fortune, Maria has to also face an inefficient bureaucratic state. All this pressure is leading her to lose control and commit adverse and destructive acts, only because she considers them to be the only solution.

Her mental state during the narrative process gradually intensifies and culminates in an emotional explosion.

> MARIA (talking in a therapy group): "Today, I want to share with you that I am absolutely unhappy. I have lived a ridiculous life. And I don't know what to do to change it. I got married when I was twenty years old, and I have three kids that I never want to see again. Neither them nor my husband. From now on, I only want to speak with strangers. Like you all. And I prefer the guilt to the life I had until this day".

According to international literature, economic and political crises are periods of intense individual and collective emotion. The conclusions of a study conducted in Greece (Chryssochoou et al. 2013) during the period of the crisis, when everyday events contributed to a changing and threatening sociopolitical environment, show that people facing a major crisis have multiple ways of reacting, ranging from radical and even violent practices to individual solutions and depression. These reactions were differently predicted by people's positions, feelings of vulnerability, grievances and the different emotions.

In these films, we also notice that the main characters feel the need to submit themselves to a constant internal search or rethinking of their life's choices so far. The apartment for Christina in $45m^2$ is not just a place to stay. It is an opportunity for both independence and discovering her own beliefs. It is also a path to the search for her real self, a path to true adulthood, which could not be completed in the paternal home.

Via the "images" of Christina's new life, which are transmitted to us through the film, after her relocation to an apartment in the center of Athens, on Acharnon Street, we watch her come in contact with a multi-cultural environment, whose daily life she enjoys observing, precisely for the same reason that she now enjoys quality music or reading a remarkable book. All these new elements make her consider things she had never thought of before and bring her closer to getting to know herself.

Giorgos and his mother Maria, in *Worlds Apart*, Maria in *A Blast* and Tzortzina in *Success Story* review their lives and consider their pasts with stricter standards this time. This process involves an internal analysis of the parts of all the characters and is directed at the viewer through a voice-over, dialogues, or the power of the cinematic image that transmits the emotions of the actors to the audience. This (process) leads the characters to ultimately challenge their previous choices.

In terms of *family relationships*, we observe domestic conflicts in all the movies analyzed. Physical and verbal violence prevail. There are also conflicts that start with the traditional Greek family refusing several times to let their adult children live independently, believing that this would mean losing them. Parental insecurity acts as a deterrent to children's autonomy, creating dependent adults.

In this fact, the traditional character of Greek family may play an important role as the Greek retirees support their young members, even for many years until they find a job (Zyga 2015), often reaching the point of depriving themselves of necessity goods and products (such as medicines).

Christina ($45m^2$) wrangles with her mother all the time about the same issues:

> (*Christina's dialogue with her mother*)
> MOTHER: "If I die, your father's pension goes with me".
> CHRISTINA: "You've been dying forever, but here you still are. You'll be the death of me! Then you finally be at peace!"
> (*Christina to her friend*)
> CHRISTINA: "I have to get my own place. I can't stand it. I'm not sure if I do things for me anymore, or to stop her worrying (her mother)".

In the case of Maria (*A Blast*), conflicts with her family are so intense that they end up in domestic violence. Maria slaps and hits her mother when she realizes that the latter has been lying for years, hiding the store's debts. The fight with her mother results in intense physical abuse on Maria's part. Especially since her mother is in a wheelchair, the abuse shocks the viewer and brings to mind the violation of human rights.

Marital or relationship conflicts are also very common. In *What If*, we see the couple of protagonists (Dimitris and Christina) mostly fighting about things that are relevant to the effects of the crisis. We could say that it is clear to the audience that the couple's conflicts arise from deeper causes, such as the insecurity and stress caused by the difficult socio-economic situation.

In *What If*, we observe also the couple being equally emotional in how they express their feelings toward each other. The same happens also in their "outbursts" of anger.

> CHRISTINA: "Have you noticed the billion times I have asked you to care for me?"
> DIMITRIS: "You want to control and approve everything and I have to apologize for everything. Because I have no job, no money..."
> CHRISTINA: "Why do you believe that all our problems occur from money? Why everything has to do with money? Is this our problem?"
> DIMITRIS: "Plus this..."

In *Worlds Apart*, self-employed Minas, who has been hit by the crisis, comes into conflict with his wife, accusing her and their children of being responsible for his failure.

> MINAS: "Why do you think I'm doing all this?"
> MARIA: "Because you failed at everything else".
> MINAS: "Everything is gone..."

Giorgos, in the same film, seems to be trying to escape the verbal violence of his wife, and for this reason, he tends to lock himself inside his office, put on his headphones and turn on loud music. In the continuation of the film, we see him "escape" through the use of antidepressants and then through his affair with Elise. In the black comedy *Success Story*, there is, in addition to verbal abuse between the couple, physical violence too from both sides.

> TZORTZINA (to her husband, *Success Story*): "You don't understand what I am going through..."

Although researchers differ in opinion on whether the rates of domestic violence actually increased during the crisis, a lot of sociological research has
demonstrated the connection between this event and family upheaval. In
some studies, however, the ongoing financial crisis in Greece seems to be related to an increase in cases of physical abuse (Kontos et al. 2017: 3).

Moreover, studies show that rapidly worsening labor market conditions are
associated with increases in the prevalence of violent/controlling behavior in
marriage (Schneider et al. 2014: 1).

It is worth noting that the unemployment rate in Greece reached the level
of 27.2% in 2014 and 25.7% in 2015 (Hellenic Statistical Authority 2015: 2). The
same period, the European Institute for Gender Equality reported that in Europe, the total annual cost of gender-based violence for businesses was estimated at 258 billion euros per year (European Institute for Gender Equality
2014).

Social researches conclude that the impact of gender-based and intimate
partner violence on the economy and society is high. These costs are borne by
the whole society. This violence is detrimental to the economy in lost working
time due to injuries. It drains resources from services for which the costs are
borne publicly or collectively (Olive and Walby 2014: 115).

According to Hamilton (2018: 1), the representation and discourses of *gender* are so *deeply embedded in filmmaking* and *film viewing* that they are almost
invisible.

In the field of *gender*, men, through the movies analyzed, seem to be less
active and determined than women. In the movie *45m²* we watch Christina
decide to leave her paternal home to rent her own house and be autonomous.

The desire for independence makes her sacrifice other things, such as her
spare time (since she is forced to work two jobs to make ends meet). Au con-
traire, her boyfriend (Haris) is not thinking of taking such an action (leaving
his paternal home). The male gender (represented in this film by Christina's
boyfriend, Haris), through the film, seems reluctant to be "settled". He is stuck
in the parental nest, which may be, to an extent, related to the freedoms that
Greek parents lavishly give to a boy rather than to a girl.

> CHRISTINA: "Ever consider leaving?"
> HARIS: "What...?" "...Away from home...?" "No".

This attitude of her boyfriend, that is, to remain inactive while everything
around him changes, could be the reason which will finally lead Christina to enter a "free" relationship with a married man (Costas), much older
than her.

Moreover, the previous tenant of the apartment who had initially rebelled against his family (according to the doorman's words), eventually withdrew and returned to them. Christina was the one who suggested him leaving for the islands together, a dream he had forgotten.

The emotional world of men, as depicted in the films, seems to be more influenced than women's. Dimitris in *What If*, feels particularly bad about being unemployed, receiving financial support from his wife. This makes him break out in front of her, thus expressing how he feels about the situation he is experiencing (being unemployed). Christina, on the other hand, states that the main problem is not who brings the money home but other things, more essential for their relationship. She is missing also her personal "freedom" which had before she had her child.

Of particular interest in terms of gender is Dimitris's behavior toward his mother who is facing a mental health problem. Dimitris, in *What If*, is a caring son, which is in contrast to Maria in *A Blast*, who physically abuses her disabled mother. These two images are not in line with the stereotypes of the "tough" male and the "compassionate" female.

Furthermore, in terms of gender and employment, we observe Elise in *Worlds Apart*, holding a high position in the company where Giorgos works. She "moves the threads" and makes cuts and layoffs in order to save the business during the duration of the economic crisis "nightmare".

More examples of the reversal of gender roles are in *Success Story* and *Worlds Apart*. Panagis (*Success Story*), although he is an exception in the "male" stereotype, is the rich one of the couple (and therefore more powerful than his wife Tzortzina). He looks innocent relative to his wife, who gets to the point of orchestrating his murder to obtain his inheritance.

In addition, the personality of Maria in *A Blast* but also all her actions in the film, lead us further to the finding that the female gender is presented as more dynamic than male. Maria is the only one in the family who "does something" to change the difficult situation her family has fallen into (the possibility of losing all their assets). The men of the family (her father and her brother-in-law) seem unable to help her, even psychologically.

Moreover, the housewife (Maria) in *Worlds Apart* does not succumb to her husband's harsh words and speaks to him intensely, criticizing him for his failures, and in the end, she leaves him.

The audience is furthermore surprised to watch Maria's husband (*A Blast*), who is a sailor, giving in to his passions, enjoying sex not only with women (mostly prostitutes he meets in his travels) but also with men.

Aside from a sense of equality between the two sexes in the film *What If*, in the rest of the movies, the "woman" seems to be "stronger" than the man, and we can watch her dominating him in many areas, such as maturity, determination, and the capacity to cope with "crisis" situations, even if it means reaching the extremes (such as Maria's arson in *A Blast* and Tzortzinas's attempt to assassinate her rich husband in *Success Story*).

The above examples are inversely related to the gender stereotypes ("strong man"–"Sensitive woman"), which allows us to share the view of Murphy (2015) that "gender stereotypes" in films are making progress.

Regarding the *work sector*, we observe in all films that there is unemployment, difficulty in finding a job, low wages (*45m²*, *What If*, *Worlds Apart*, *Success Story*), and corporate bankruptcy (*Worlds Apart*, *A Blast*, *Success Story*). As with gender and employment, we can observe through the films that unemployment is an important issue with men; when a man loses his job, he loses part of his identity. In such a situation, he feels incapable of coping psychologically with the new circumstances (*Worlds Apart*, *What If*).

As it is mentioned in the international literature background, the vision of the man in pop-culture is often connected with "force", "power" and material goods. In this context seems to be justified to say that in the case of an economic crisis, the "position" of the man is in danger. Without material goods, men cannot fully present their power and force and their self-esteem is importantly decreasing (Matlak 2014: 368).

Furthermore, Greek researches showed that the economic recession and the country's fierce austerity measures had a negative impact on both sexes' participation in employment (Anastasiou et al. 2015: 44). Initially, it seemed that the crisis affected more male employment but gradually, women's employment had been negatively affected as well. In Greece, both female and male employment has kept decreasing, and the third stage of the crisis has affected women and men with equal magnitude (Périvier 2014: 82).

Regarding the films, the main issue raised in film *45m²* is that of low-wage jobs. During the film, we watch Christina who works as a store clerk in Kolonaki, dedicate her free time looking for a better job, with a better salary. After going through interviews for various jobs, without a positive result, now more disappointed than ever, she decides to work in a second job, even if this is in the evening to be able to cover her financial needs.

The difficulty in finding a job with a satisfactory salary in modern Greece is presented through the film. In fact, when one has no friends or acquaintances to "promote" him, things become even more difficult. The screenwriter clearly refers to the concept of "acquaintances" that now more than ever play a crucial role in hiring someone, to the point that employees often talk about a "war" among them.

CHRISTINA (to the employer interviewing her): "Eh, of course! My acquaintance wasn't important enough. There is Honourable Member, Minister..."

Through the film, however, we observe a kind of assimilation of Greek employees with foreigners, in terms of how they are treated by the employer regime. And we can feel how this is perceived by the first ones. Tzitzis ($45m^2$) uniquely conveys this message, using the art of graffiti, projecting in his film a slogan that Christina observes during her return from work at home after another conflict with her boss: "In front of the bosses, we are all strangers".

Moreover, Daphne's words (*Worlds Apart*) lead us to the same thought: "Because the way things are, I don't know if it's worse for a foreigner to be in Greece or for a Greek".

In 2010 some reforms in Greece dealt with the labor market imposed by the May 2010 Memorandum of Understanding (MoU) and the updated Memoranda (August 2010, November/December 2010) between the Greek government and the EUROPEAN Government-DNT (Troika). These amendments comprised institutional changes in wage processes. The reason they were adopted was to increase labor market flexibility and productivity. Unfortunately, these reforms had finally a direct impact on workers' wages as they included, among other things, reducing the minimum wage to facilitate young people entering the labor market, reducing overtime pay and wages, and reducing also redundancy costs (Papapetrou and Bakas 2012).

Many employers, on the occasion of these modifications, found the opportunity to make significant reductions in wages (even if they were about healthy businesses) and to take a very strict stance against any staff requests, knowing that, due to the rising unemployment rate (the national unemployment rate rose from 11.0% in the first quarter of 2010 to 16.7% in the second quarter of 2011) (Papapetrou and Bakas 2012: 5), there was a huge supply of demand.

Through the dialogue between Christina ($45m^2$) and her employer, it is clear that the latter is taking advantage of the situation.

CHRISTINA'S EMPLOYER (to Christina, $45m^2$): "So you want a raise because we bought a house in Mykonos? It's my fault for sharing with you. Some friend you are!"

The threat of unemployment plays an important role in *Worlds Apart*, too. "Problematic" companies are making massive layoffs, which the employees are not able to withstand. This situation has painful consequences for the staff.

GIORGOS' COLLEAGUE (to Giorgos, *Worlds Apart*): "...And then comes a day when we hear that our friend who got fired killed himself..." "...Odysseus' wife just called. They found him this morning. He was hanged".
MINAS (*Worlds Apart*): "I had three stores. Three ... I had my family, my job, my life, my dignity and now I'm struggling to survive..."

The link between the financial crisis and mental disorders has long been apparent. Unemployment and average income are the two components of the financial crisis that appear to be linked the closest with mental health (Efthimiou et al. 2013; Katsas 2011).

Greek data on suicides, unemployment, and other macroeconomic and behavioral factors showed a significant yearly increase after 2008, the year of the onset of the financial crisis, providing evidence for a strong association between unemployment and suicides (Madianos et al. 2014).

Regarding the *impact of the crisis on society*, we get a picture of the main characters in all five cases experiencing economic weakness and a loss of hope, with some of them expressing racism and xenophobia (*Worlds Apart, A Blast*). We also become aware of people embracing neo-Nazism (*A Blast*).

MINAS (to the members of the extremist group he has joined): "You know how much I owe for the damage they did to me a year ago? My bank took it all away. I have nothing".

Minas in *Worlds Apart* and Costas in *A Blast* are looking for other ways to escape from this unpleasant situation of the debt crisis and their dissatisfaction of their expectations, turning to fascism. During the film, we observe Minas curses the immigrants and refugees to the members of the extremist organization has joined, blaming them not only for his own professional failure but also for the downfall of his country. He later claims the same to his wife.

MINAS (to a refugee, *Worlds Apart*): "Get out of my sight! Go to hell, scamps! Stinkers!"
MINAS (to the members of the extremist group he has joined, *Worlds Apart*): "Wherever I go ... Wherever I look ... The streets are full of those gross people. I can't take it anymore ... ... I want them gone...! ...I want them to disappear from our country!"

He becomes a member of an extremist anti-immigrant group and hits innocent immigrants at nights to vent his anger at being "a loser". Putting the blame on them initially gives him relief, but then his odium leads to a vicious circle, which closes tragically when he loses his daughter in an attack he organizes against the immigrants.

On the other hand, the garbage manager (Costas) in *Blast* has flooded his room with Nazi symbols, which he does not take care to cover even when his minor-age nieces are in his house. Scenes from the two films refer to the inclusion of a portion of citizens in extremist groups. We could also say that there is an indirect reference to the rise of the far-right party in Greece.

A party whose "political and ideological discourse combines extreme racism, nationalism and authoritarianism along with traditional conservative positions, mainly about traditional family roles and values and the Greek Orthodox Church" (Sotiris 2017: 215).

During the recession, some citizens put faith in—mainly due to the immigration issue in the wake of the economic downturn and its aftermath –, the extremist right-wing Greek Golden Dawn (GD). Favored by these circumstances, GD gained power firstly in the capital of Greece and then in the region (Papaioannou 2013).

> MINAS (to the members of the extremist group he has joined, *Worlds Apart*): "Those who I believed, those who I trusted, they left me. They're all useless. Operators, political parties, state, everyone..."

Political scholars noted that the main way in which this political party gained power was through capitalizing on the de-legitimation of Greek political institutions and through its organizational activity and functioning as a socially legitimate anti-system alternative. They also pointed out that a more careful re-examination of the political developmental factors, explaining why such a violent and authoritarian political party seems to have taken root in an established democracy, is imperative (Ellinas 2015: 16).

In relation to the immigrants who live in the country, the case of *45m²* is of particular interest. The doorman suggests leaving the house in Christina at a cheap price so that "foreigners" do not come to rent it. On the contrary, the company that has taken over the rent of this apartment shows a particular preference for immigrants, as they have the opportunity to spend more money than Greeks. So, the immigrant is accepted when he can pay more. Of course, during the time the film was made, as we mentioned above, Greece had not entered yet into the crisis "deeply".

As for the youth, and especially those in their 20s, we could say that we observe them showing a more positive attitude towards the immigrants and refugees in the films (Daphne and her colleagues in *Worlds Apart*, Christina in *45m²*) than we observe older people showing.

(Presentation of the crisis by the Broadcast Media, *Worlds Apart*)

"The objections regarding the economic politics employed by the European Union against the southern European countries have risen ... A distinctive example is Greece which for many acts as the guinea pig of cruel financial politics which gradually starts to expand to the rest of Europe. Suicide, a previously non-existing phenomenon in Greece is now reaching high-sky levels..."

Unemployment and business bankruptcy (*A Blast, Worlds Apart, Success Story*) are observed in the movies as it concerns the labor sector while in terms of society in general, there are phenomena of violence and crime (*What If, A Blast, Worlds Apart, Success Story*), of suicide (*A Blast, Success Story, Worlds Apart*), a tendency toward illegality to be financially secure (*Success Story, A Blast*) while to a lesser extent there are demonstrations/protests by the citizens (*What If*).

5   Conclusion

Film as a medium plays an important role in constructing social representations. Furthermore, according to the theoretical framework, the changing trends in films are used to reflect the changes taking place in society, confirming that an interaction exists between social context and filmography, especially in times of great changes such as economic crises.

Whether they come from commercial cinema or artistic cinema, the images of Greek society that are transferred to the audience through the films analyzed reveal citizens in despair who are trying to redefine themselves in their unfavorable situations.

Unemployment, small-business bankruptcy, depression, suicide, and dysfunctional relationships prevail among Greek families not only in the movies but also in citizens' everyday lives. This is revealed in a number of studies -some of which we refer to- which relate these phenomena to the crisis.

In addition, stereotypical views and traditional perceptions of gender that prevail in Greek society and are resistant to change seem to be challenged through the films. This is the case where the "male gender" seems, to some extent, to be powerless in the face of the onset of the economic crisis. To a lesser extent, we observe the phenomenon of racism, mainly as a result of the citizens' frustration with the state, which is unable to support them efficiently.

The main component that all five films share that we could say highlights a positive element of the crisis is the protagonists' need for change through which they are given the opportunity to learn things and become stronger. Of course, this is a change that nobody knows—in all five cases—whether it will lead to a happy end to their trials, just as an entire society does not know what to expect during a crisis or after it.

Cinematic representations reinforce a "negative" image of the recession in Greek society. Throughout the study of the five cases, we can view a society in crisis in the narration of films reflecting the devastating economic and social circumstances in the country; unpleasant feelings, family conflicts, unemployment, gender-related issues, and social dysfunction are the main issues depicted as the effects of the crisis.

6   Appendix: Presentation of the Films

6.1   *45m²*

The theme of Stratos Tzitzis' film is the struggle of a 23-year-old girl (Christina) in overcoming financial constraints, which prevent her from living the life she desires. With the few financial means she has, she rents a 45m² apartment which she manages to maintain for about two months. During this period, she explores her true self, while at the same time coming into contact with a more liberal culture, exploring the belongings of the young man (Fotis) who rented the apartment before her.

The film premiered in cinemas on 1/20/2011 and won the Best Screenplay Award at the 4th Annual London Greek Film Festival (LGFF). It addresses issues related to the Greek economy, employment, family, and gender. Although the film was created, as the author stated in an interview, a year before the financial crisis, and that, in fact, it is not a film about the crisis itself (Newsville.be 2012), it is a reference to economic constraints, which often become a "brake" on our personal development. These restrictions, according to the author, became even more "suffocating" during the economic crisis.

6.2   *What If*

This is a story that is presented from two sides. Dimitris, a financially independent director, is called upon one ordinary night to make a simple decision on whether to take his pet out. If he makes the small decision to go out, this exit will lead him to meet the love of his life. If not, he will continue to live alone, and the course he will take will be different.

In this film, there is an abundance of emotions such as fear, sadness, anger, anxiety and the feeling of loneliness flooding the protagonists, who are at their most productive age during the crisis and are trying to survive in a Greece in which unemployment is skyrocketing and layoffs are on the rise.

Couple conflicts, protests of the citizens in the town center and the factor of crime as a result of the crisis are projected through the film alongside shots of a beautiful Athens that fascinates.

The film received two award nominations from the Hellenic Film Academy, one for best direction and one for best sound, eventually securing the latter award. It was the second most commercially successful Greek film (553,314 tickets[2] sold; release date: 11/29/2012) of the 2010–2019 decade, after the film *Worlds Apart* (2015).

6.3   *A Blast*

During the financial crisis, Maria, a mother of three, takes over the indebted small family business and is forced to make difficult decisions regarding the future of the family, resulting in her being out of control.

Through the film, the portrait of modern Greek pathogenesis emerges. It premiered at the International Competition of the Locarno Festival in 2014 and had an excellent run at international festivals.

6.4   *Worlds Apart*

The film presents three stories of different generations of Greeks who fall in love with foreign citizens. Student Daphne meets Fari, a Syrian refugee, when some of her compatriots attack her to steal all her belongings. Giorgos, a 40-year-old executive of a multinational company, meets the Swedish, Elise, in the same period, and realizes that he is unhappy with his marriage. Maria, a 60-year-old housewife, meets the German, Sebastian, at the supermarket. This event prompts her to revisit her life.

From beginning to end, the film refers to love and the second opportunity that each person has to find true love, as the protagonists face difficulties and dilemmas in Greece throughout the financial crisis.

This movie, due to the three stories it contains, gives us a wide perspective on the impact of the economic crisis compared to other movies of the same theme. Moreover, it addresses issues related to love and the liberating power it has across all ages, while also touching on unemployment, crime, racism and xenophobia.

---

2   Data received upon the author's request for information from the film's distribution company, Village Films, in May 2019.

The film was also distributed in Switzerland, Austria, Germany and Zurich. It eventually became the highest-grossing film of 2015 (668,909 tickets;[3] release date: 12/17/2015) and also the most commercial Greek film of the 2010–2019 decade (Naftemporiki 2017).

6.5   Success Story

The film is a love story of a wealthy psychiatrist (Panagis) and an unemployed actress (Tzortzina). The two fall in love and get married despite their differences. The abrupt changes in financial terms, Panagis's involvement in politics and, a suicide, increase their disputes. Their love story becomes a tale of revenge and hate.

This movie is a satire of modern Greek reality that touches on the issue of the economic crisis that the country is experiencing. Through it, issues related to the consequences of the crisis, which reach not only the poor but also the rich, are raised: insecurity, fear, anger, marital conflict, drug use, bankruptcy, and suicidal attempts.

Bibliography

Allen, R. and Gomery, D. (1985). *Film History: Theory and Practice*. New York: McGraw Hill.

Anastasiou, S., Filippidis, K. and Stergiou, K. (2015). "Economic Recession, Austerity and Gender Inequality at Work. Evidence from Greece and Other Balkan Countries". *Procedia Economics and Finance* 24: 41–49.

Basea, E. (2016). "The 'Greek Crisis' through the Cinematic and Photographic Lens: From 'Weirdness' and Decay to Social Protest and Civic Responsibility". *Visual Anthropology Review* 32: 61–72.

Chryssochoou, X., Papastamou, S. and Prodromitis, G. (2013). "Facing the Economic Crisis in Greece: The Effects of Grievances, Real and Perceived Vulnerability, and Emotions Towards the Crisis on Reactions to Austerity Measures". *Journal of Social Science Education* 12(1): 41–49.

Constantopoulou, Ch. (2009). *Sociology of Everyday Life* (in Greek). Athens: Papazissis.

Efthimiou, K., Argalia, E., Kaskaba, E. et al. (2013). "Economic crisis & mental health. What do we know about the current situation in Greece?" *Encephalos* 50: 22–30.

---

3   Data received upon the author's request for information from the film's distribution company, Village Films, in May 2019.

Ellinas, A.A. (2015). *Neo-Nazism in an Established Democracy: The Persistence of Golden Dawn in Greece*. South European Society & Politics. Available (consulted 10 September 2019) at: https://doi.org/10.1080/13608746.2014.981379.

Ferro, M. (1988). *Cinema and history* (trans. N. Greene). Detroit: Wayne State University Press.

Fritsche, M. (2013). *Homemade Men in Postwar Austrian Cinema: Nationhood, Genre and Masculinity*. New York: Berghahn.

Hamilton, A. (2018). "Gender and Cinema, Anthropological Approaches to". In Callan H. (ed.). *The International Encyclopedia of Anthropology*. Available (consulted 10 December 2019) at: https://onlinelibrary.wiley.com/action/showCitFormats?doi=10 .1002%2F9781118924396.wbiea1946.

Hellenic Statistical Authority (ELSTAT). (2015). Press Release (Workshop Research, January 2015). Available (consulted 10 September 2019) at: https://www.statistics.gr/ documents/20181/9b33eddo-1c51-41e6-ab81-401c29681599.

Huda, A. (2004). *The Art And Science Of Cinema*. Atlantic Publishers & Distributors Pvt Ltd.

Karalēs, V. (2012). *A history of Greek cinema*. New York, NY: Continuum.

Katsas, G. (2011). "Depression as a social phenomenon: Alienation and apathy". *Encephalos* 48(4): 143–145.

Kontos, M., Moris, D., Davakis, S. et al. (2017). "Physical abuse in the era of financial crisis in Greece". *Annals of translational medicine* 5(7): 155. DOI: 10.21037/ atm.2017.03.26.

Lykidis, A. (2015). "Crisis of sovereignty in recent Greek cinema". *Journal of Greek Media & Culture* 1: 9–27.

Madianos, M.G., Alexiou, T., Patelakis A. et al. (2014). "Suicide, unemployment and other socioeconomic factors: Evidence from the economic crisis in Greece". *European Journal of Psychiatry* 28(1): 39–49.

Matlak, M. (2014). "The Crisis of Masculinity in the Economic Crisis Context". *Procedia Social Behav. Sciens* 140: 367–370. Available (consulted 1 March 2020) at: https://doi. org/10.1016/j.sbspro.2014.04.436.

Matsaganis, M. (2013). *The Greek Crisis: Social Impact and Policy Responses*. Berlin: Friedrich Ebert Stiftung.

Mavridis, S. (2018). "Greece's Economic and Social Transformation 2008–2017". Social Sciences, MDPI, *Open Access Journal* 7(1): 1–14.

McQuail, D. (2005). *McQuail's Mass Communication Theory* (5th Edition). London: Sage Publications Ltd.

Mikos, L. (2014). "Analysis of film". In: U. Flick. *The SAGE handbook of qualitative data analysis*, pp. 409–423. London: SAGE Publications.

Moscovici, S. (1961). "La psychoanalyse, son image et son public. Etude sur la representation sociale de la psychoanalyse. Paris, France : Presses Universitaires de France".

In: Terri Mannarini, Giuseppe A. Veltri, Sergio Salvatore (eds.). *Media and Social Representations of Otherness: Psycho-Social-Cultural Implications*. Cham, Switzerland: Springer Nature.

Moscovici, S. (1984). "The phenomenon of social representations". In: R. Farr and S. Moscovici (eds.). *Social Representations*, pp. 3–69. Cambridge: Cambridge University Press.

Moscovici, S. (2001). *Social representations: Explorations in social psychology*. New York: New York University Press.

Moscovici, S. (2007). *Psychoanalysis. Its Image and Its Public* (first published 1961). Oxford: Blackwell Publishing.

Moscovici, S. (2008). *Psychoanalysis: Its image and its public*. Polity Press.

Murphy, J.N. (2015). "The role of women in film: Supporting the men. An analysis of how culture influences the changing discourse on gender representations in film". Journalism Undergraduate Honors Theses. Available at: https://scholarworks.uark.edu/jouruht/2 (consulted 26 March 2020).

Naftemporiki. (2017, October 1). "Worlds Apart" crosses the borders of our country again. Available at: https://www.naftemporiki.gr/story/1191608/enas-allos-kosmos-perna-kai-pali-ta-sunora-tis-xoras-mas (consulted 5 October 2019).

Newsville.be. (2012, September 26). *Stratos Tzitzis about the 45m²* [Video File]. Available at: https://www.youtube.com/watch?v=kjq8sv9AW64 (consulted 8 October 2019).

Nikolaidou, A. (2020). "Self-Exoticism, the Iconography of Crisis and the Greek Weird Wave". In: Panagiotopoulos P., Sotiropoulos D. (eds.). *Political and Cultural Aspects of Greek Exoticism. Reform and Transition in the Mediterranean*. Cham: Palgrave Pivot.

Olive, Ph. and Walby, S. (2014). "Estimating the Costs of Gender-Based Violence in the European Union. European Institute for Gender Equality". Luxembourg: Publications Office of the European Union. Available at: https://eige.europa.eu/sites/default/files/documents/MH0414745EN2.pdf (consulted 1 October 2019).

Papadimitriou, L. (2014). "Locating Contemporary Greek Film Cultures: Past, Present, Future and the Crisis". Filmicon: *Journal of Greek Film Studies* 2: 1–19.

Papadimitriou, L. (2015). "Greek media and culture at a new juncture". *Journal of Greek Media & Culture* 1(1): 3–7.

Papaioannou, K. (2013). *The Clean Hands of Golden Dawn. Application of Nazi Purity* (in Greek). Athens: Metaixmio.

Papakaliatis, C. (Director). (2012). *An.../What If...* [Video file] Greece: Village Plus Productions.

Papakaliatis, C. (Director). (2015). *Worlds Apart*. [Video file] Greece: Plus Productions S.A.

Papapetrou, E. and Bakas, D. (2012). "Unemployment in Greece: Evidence from Greek Regions". Working Papers 146, Bank of Greece.

Perakis, N. (Director). (2017). *Success Story*. [Video file] Greece: View Productions.

Périvier, H. (2014). "Men and women during the economic crisis: Employment trends in eight European countries". Paris: *Revue de l'OFCE—Débats et Politiques* 133(2): 41–84.

Purkhardt, S.C. (1993). *Transforming social representations: A social psychology of common sense and science*. London: Routledge.

Schneider, D., McLanahan, S. and Harknett, K. (2014). "Intimate Partner Violence In The Great Recession". Working Papers, wp14-04-ff. Princeton University, Woodrow Wilson School of Public and International Affairs, Center for Research on Child Wellbeing.

Scott, A.O. (2010 June 25). "A Sanctuary and a Prison". *The New York Times*. Available at: https://www.nytimes.com/2010/06/25/movies/25dog.html (consulted 7 September 2019).

Sotiris, P. (2017). "Political Crisis and the Rise of the Far Right in Greece: Racism, nationalism, authoritarianism and conservatism in the discourse of Golden Dawn". In: Kopytowska, M. (ed.). *Contemporary Discourses of Hate and Radicalism across Space and Genres*. Amsterdam/Philadelphia: John Benjamins Publishing Company, 215–241.

Sotiropoulos, D.A. (2014). "The social situation of Greece under the crisis". *Basic socio-economic data for Greece, 2013*. Berlin: Friedrich Ebert Stiftung.

Tzitzis, S. (Director). (2010). *45m²* [Video file]. Greece: Feelgood Entertainment.

Tzoumerkas, S. (Director). (2014). *A Blast*. [Video file]. Greece: Homemade Films.

Varmazi, Eleni. (2019). "The Weirdness of Contemporary Greek Cinema". *Film International* 87: 40–49.

Žižek, Slavoj. (2008). *Violence: Six Sideways Reflections*. New York: Picador. In: Lykidis, A. (2015). "Crisis of sovereignty in recent Greek cinema". *Journal of Greek Media & Culture* 1: 9–27.

Zyga, E. (2015, December 10–12). *The social and economic contribution of the elderly to the support of the Greek family during the crisis*. In: Koniordos S. (ed.). Paper presented at the 5th Conference of the Hellenic Sociological Society: The Greek Society at the crossroads of the crisis—six years later, pp. 148–156. Athens, Greece.

CHAPTER 10

Developing Educational Discourse on Refugees: from the "Others" to Cinema Meta-language on Refugee Citizens

Evaggelia Kalerante and Calliope Tsantali

1 Introduction

Migrant communities had existed across European nation-states long before the refugee flow of the past years. Proof of this is the textual narrative of nation-states regarding the migrant-related policy of rights. It seemed that they were able to handle migrant population mobility, settlement and integration into their societies. Relevant European Union guidelines (Council of Europe 2000) and reports of international organizations (UNESCO 2019) attempted to create suitable conditions for migrant integration and the transformation of societies so that eventual social inequalities could be mitigated.

This situation has been reversed by far ever since the beginning of the Syrian war and the immense refugee flow to European nation-states. The already formed normality has been challenged by the refugee presence since Europe has been found unprepared, in terms of legislation, normative discourse and welfare benefits to handle the massive refugee arrival.

Two different governments, with completely different standpoints and policies regarding refugee population, have been responsible for the management of the refugee issue in Greece. The former government of SYRIZA from 2015 until 2019 (Kouvara n.d.) was a left political party whose policy was tied to welfare state, the policy of rights and controlled liberalization of the economic system. In this respect, emphasis was placed on policies conducive to refugee integration through the gradual change of legislation. For instance, they developed policies for refugee education based on learning the language of the reception country and familiarizing with the culture.

In 2019 New Democracy won the national elections and took reign of the country. This right wing political party is distinctive of political principles towards the development of the private economic sector and concurrent shrinking of the welfare state. Moreover, they manifest a radical right perspective against refugees as threat to the national identity and decreased economic resources for natives. On the basis of these principles, they have followed the expanded European Union policy about the limitation of refugee entry to European countries. As a result, these conditions have favored an on-going opposition against refugees in Greece, especially at a time period characterized by the acute relations with neighboring Turkey.

The Mass Media (Krishna-Hensel 2018; Soules 2015), television and social networks in particular, have formed discourse on the promotion of the country, the nation and on securing the value system. In this frame, refugees have been classified as the "others", the "invaders" to another country and culture. In particular, the refugee is perceived as the foreigner to distort the European lifestyle. More generally, population mobility has been seen as an external phenomenon of history, fractures of normality both for nation-states and the European history (Gatrell 2019). At the same time, the refugee differentiation has been put forward in terms of religion, considering the construction of Christian identity in contrast to the "lesser" Islamic religion. This discourse on refugee exclusion has been characterized by different content that is the refugee right to better living conditions. The Mass Media has regarded certain refugee groups as non-refugees in the sense that their countries have not been at war or that these people did not need to move to another country. Throughout this time period up until today, refugee expulsions have been orchestrated along with a limitation to refugee entrance both from Syria and other countries, as a consequence of both the European and Greek relevant policy.

It is noteworthy that political discourse on refugee rights has been limited, while international organizations have been apparently unable to focus on the projection of refugee policy of rights. The Mass Media and social networks discourse is characteristic in that refugee removal, and not their rescuing, is perceived as success.

Cinema seems to be a different kind of discourse, as it formulates a different narrative about issues that have not been highlighted by the dominant networks in terms of constructing a value-normative model and political social identity. A new generation of directors utilize New Technologies and develop discourse through cinema. There is a gradual liberation from the limitations set by the dominant cinematic discourse that seeks to withhold both social problems and the rejected discourse of underprivileged social groups (Mendik and Schneider 2002). Film production has become somehow independent from the general political and social principles of commercial film industry. Moreover, films about social problems are potentially distributed and shown by social networks that articulate a different discourse on the refugee policy of rights. The creators of these films are theoretically liberated by putting forward discourse mainly opposed to far right policies that are the real threat to democracy and democratic institutional and social organization. This liberating

cinematic discourse may be conducive to legalizing other policies on a different political function of the European Union nation-states. Put differently, the
development of a globalized democratic culture could acquire a new political
content characterized by humanism and political morality (Tahvildaran 2010).

2 Theoretical Framework

Greek policy has been concerned with the refugee issue since 2015 when,
amidst the economic crisis, the refugee flows in Greece have burdened the economic, social and political conditions of the country. In other words, the welfare state has born further responsibilities to meet the needs of more vulnerable groups, the refugees in this case. At the same time, racist behaviors and
incidents have been increased because social structures have been unable to
meet the requirements of an organized effective system toward refugee inclusion. The on-going civil conflicts and war in Syria have been conducive to increasing the number of refugees during a time period when their mobility to
other European countries was limited due to their gradually intensified policies on refugee exclusion (European Commission 2017; European Council 2011;
Kermani, Saman and Crawford 2019; Wanrooij 2019). Despite the efforts of the
European Union and international organizations to put forward the refugee
policy of rights (da Costa 2006) there have been intensified reactions by nation
states against refugee inclusion in their territories. At present, the Greek migration policy focuses on the continuous upgrading of legislation; yet, not supported by corresponding practical implementation (L.4587/2018; L.4636/2019).

The refugee issue was primarily handled by the left government of SYRIZA
(Takis 2015) in an attempt to put forward the principles of political morality
and political humanism, while highlighting the concept of the citizen-refugee.
Throughout 2015–2019, during the SYRIZA governing, a number of policies to
reinforce the refugee educational capital were in effect, in an attempt to showcase the refugee culture, while reversing the stereotype of the refugee–radical
Islamic entity (Greek Parliament 2019; Panagos, Nagopoulos and Rantos 2017).
Education directly served as the means by which children could be initially
included in the Greek education system, while adolescents could be included
in it later in time. There were acute reactions by local communities resulting in
generating racist stereotypes, obsolete up to that moment, regarding race purity, nationalism and the potential reversal of the Christian model. That condition was further enhanced by the far right political discourse of Golden Dawn
and other corresponding far right constructs. As a result, refugee reception
classes, Greek language tutorial departments and the Reception Structures for

Refugee Education (R.S.R.E.) did not work effectively. That meant that only a limited number of refugees attended those educational structures resulting in a slow-moving refugee inclusion in the local community. The migrant and refugee communities were further polarized due to exclusion from education, as they experienced feelings of entrapment within a country that seemed weak to support their personal goals for progress and prosperity, given that the country's economic conditions and the state's structures were unable to meet their needs. Besides, it was made clear from the beginning that their presence in Greece would be temporary, as part of their transfer to other European countries.

New Democracy, a center-right government that took the reign in 2019, developed political discourse on limited refugee access to Greece. Their policies focused on decreased refugee flows and ways to send refugees back to their countries of origin. These extreme policies have been apparently non-implementable, while the government has attempted to make positive impression among conservative citizens by implementing measures of safeguarding the Aegean Sea through deterrents to refugee access to the Greek shores. As a result, an escalating condition of targeting refugees has also been developed by Mass Media. On the other hand, political issues tied to the causes of refugees fleeing their homelands have not been showcased namely wars, civil wars, economic or political turmoil or environmental crises. The far right discourse (Kalerante 2015), already diffused across Europe has also affected other Greek parties' political discourse resulting in further biased attitudes and behaviors against refugees. The initial refugee educational programs have not been obviously enhanced and the same applies to corresponding programs for adolescent refugee education. A condition of entrapped people in unsuitable areas has been gradually emerging. In other words, isolated invisible groups of people have been abandoned because of a vague political objective to send them back to their countries of origin. At the same time, the asylum committees for refugees are also weak in processing asylum applications. Within an environment of migration policy crisis, responsibilities are shifted to NGOs, instead of the European political apparatus, by intending to pass a law on monitoring the actions of NGOs involved with refugees in Greece.

Everyday life scenarios of people in reception camps have unfolded and ignited new discourse developed by free networks of art with focus on the effects of a negated refugee policy of rights. The latent social consequences on the individual-refugee are highlighted through the cancellation of the present and future opportunity structures relevant to their personal fulfilment based on education, work and family as well as on personal pleasure deriving from the right to art and other cultural achievements. The refugee is gradually becoming the "other" of the system. The refugee issue has been handled in the same way like all economic crisis effects such as impoverishment, acute social inequalities and upper social strata reinforced privileges, meaning that it has been "silenced", while political responsibilities have been concealed.

Cinema becomes particularly important within a period of prolonged silence. One could wonder about the intellectuals' attitude, the schools of thought that should put forward the citizens' policy of rights along with manifesting the causes of wars. Besides, one could wonder about the scientific discourse that could shift the interest from the necessity of excluding individuals to people's functional co-operation toward addressing and handling the real political outcomes of the uncontrollable course of capitalism and neoliberal policies on shrinking citizens' rights.

The Mass Media and the popular dominant social networks shape piecemeal representations of the refugee issue effects by putting the blame on refugees. The refugee is portrayed as the "other", the foreigner, the savage, the uncivilized, the threat to the political rational operation of the Western system. These perceptions can be further reinforced due to lacking educational capital, since all educational grades are distinctive of the absent discourse on shaping the notion of the citizen-refugee within the collective "we"—the victims of the economic crisis, of the political and social instability and the dysfunctional democratic institutions (Arlt and Wolling 2016). At the same time, the media and social networks do not tend to develop discourse corresponding to scientific views on social inclusion, social coherence and opportunity structures for citizens-refugees in the way they have been shaped by social sciences. Thus, refugee exclusion is intensified, while anomic behaviors within the refugee communities are reinforced. It is noteworthy that any dysfunctions or anomic phenomena within refugee communities are reported as incidents generated by persons of a lesser culture and not as the outcome of the dysfunctional political system (Galikhuzina, Penkovtsev and Shibanova 2016).

Within this framework, cinema directors, representatives of different schools of thought and distinctive of high educational capital and political discourse, attribute to cinema a completely new content by putting forward competing discourse. As will be seen below, these directors represent a different ideological capital that combines political and social textual analysis. Thus, the intervening cinematic discourse is showcased by transcending the limited belief that cinema is merely a means for leisure.

During this period, the cinema is transformed into the other discourse that originates from art and instrumentally uses the scientific rationalism, memory, emotion and image. Scientific rationalism encapsulates political discourse that puts forward human existence, life and the right to happiness as common features of all social individuals. The isolated aspect of refugee political rights is incorporated in the general aspect of the policy on human rights. Each time refugees describe painful conditions these are interpreted as loss of human rights with certain outcomes, so that non-refugees can identify themselves with refugees as excluded and deprived entities of various socio-political rights. As a result, "we" is shifted from fictitious nationality or religion-based identifications to real identifications of individuals excluded from opportunity structures. As a result, any deficits of democracy and the effects of single-sided economic choices are underscored. The refugee issue triggers the causes of the irrational political system that generates exclusions and legalizes social inequality and racism through the dominant institutions.

The interface between present and past is a powerful tool of cinematic discourse. This is an artificial invocation of memory toward utilizing history as an area of consideration in order to underline historical continuation. For example, Greek documentaries on the refugee issue (Kaltsidou 2016) showcase historical memory, as in the case of refugees fleeing to Greece after the distraction of Asia Minor in 1922. Transfer to historical moments is reinforced by rekindled memory and the refugee issue is eventually depicted as normality of political dysfunctions. This phenomenon is neither new nor predictable, or fatal of one people or a limited group (Balta 2014; Carlsten and McGarry 2015; Neiger, Meyers and Zandberg 2011).

Cinema uses the scientific rational capital. The principles of Policy, Sociology, Psychology and History are integrated into the cinematic screenplay and enriched with emotions (Stam 2005). These are actually functional transpositions within a system of political exclusions that causes negative social emotions, like range and hatred conducive to violent reactions (Giannetti 2011; Smith 2003). Emotions are reformed based on a screenplay of reversed stereotypical racist discourse in the sense that negative social feelings are transformed into positive ones. Thus, love and solidarity are developed in the form of a democratic humanistic proposal in a society that could be based on love, solidarity and respect in relation to the personality of other people. Therefore, progressive cinema seeks to create intense emotional bindings deriving from DISCOURSE dynamics. Distanced from infertile instruction, cinema can create intense emotions beyond simplified expressions of sorrow that would eventually trigger philanthropy and mercy by using the scientific capital of humanism. In this respect, each individual's political responsibility could mean a sensitized civil society that could bring the debate back to the political resolution of issues through promoting corresponding requests.

Cinema is based on image (cinema, image, music, photography, etc.). Screenplay as discourse is transformed into signs that convey meaning in the form of image. Consecutive images create meanings that lead to discourse development. Textual discourse is enriched with colors, faces, motion and music. Nothing is accidental or piecemeal. Everything is part of a reinforced mission beyond limited instruction since the focal point is the art of cinema (Heath 1990). The limits are delicate when referring to cinema as art and cinema as mission. The theme under exploration is supported by films that fulfil both criteria of art and mission, as will be shown in methodology below. This is not commercial cinema, but rather one engaged with political issues in order to showcase the political dimensions emerging from broader socio-political readings of the protagonists through their interaction with broader socio-political spaces. No solutions are presented in these films. The audience is left with a consideration and question, as the end of these films enables them to "revisit" the screenplay (Terzis 2016).

The films repertoire seeks to unveil contemporary socio-political conditions such as lack of democracy, individual political rights, expanded social inequality and new forms of social exclusion and marginalization. According to these conditions, people are perceived as waste and other groups of population are transformed into masses of individuals that move in the parallel setting of an invisible population of "failures".

3   Methodology

The films under exploration are distinctive of the period from 2016 until 2019 and focus exclusively on the refugee issue. The directors could be characterized as those seeking to showcase political discourse. They belong to a school of cinema in which discourse and art interact in order to convey social messages. They apparently develop political discourse focusing on the policy of rights, the transgression of simplified patterns pertaining to refugee = an isolated incident. Through these films an effort is made to highlight institutional dysfunctions of nation-states as well as the broader institutional dysfunctions of the European Union and the international community.

The selection criteria of films were based on their recognition in film festivals and not only on their theme and dynamic show. Semiotic analysis was applied (Monaco 2000) in order to underline elements tied to textual discourse, screenplay and the means (photography, music) so that the specific discourse is highlighted along with the creation of emotion and social experience. In each film, the themes that emerged regard (a) the individual-refugee, (b) their position in the refugee community, and (c) the socio-political environment of the reception country (Hamenstädt 2019).

As regards the category individual-refugee, characteristic features of their culture and personal pursuits are portrayed along with specific features of their social identity shaped by the educational, economic, social and cultural capital. This means that the concept of the refugee is approached in direct correlation with the identity of the social subject as this was shaped back in their homeland. In this respect, all refutations and reversals regarding their personal expectations and trajectories are showcased.

There is a gradual shift from the individual aspect and its social dimensions to the collective aspect of the social group shaped under new conditions within the reception camp. This leads to defined dimensions of the new social environment in the reception country where camps become the new social environment, the new community distinctive of cultural features from the homeland combined with value and normative models shaped within uncommon conditions of co-existence. In this framework, the previous social identity is reconstructed within new social representations.

These social representations evolve within the socio-political environment of the reception country. The social representational environment of the films seeks to put forward cinematic moments as transitions—indications of the social space that reconstructs social identity, readjusts choices, either entrapped or developed within a dynamic interconnection of space–time–historicity. In this framework, the social subjects are the protagonists in a space in which they lack discourse; yet, there are open interpretations about them, but without them. Thus, one could refer to opposing cinematic discourse through which refugees are attributed speech and roles in order to interpret any new situations. At the same time, this discourse works as opposing discourse against racism and the far right perspective highlighted by the popular and dominant Mass Media (Salti 2007).

Focus is not placed on inner differentiations of social inequalities like gender, etc., as the intention is to highlight the concept of the refugee without being fragmented into other patterns that probably disorientate textual readings irrelevant of the films chosen (Berger 2016; Brennen 2017).

It should also be mentioned that the focal point of the study is the qualitative semiotic analysis of the emerging themes; thus, the data were not quantified. On the contrary, they were utilized to portray the intensity of the phenomena, the description of the refugee as well as unfolding of supplementary supportive tools like photography, music, motion, setting, clothing, body language and acting techniques (Terzis 2016).

4   Presentation of the Narrative and Cinematic Discourse of the
     Three Films

"Survivor" is a short film produced in 2016 by Mazen Haj Kassem, a Syrian film director. Kassem used to work for the television in Syria before the war, but he had to flee his country, so he moved to Denmark to save himself. He left his father behind with whom there was no contact. The film focuses on Syrian refugees, children and adults, who flee their war torn country in hopes for a better life in a safe place. It is a combination of past and present, as it portrays images of Syrian life prior to war, when people used to lead a normal life and children were dreaming of their future without the slightest idea of what was about to follow.

However, due to riot outbursts against the Syrian government and people's arrests and tortures, normal life seems to be derailed and the future of Syrians is more than uncertain and unpredictable. The once beautifully constructed Syrian cities turn into ruins and tombs for thousands of innocent people. Shootings of bombarded houses and neighborhoods are powerful connotations of derailed and wretched lives, the violent shift from ordinary and normal life to war and reversed reality. The route to a safer place seems to be long for those who survived bombs, yet they must struggle all the way to a European country, amidst threatening journeys on the sea and hostile reactions of native populations in their attempt to settle down to a safe and peaceful place.

"The Refugee Project", the second film of this study, is an award-winning documentary by Matthew K. Firpo. Firpo is an American film director, screenwriter and photographer, winner of several festival documentaries. The film was produced in a reception camp in Greece in 2016 and was based on the interviews of Syrian refugees who volunteered as protagonists. It is actually a multimedia chronicle of human stories narrated by Syrian men and women who were forced to flee their homeland with their families to save themselves. Detailed narrations are unfolded by the protagonists sitting in front of a piece of black cloth. The black color is strongly associated with death, sorrow and despair, signifying, in this case, aspects of refugee life courses. To this end, the protagonists provide details about leaving their homes and properties behind to escape from the massacre. Black symbolizes dead family members, sorrow about their wretched lives and despair about the current situation and what will happen in the future. At the same time, individual narrations are framed by images of bombarded Syrian cities.

The director focuses on the individual-refugee and their struggle for survival either by leaving their war torn hometowns or by struggling to survive the long and threatening voyage until they settle down in a reception camp. This is enhanced by images from refugees stepping their foot on the Greek shores. Emotions are intertwined with memories. Past and present are combined to portray life stories of people trying to make a new beginning within the reception camps, while they are nostalgic about their life back home. Within the refugee community as this has been established in the reception camp, they try to portray on camera their hopes for a better future. Parents dream of a better life for their children within a safe and welcome environment. Their words are framed by images of children carrying schoolbags, implying parents' expectations and hopes for their offspring. The fact that they are characterized as second class citizens implies stereotypes and bias against what is different from the mainstream culture. On the other hand, the words of a refugee woman are noteworthy when she says *"maybe with our stories people will get to know us and realize we are not extremists"*. Socio-political aspects related to human rights, social equality and access to opportunity structures are showcased through the narrations, while the democratic principles are strongly tested by the broader refugee crisis.

"Stars" is a film on refugees produced in Holland in 2017 by the Dutch director, producer and cinematographer Lara Sluyter. She has directed a number of films that focus mainly on the visual aspect of reality. Through her film, she tries to communicate her socio-political beliefs on social equality. This is why most of her films portray the hardships of socially vulnerable groups of people. In the specific film, she focuses on the life of a young Syrian refugee, Jara, who had to flee the Syrian war to save her life. Jara is hosted by a Dutch family, a middle-aged couple in particular. From the very first moment she has been welcomed with love and warmth by the host family. She has enrolled in a Dutch high school where she feels accepted as she quickly makes friends with a Dutch girl. A major characteristic of the film is that the protagonists do not talk. The only sound is that of music which emphasizes Jara's emotions as they follow a certain course from a negative to a positive state. What is more, the power of body language is indicative of emotions, dreams and expectations.

The director makes an attempt to send a powerful socio-political message about tolerance and open-mindedness as factors that can help make a better society and a better place for everyone regardless of their ethnic, social or racial background. The refugee girl and her feelings are put forward by close angle shootings to her face in an attempt to highlight her mixed feelings. It is noteworthy that every night when Jara goes to bed she fixes her eyes on the sticker stars on the ceiling of her bedroom. Nostalgia for her homeland and the consequent sadness when she reads about the killings back home overwhelm her. Her adjustment to her new life is showcased by her getting out of the house and looking at the real stars in the sky. Additionally, her position in the refugee community is not referred to at all. The director, in contrast to the other two films, intentionally moves on highlighting the refugees' inclusion in the civil society and their right to life and opportunity structures. Sluyter chooses to shoot wider angles when Jara is found among other members of the Dutch community and, this way, conveys the message of acceptance, mutual respect and solidarity, in an attempt to underscore and value the essence of democratic institutions.

The screenplay helps unfold images, situations and emotions in all three films. Multiple meanings are communicated to the audience. Multiple meanings are made by the audience. Moments are symbolized within a new dimension of time which includes past, present and future (Miltry and King 2000; Wildfeuer and Bateman 2016).

5   Semiotic Analysis of Films

Each film was broken down to individual themes such as (a) the individual-refugee, (b) their position in the refugee community and (c) the socio-political environment of the reception country (Hamenstädt 2019).

Three functional categories are distinguished in terms of thematic content in the films illustrated above. Thus, it becomes clear that, besides their particular content, the films have unified perceptions reflecting their common socio-political questioning about the refugee identity. In this respect, the refugee issue and refugee identity are conceptualized within a dynamic field of socio-political conditions beyond the borders and peculiarities of nation-states.

The first thematic category, the "individual-refugee" predominates in all three films. In the first film the refugee is visible through their culture in which the place, their country is defined in terms of the policy of rights, life, enjoyment, prosperity. The refugee is perceived as a human being with personal pursuits for the future and the interminable process toward their personal fulfilment within a context in which the war was totally unexpected. The film portrays incidents escalating from the peaceful period to the beginning of the war in an attempt to highlight ruptures and turnovers due to war.

The second film, somehow a continuation of the first one, focuses on particular refugee experiences. The past is unfolded through social experiences of Syrian refugees. People of different ages recall life moments back in their country of origin, as they strongly feel the need to put forward their culture, to approach the "western" culture through a flowing discourse. The director has intentionally put all protagonists in front of a piece of black cloth in order to cancel the perception of space and put forward the emptiness as a means of strong bonds to the past. In this sense, the refugees-protagonists of the film become the mediators between the two cultures, between past and present. Spotlights are on them. Their faces are nothing more than everyday familiar faces. Their oral discourse is visualized and the audience is captivated by its flowing power since there is only discourse and people wishing to communicate (Staiger 1992). The verbal biographical discourse of refugees is gradually enhanced with life incidents from their arrival in Greece. Contrasts, cancellations and expectations are all visualized by strong frames. This way, the biographical analysis of refugee discourse is in line with readings about life moments in the reception country.

In the third film, a Syrian refugee woman, an adolescent, represents, through her narrative, the expectations of a lost generation of refugees who perceive their future as something inauspicious. This means that they are marginalized due to their refugee identity, while the content of knowledge, professional aspirations and progress seem inaccessible to them (Akil 2016). The issue of inequalities is put forward so that, besides refugees-natives differentiations, gender identity differentiations are also highlighted. The director attempts to make a transition from the fragmentary refugee issue to the holistic approach to the policy of rights; a message that the "others" of the system are becoming more and more.

As regards the second thematic category about the refugee position in the refugee community, the first director showcases the refugee identity through the unified elements of death avoidance, survival and interpretation of needs based on instinctive reactions, suggestive of their desire for life. These common pursuits gradually highlight substantial privilege differentiations of different refugee groups based on their economic, social and educational capital. Thus, refugee roles are defined differently in terms of pursuits, choices and expectations. In other words, besides the unified narrative of common identity, every social subject represents a different status depending on being socially privileged or underprivileged in the country of origin. The narrative discourse, the particular linguistic code represents cultural elements of different social classes. Information management, the content of knowledge and personal choices in the reception country are proof of the fact that nothing is accidental and social subjects depend on their educational, social and economic capital, rather activated to enhance privileges especially throughout crises. Moreover, the profound attention to underprivileged persons in the reception country is not accidental, while they attempt to move on with their lives, yet in the margins of society (Woolley 2014).

In the second film, the black cloth of uniformity regarding refugee identity reflects each and every one's different identity in terms of semiotics. The negation of rights differs between the privileged and underprivileged refugees. Life incidents back in the homeland have different content depending on the possibilities offered to citizens by the state. Social inequality is a lived experience and normative condition both in the country of origin and the reception country. Organizing their life in the reception country is different among people of different social classes. The same applies to their expectations, which are not dreams empty of social content. On the contrary, they stem from different readings, in social terms, about the role of social subjects, their rights and their differentiation based on their social class. The unifying negative consequences of the refugee status do not cancel the differentiations among refugee groups. In this respect, the director attempts to showcase the marginalization of refugee lower social classes which will be intensified more in a context of denied access to educational capital, the only factor to upward social mobility.

In the third film, the privilege of refugee upper social class in terms of choices is visualized meaning that the adolescent refugee girl will continue being educated. Education is put forward as privilege considering the fact that in Greece refugee education is either deficient or procedural, only to learn the language of the reception country, or totally absent (Kalerante 2020). Therefore, both Holland, the reception country and its organized social system to provide opportunities for refugees, despite racist incidents, is a positive fact of opportunity structures. The place, Holland, is interpreted as a privileged socio-political context, rather diversified from massive refugee groups in Greece or Turkey. The director's discourse refers to a new market of opportunities for refugees, established in western countries for the privileged ones.

The third thematic category includes analyses of interpretations deriving from natives in an attempt to shed light on the socio-political context of the reception country. All three films are distinctive of lacking intercultural capital depicted through tensions and shaped criteria of accepting the "other". Within postmodern conditions, the confined systems of nation-states lead to exclusions, while making new meanings about diversity, the non-purity of the "others" along with the emerging argumentation about the limited economic capital of the native population. Therefore, the refugee-migration issue is also part of the economic paradigm in which the "other" is threat to the economic development and progress of a state. The fact that this argumentation is further reinforced by the attitudes of native marginalized underprivileged people is rather oxymoron. A considerable number of important issues are visualized by the three films such as political humanism, democratic operations of states, focus on movements toward the democratization of societies, mitigation of social inequalities along with the highlighted causes of migration. This has been particularly evident over this period due to the acute contradiction between Greece and Turkey, as the neighboring country has breached the conventions with the European Union. Moreover, Turkey does not cater for establishing refugee reception camps, but rather manipulates refugee transfer to Europe through Greece.[1]

6   Discussion and Considerations: cinematic Discourse in a Different Political Narrative

Amidst a period characterized by the acute refugee issue, the cinema focuses on its causes and effects. Mass Media selectively show war, domestic conflicts and environmental crises incidents by sorting political discourse. Moreover, they mask the causes of other states' involvement in this issue, as they explicitly or implicitly benefit from this situation. The political discourse is portrayed through confined arguments so that the non-normality of human life is perceived as an anticipated condition that should be handled by persons only. In this sense, the refugee or migrant becomes the "other", exclusively responsible to deal with their own problems without disturbing native populations. Despite the existence of international organizations and the European Union, provisions to refugees are being limited, whereas there is an emerging political philanthropy, rather piecemeal and disengaged from the policy of rights. Thus, the refugee or migrant is no longer deemed as citizen. They are gradually perceived as potential threat since the weak protection of the political system showcases identity peculiarities. This means that parts of their identity are coined in such a way so as to legalize and naturalize their marginalization (Minh-ha 2011).

Within the context of isolation and marginalization, cinema brings the discussion back to the causes and effects of the refugee issue (Wessels 2017). All three films presented above showcase the refugee identity in an attempt to negate the political discourse that shapes the refugee as enemy and invader to the native culture and everyday life. All three films seek to associate the intercultural element with emphasis on understanding, recognizing and promoting

---

1   At the time when this chapter is being prepared, a number of issues have risen regarding massive refugee flows towards Greece, while negotiations between Greece and the European Union are taking place. It is obvious that there is not explicit European policy on the refugee issue and the European countries are not willing either to host refugees or address the causes of the refugee issue. At the same time, humanity is facing the pandemic of Coronavirus, which reminds us that we live in risk societies, rather vulnerable despite their technological and economic growth. These conditions can spark new considerations for the scientific community in the future, such as the new construction of "others" in societies.

diversity toward society enrichment. The body language, discourse and color are conducive to forming a different narrative for these people attempting to redefine their life through assembling pieces of both their past and present social space (Celik 2015). Therefore, any information about who these people are is very important. This way, natives can get to know where they come from, what their culture represents and which unified elements can help enrich contemporary societies, while highlighting the dysfunctional economic and political system. In other words, transgression of natives-refugees internal contradictions can lead to a new space, not merely that of typical co-existence, but rather of substantial involvement in a different model. Based on this model, both natives and refugees can interpret situations, go beyond limitations, deal with contemporary problems and define their future through participation in expanded groups without national or religious discriminations. These identities generate only rivalry and hatred, while concealing the socio-political dimensions of opportunity distributions to the poor within a context of institutions serving the dominant economic system.

The distinctive feature of the three films is their systematic processing of ideas. Their combination with the dynamics of technical features is conducive to the visualization of opposing discourse against the dominant political discourse by reflecting the human side of refugees and migrants. This dynamic discourse is not consumed with instrumental propagandistic projections. To this end, the films chosen do not belong to the politically commercialized film industry. They represent different schools of thought which incorporate political discourse through a different perspective that puts forward political humanism and democratic institutions instead of segregating or banishing politicians or highlighting specific political parties (de Valck 2016). Within a period of intense anti-democratic rhetoric, cinema criticizes capitalism because the capitalist development casts democracy out. Therefore, the connection between democracy and capitalism comes to an end, as limitless collective progress vanishes due to unsolved social issues (Streek 2016).

Were the three films to be connected in a unified screenplay, a different story could possibly unfold. In other words, the first film familiarizes the audience with the country of origin, Syria, where the persons' biographical discourse through human portraits showcases social spaces, social fields of regularity and the negation of war. It is noteworthy that the western audience, speaking of age, do not have memories of war. They simply rely on historical data or literature in order to understand the consequences of war. Therefore, it is essential to present what war is like, with its emphasized consequences on human beings, especially in a time period when war is mostly linked to profit and loss, territories and their resources. In this respect, the film utilizes different

discourse to focus mostly on people. This means that the audience is familiar-
ized with the real defeated entities of war, human beings who experienced loss
and negated rights at the same time (Rastegar 2015).

According to this modular study, the second film associates past and present within a refugee reception camp. These places open up to the audience,
faced with the concealed narratives of the people living there. The migrants
and refugees who reside in the outskirts of towns or frontiers acquire discourse
and character through the screenplay and become visible. Therefore, the second film could work as a continuation of the first one, highlighting the transition from past to present and the actual lacking policy of the European Union
and international organizations. The audience is confronted with people
heaped, isolated and marginalized in the secluded reception camps as if they
are a temporary phenomenon, material to be disposed or undesired material,
continuously under surveillance. In conditions of "specified emergency", their
privacy does not exist, as they are under surveillance as mass. At this point the
role of technology becomes important because the Mass Media-related technology of persuasion coincides with control through technology (Zuboof
2019). The refugee routes are being tracked and their choices are being limited
by nation-states in their attempt to control refugee "spread", perceived as
threat to Europe. According to Bauman's terms, they are deemed as contemporary waste. Thus, the second film is an attempt to reverse this perspective and
put forward refugees as precious, yet different, human beings who could contribute to a different social model (Bauman 2004).

Our screenplay is completed with the third film illustrating the stage of maturity through the process of social inclusion in the reception country. This is,
perhaps, an exemplary proposal or challenge to a different model of social co-
existence that concurrently highlights other social inequalities, possibly mitigated with the refugee-migrant contribution. The film implies that the notion
of the "others", reinforced biased perceptions about individual or groups exclusions and the overall promotion of far right policies supporting infertile nationalism through classifications in natives and non-natives are nothing more
than political constructions.

The common cohesive element of the three films is the promotion of social
environments that include migrants-refugees through the creation of social
representations for the audience. In other words, the audience perceives them
as a population, a sort of established reality in globalized societies within a
model of democratic co-existence and humanism. The audience is familiar-
ized with the "other" through a process of identification and understanding.
Along the administrative condition of tolerance, a new condition of accepting

the "others" emerges in terms of their distinctive cultural characteristic features. Even though the mainstream cinematic representation creates negative models of inferiority for this distinction, underground cinema puts forward a positive distinction by highlighting the culture of the "others" in the form of people's cultural enrichment (Ehrat 2005). Therefore, the concepts of cultural purity, racial characteristics or religious discriminations that lead to the migrant-refugee rejection and the political reinforcement of anti-democratic attitudes and behaviors conducive to far right policies are in contrast to underground cinema, a means of reinforcing various social representations that strengthen the democratic narrative and humanistic completion through the co-existence of different cultures.

The cinematic discourse of the films under exploration is part of underground cinema; theoretically speaking a marginalized cinematic discourse. This means that it exists off the mainstream cinema schools, the official cinema festivals, cinema awards and distribution of cinema films. The dominant cinematic discourse focuses on the selective promotion of migrants-refugees perceived either as a problematic situation in which they are presented as crowd or mass, or as individuals with special features included in western societies or completely ignored and silenced; a population group with whom nobody wishes to engage. One could refer to the dynamics of a medium that creates social representations similar to those of Mass Media and shapes visual fields conducive to certain choices, attitudes, behaviors and perceptions. It can be said that cinema becomes part of the dynamic environment of meaning-making through the narrative, legalized discourse and emotional enrichment, eventually evolving to political text (Constantopoulou 2015).

Considering the above, in the first case, the crowd or mass is not diversified, but rather portrayed as a dangerous, unpredictable and detrimental situation for western culture, economy and religion. In the second case, individual migrants or refugees, distinctive of their characteristic features, are portrayed in the sense of benefited individuals by western philanthropy. In this case, one could refer to developing love and mercy scenarios in which migrants and refugees are accepted by the western population and identify with western values. In the third case, the migrant-refugee issue is neither part of the cinematic narrative nor cherished by screenwriters and directors. Thus, the films under exploration are included in the marginalized cinematic narrative, the selection of certain screenwriters and directors whose political attitude and social awareness represent different knowledge and perceptions of the migrant-refugee identity. This cinematic discourse, as theme, is also marginalized by an audience characterized by their limited social representations because of absent educational discourse on the humanistic and democratic approach to the migrant-refugee issue as well as the disempowered democratic political narrative of Mass Media and syndicalist bodies.

7   Educational Discourse through Cinema as Content of a Different Social Narrative

Cinematic discourse on refugees is actually a form of differentiated opposing discourse because it focuses on procedures that highlight the refugee identity and the corresponding policy of rights. On the basis of the perspective that the number of new technologies users is constantly increasing in western societies, this different cinematic discourse is reinforced by similar supplementary discourse on the Internet. Through special platforms, cinema functions as public discourse beyond its showing in cinema halls. Therefore, its dynamics is related to potential penetration in an audience beyond the nation-state by shaping political readings for culturally diverse population groups (Ottley 2011; Sealy 2008).

The young population is part of this expanded audience and potentially understands the political discourse that differs from the far right political discourse. Thus, this kind of cinema contributes to political socialization by putting forward democratic values and political humanism. The cinematic political discourse should be based on the educational discourse developed in formal education. As a result, adopting democratic political values tied to the refugee policy of rights can be further reinforced in democratic societies. New readings about democracy, globalized values and humanism should be enhanced by education. Therefore, this kind of cinematic discourse could be instrumentally integrated into teaching methods about democratic values in all educational grades (Information Resources Management Association 2018).

A broadened audience, that can watch, interpret and consider social situations as such expressed through art, needs a different educational model. Therefore, the dominance of far right political discourse on the policy of rights, the promotion of ideologies about race purity and religious superiority or inferiority that had allegedly disappeared from societies, come back in different terms, targeting refugees through the construction of the "others". It should be noted that along with the "others", some other "traditional" categories of "others" come back, namely the Jews, Muslim, etc. Apparently, a cinema "school" that showcases people's rights is not enough in case individuals have not been educated in recognizing these codes of theoretical narrative. Therefore, cinema should become part of the education system so as to reinforce narratives about democracy. Cinema, as all forms of art, should not be considered an elite product when it comes to teachers' training, but rather a means of political enlightenment within a model of rational function of societies (Noddings 2013).

A large number of individuals, mainly from underprivileged social groups, shape their social and political identity in contrast to the "others". This perhaps explains the dynamics and radicalization towards far right of those individuals who have not shaped their political identity through education. Thus, education could be the means by which people could recognize the others by adopting political values about the rights of the others and through understanding different cultures (Sensoy and DiAngelo 2017).

Films, that highlight the narrative about the refugee rights through their content, bring up to date issues of exclusion and marginalization of population groups who are perceived as "invisible" by the conservative political systems. A different type of education is necessary so that this cinematic discourse predominates and interest in this type of films is increased. A new kind of literacy is needed to put the human being at the epicenter and investigate issues of social inequality in relation to the consequences of war and the effects of the neoliberal economic paradigm. Within the new educational model, knowledge about the economic system and labor market can be transformed into knowledge about the humanistic function of societies (Herrick 2005; Seymour and Levin 2004).

As Luigi Zoja (2009) puts it, love is what is needed, that kind of love whose content is truth and truth is related to morality. Morality of love includes morality of otherness which shapes the "being" as a whole in which the others are included. In the risk society (Beck 1992) characterized by unawareness, different meanings and fear, cinema and education can work together toward the negation of constructed uncertainty, attempting to reconstruct the public sphere by replacing fear with love.

Bibliography

Akil, H.N. (2016). *The Visual Divide between Islam and the West: Image Perception within Cross-Cultural Contexts*. New York: Palgrave Macmillan.

Arlt, D. and Wolling, J. (2016). "The refugees: threatening or beneficial? Exploring the effects of positive and negative attitudes and communication on hostile media perceptions". *Global Media Journal. German Edition* 6(1).

Balta, E. (2014). *The Exchange of Population—Historiography and Refugee Memory*. Istanbul: Istos Yahin.

Bauman, Z. (2004). *Wasted Lives: Modernity and Its Outcasts*. London: Blackwell Publishing Ltd.

Beck, U. (1992). *Risk Society. Towards a New Modernity*. London: SAGE Publications.

Berger, A.A. (2016). *Media and Communication Research Methods: An introduction to Qualitative and Quantitative Approaches* (4th ed.). Los Angeles: SAGE.

Brennen, B.S. (2017). *Qualitative Research Methods for Media Studies* (2nd ed.). New York: Routledge.

Carlsten, J.M. and McGarry, F. (eds.). (2015). *Film, History and Memory*. New York: Palgrave Macmillan.

Celik, I.A. (2015). *In Permanent Crisis: Ethnicity in Contemporary European Media and Cinema*. Ann Arbor, MI: University of Michigan Press.

Constantopoulou, C. (ed.). (2015). *Social representations. Communicative media and authority*. Athens: Papazisis. (in Greek).

Council of Europe. (2000). *European Convention on Human Rights*. Strasbourg: Council of Europe.

Da Costa, R. (2006). *Legal and Protection Policy Research Series: Rights of Refugees in the Context of Integration; Legal Standards and Recommendations*. New York: United Nations High Commissioner for Refugees.

De Valck, M. (2016). "Film festivals: mediating the mainstream and marginal voices". In Tzioumakis, Y. and Molloy, C. (eds.). *The Routledge Companion to Cinema and Politics*. New York: Routledge.

Ehrat, J. (2005). *Cinema and Semiotic. Peirce and Film Aesthetics, Narration, and Representation*. Toronto: University of Toronto Press.

European Commission. (2017). *European Agenda on Migration: Consolidating progress made*. Brussels: European Commission.

European Union. (2011). *DIRECTIVE 2011/95/EU OF THE EUROPEAN PARLIAMENT AND OF THE COUNCIL of 13 December 2011 on standards for the qualification of third-country nationals or stateless persons as beneficiaries of international protection, for a uniform status for refugees or for persons eligible for subsidiary protection, and for the content of the protection granted (recast)*. Official Journal of the European Union.

Galikhuzina, R.G., Penkovtsev, R.V. and Shibanova, N.A. (2016). "The image of refugees in the communication mass media: A source of conflict or cooperation?" *Academy of Marketing Studies Journal* 20: 27.

Gatrell, P. (2019). *The unsettling of Europe: How Migration Reshaped a Continent*. New York: Basic Books.

Giannetti, L. (2011). *Understanding Movies*. (12th ed.). New Jersey: Pearson Education, Inc.

Greek Parliament. (2019). *Dilemmas and contexts of the refugee issue*. Athens: Greek Parliament Foundation. (in Greek).

Hamenstädt, U. (2019). "Movies and Social Science". In: Hamestädt, U. (ed.). *The Interplay Between Political Theory and Movies*. Springer: Cham.

Heath, S. (2990). *The Semiotics of Cinema*. Athens: Aigokeros. (in Greek).

Herrick, J. (2005). *Humanism: An Introduction*. New York: Prometheus Books.

Information Resources Management Association. (2018). *Social Media in Education. Breakthroughs in Research and Practice*. Hershey, PA: IGI Global.

Kalerante, E. and Galanis, K. (2015). "The educational discourse policy of the Greek far right party "Golden Dawn" in their propagandistic gazette: Conceptualisation of culture and national political area". International Conference: *Cultural Diversity, Equity and Inclusion: Intercultural Education in 21st century and beyond*. Ioannina.

Kalerante, E. (2020). "Policy on refugee education: Textual discourse and educational structures". *Preschool and Primary Education*. (in press).

Kaltsidou, A. (2016). "The Refugees". Drama Film Festival. Retrieved 20/12/2019. Available at: https://flix.gr/articles/drama-ffest-2016-the-refugees.html (in Greek).

Kermani, N., Saman, M. and Crawford, T. (2019). *Upheaval. The refugee trek through Europe*. Cambridge: Polity Press.

Kouvara, V. (n.d.). Welfare State. Retrieved 20/03/2020. Available at: https://www.syriza.gr/article/id/67020/Koinwniko-Kratos.html.

Krishna-Hensel, S.F. (2018). *Migrants, Refugees, and the Media: The New Reality of Open Societies*. New York: Routledge.

Law 4587/2018. *Urgent regulations of the Ministry of Migration Policy and other provisions*. Government Gazette 218/A/24.12.2018.

Law 4636/2019. *About International Protection and other provisions*. Government Gazette 169/A/1.11.2019.

Mendik, X. and Schneider, S.J. (2002). *Underground U.S.A. Filmmaking Beyond the Hollywood Canon*. New York: Columbia University Press.

Mitry, J. and King, C. (2000). *Semiotics and the Analysis of Film*. U.S.A.: Indiana University Press.

Minh-ha, T.T. (2011). *Elsewhere, within here. Immigration, refugeeism and the boundary event*. New York: Routledge.

Monaco, J. (2000). *How to read a film: the world of movies, media, and multimedia: language, history, theory*. U.S.A.: Oxford University Press.

Neiger, M., Meyers, O. and Zandberg, E. (eds.). (2011). *On Media Memory. Collective Memory in a New Media Age*. New York: Palgrave Macmillan.

Noddings, N. (2013). *Education and Democracy in the 21st Century*. New York: Teachers College Press.

Ottley, C.D. (2011). *The Cinema in Education. A Handbook for Teachers*. London: Redgrove Press.

Panagos, N., Nagopoulos, N. and Rantos, C.V. (2017). *The refugee-migrant issue in Lesvos and the local community: Attitudes and behaviours*. Athens: Tziola. (in Greek).

Rastegar, K. (2015). *Surviving Images: Cinema, War, and Cultural Memory in Middle East.* Oxford: Oxford University Press.

Salti, R. (2007). *Insights into Syrian Cinema: Essays and Conversations with Contemporary Filmmakers.* New York: Rattapallax Press.

Sealy, K.S. (2008). *Film, Politics and Education: Cinematic Pedagogy Across the Disciplines.* Bern: Peter Lang Inc.

Sensoy, O. and DiAngelo, R. (2017). *Is Everyone Really Equal? An Introduction to Key Concepts in Social Justice Education.* (2nd ed.). New York: Teachers College Press.

Seymour, M. and Levin, H.M. (2004). *Educating for Humanity: Rethinking the Purposes of Education.* New York: Routledge.

Smiths, G.M. (2003). *Film structure and the emotion system.* Cambridge: Cambridge University Press.

Soules, M. (2015). *Media, Persuasion and Propaganda.* Edinburgh: Edinburgh University Press Ltd.

Staiger, J. (1992). *Interpreting Films.* New Jersey: Princeton University Press.

Stam, R. (2003). *New vocabularies in film semiotics.* London: Routledge.

Streek, W. (2016). *How will Capitalism end? Essays on a Failing System.* New Westminster, CA: Post Hypnotic Press Inc.

Tahvildaran, J.R. (2010). *Democracy and Difference Through the Aesthetics of Film.* Iowa: Kendall Hunt Publishing.

Takis, A. (2015). *The refugee issue of 2015: The chronicle of a portend crisis.* Retrieved 20/12/2019. Available at: https://gr.boell.org/el/2015/12/04/prosfygiko-2015-hronikomias-proanaggeltheisas-krisis (in Greek).

Terzis, N. (2016). The semiotic analysis of a film. 10th International Conference: *Changing Worlds and Signs of the Times.* Volos: The Hellenic Semiotics Society.

UNESCO. (2019). *UNESCO guidelines on intercultural education.* Paris: UNESCO.

Wanrooij, B. (2019). *Displaced. Europe and the global refugee crisis.* London: Independent Publishing Network.

Wessels, J.I. (2017). *Documenting Syria: Film-making, Video Activism and Revolution (Library of Modern Middle East Studies).* London: I.B. TAURIS.

Wildfeuer, J. and Bateman, J. (2016). *Film Text Analysis: New Perspectives on the Analysis of Filmic Meaning.* London: Routledge.

Woolley, A. (2014). *Contemporary Asylum Narratives: Representing Refugees in the Twenty-First Century.* New York: Palgrave Macmillan.

Zoja, L. (2009). *La morte del prossimo.* Torino: Giulio Einaudi. (in Italian).

Zuboff, S. (2019). *The age of surveillance capitalism.* New York: Hachette Book Group.

Index

CPSIA information can be obtained
at www.ICGtesting.com
Printed in the USA
JSHW032028281021
19962JS00005B/9

9 781642 596151